The Sociology of Minority Group Relations

Graham C. Kinloch

Florida State University

Prentice-Hall, Inc., Englewood Cliffs, N.J. 07632

Library of Congress Cataloging in Publication Data

KINLOCH, GRAHAM CHARLES.
  The sociology of minority group relations.

  (Prentice-Hall series in sociology)
  Includes bibliographies and indexes.
    1. Minorities—Social aspects. 2. Social groups.
3. Social interaction. 4. Civil rights. 5. Minori-
ties—United States. I. Title.
HM133.K52   301.45   78-12274
ISBN—0-13-821017-9

Prentice-Hall Series in Sociology
Neil J. Smelser, Editor

Printed in the United States of America
10 9 8 7 6 5 4 3 2 1

Editorial/production supervision by Joyce Turner
Manufacturing buyer: Nancy Myers

Prentice-Hall International, Inc., *London*
Prentice-Hall of Australia Pty. Limited, *Sydney*
Prentice-Hall of Canada, Ltd., *Toronto*
Prentice-Hall of India Private Limited, *New Delhi*
Prentice-Hall of Japan, Inc., *Tokyo*
Prentice-Hall of Southeast Asia Pte. Ltd., *Singapore*
Whitehall Books Limited, *Wellington, New Zealand*

To a saner and more humane world

Contents

Section Two
DEFINITIONS AND THEORIES

Section Three
A GENERAL CONCEPTUAL FRAMEWORK

Section Four
AN ANALYSIS OF MINORITY GROUP RELATIONS

Section Five
TOWARD HUMAN LIBERATION

Preface

Recently the field of minority group relations has expanded to include women as well as subordinate racial and ethnic groups. Increased visibility of minority group reaction and awareness of the "minority problem" has also made the topic more popular and relevant than it has been in the past. However, the field remains restricted to these three groups for the most part and reflects a predominantly descriptive approach.

Reacting to these developments and limitations, this work has two major aims: (1) expansion of the notion "minority" to include age based, economic, and behavioral groups which are subject to discrimination and, (2) an attempt to develop a general theory which accounts for the origins and emergence of minority groups both in the United States and world-wide. The result of this is a structural, demographic-economic theory of minority group relations which focuses on their evolution through a number of specific stages. Major advantages of such an approach include its broad scope which covers most major groups in society and its potential for accounting for a wide range of social phenomena in terms of underlying social processes. This gives the analysis both scope and unity.

As with any macroscopic framework, however, a number of limitations are clearly evident. The general theory advanced is extremely broad and tentative, requiring refinement and extensive testing; the approach taken to each minority is analytical rather than encyclopaedic, while the comparative analysis is illustrative rather than detailed. Consequently, the author readily anticipates charges concerning broad generalizations, weak specifics, and the "Bongo-Bongoist" mentality which argues that this framework is "all very well" but does not apply specifically to the case of Bongo Bongo.[1] In response I would emphasize my awareness of these problems but my greater concern for uncovering underlying factors and the processes relating to social differentiation and domination. As a result my concern is with macroscopic societal processes related to stratification as a whole in order to highlight basic causes of, and possible solutions to, this crucial social problem in contemporary society. The approach developed is macroscopic and analytical rather than microscopic and descriptive. Its limitations are readily apparent but I would argue for its distinct advantage of delineation of societal factors behind the general process of social stratification. Such concerns are vital to the important issue of "human liberation" if contemporary society is to move away from its preoccupation with material development and dehumanization toward a concern for the utilization of material resources for human needs in the context of values that emphasize assumed equality rather than inferiority. Reformist and descriptive approaches appear to offer little help in this. A structural, process-oriented framework is offered, despite its limitations, in the hope that it might prove useful, if only in a preliminary fashion, in developing awareness of the scope of this problem and its possible solutions.

I would also emphasize that in this analysis by "minority" I imply a group singled out on the basis of specific distinguishing characteristics and subject to specialized, institutionalized discrimination and exploitation. It is obvious that poverty, deviance, sexual and age differences, and ethnic prejudice have existed for many centuries; however, this does not automatically imply specialized, institutionalized minority group status. I am using the term in a *specialized* manner.

---

[1]For a discussion of this see M. Douglas, *Natural Symbols* (New York: Vintage, 1970), pp. 15–16.

I am most grateful to the following individuals for their encouragement and help in the development of this work:

To students, both graduate and undergraduate, for their enthusiasm and help;

To Ed Stanford, my editor, for his enthusiasm, patience, and insight;

To Crismas Carroll, for her encouragement;

To Beverley, for her patience and understanding;

To Barbara, for her forbearance and painstaking typing of the manuscript. My thanks are due them all.

Graham C. Kinloch

Section One

THE UNIVERSALITY OF MINORITY GROUPS

1

Dimensions and Criteria

Minority groups appear to have been an integral part of society from the beginning of human existence. This emphasizes the extent to which inequality and domination are apparently universal processes. The widespread existence of a range of minorities in contemporary society—racial, sexual, age-based, social class, ethnic, and behavioral deviants—highlights the pervasive nature of majority-minority group relations throughout the world.

Minorities have become increasingly visible as they have channeled their rejection of majority group discrimination into well-organized social movements—black nationalism, women's liberation, ethnic power, gay liberation, and concern with children's rights. Thus, awareness of the oppressive nature of modern society has increased markedly within the last decade as has rejection of exploitation by subject minorities. Rather than moving toward increased levels of social, political, and

3

economic assimilation, contemporary society, particularly in the United States, appears to be increasingly differentiated by the dimensions of race, sex, age, culture, class, and behavioral deviance as these subgroups become more vocal and organized.

While the social sciences have recently been deluged with texts relating to minority group situations, it can hardly be claimed that they have been in the forefront of minority group protest. In the past they have tended to be elitist, assimilationist, and generally biased in orientation, with little awareness of the extent to which this society is based on a wide range of discrimination. They believed in the Horatio Alger myth of an "open" society where opportunity is accessible to all who desire it, and moved toward a "melting pot" utopia where background differences were no longer significant. Early works on particular minorities tended to reinforce rather than to reject predominant prejudices and stereotypes of the day.[1]

More recent works on minority group relations are subject to different limitations. They tend to focus on a narrow range of minorities, primarily the racial and ethnic, thereby ignoring groups such as women, children, and the mentally ill. They de-emphasize or overlook characteristics of the historical evolution of these groups, ignore majority-minority group relations in societies other than the United States, and continue until very recently, to be written by and therefore represent the views of majority group members.[2] Such problems severely limit the insight and utility of such works.

Sociology, however, has much to offer to the understanding of minority group relations. It is applicable to a very wide range of such groups in contemporary society, highlights the underlying causes of minority group differentiation in both historical and comparative perspective, and is able thereby to suggest varying solutions to the "minority group problem." It is with such possible insights that this book is concerned as we attempt to analyze the major sociological factors behind many minority groups and their relations both within and outside American society. In this chapter we are concerned with characteristics of the approach we shall take, the model and terminology to be used, and an outline of the major sections and chapters to follow.

[1]A useful analysis of this is Frazier's discussion of the manner in which nineteenth-century treatises on the subject of race were concerned with rationalizing the system of slavery as functional and right. Early sociological writers also highlighted the racial caste system and intellectual differences. See E. F. Frazier, "Sociological Theory and Race Relations," *American Sociological Review,* 12, (1947), 265–71.

[2]An example is A. G. and R. J. Dworkin, eds., *The Minority Report. An Introduction to Racial, Ethnic, and Gender Relations* (New York: Praeger, 1976).

APPROACH

We shall deal with minority groups such as blacks, Indians, Chinese-Americans, women, children, the aged, the lower classes, Irish-Americans, and the mentally ill. These minorities represent groups of people who are defined as different from the majority on the basis of *assumed physical, cultural, economic,* and *behavioral criteria* and are controlled and treated in a negative fashion. The basic questions we shall ask include, "Why is this so? Why and how do these groups emerge and become subject to control and discrimination? Why are they defined as different and inferior in comparison with majority groups? What keeps them in such invidious positions? In what manner do they relate to each other and the majority elite? Finally, how and why do these *relations* change over a period of time?"

In response to such issues we shall attempt to analyze the major societal, group, and individual factors behind minority groups and their relations with respect to six major dimensions:

1. *The historical dimension:* How did they emerge and develop both in America and other societies? What is their foundation and evolution?

2. *The demographic dimension:* What are their characteristics with respect to group size, geographic distribution, economic and health characteristics, and so forth. What are their demographic and socioeconomic conditions as compared with majority groups?

3. *The attitudinal dimension:* What are the major attitudes and stereotypes concerning each minority among its own members and those of the majority?

4. *The institutional dimension:* What are the political, social, and economic institutions in society that reinforce attitudes toward, control of, and relations among minority groups? Examples will include political exclusion, salary inequities, unequal educational opportunity, media stereotypes, and legal discrimination. All these are aspects of the institutionalized control of minority groups.

5. *The social movement dimension:* What are the reactions of minority groups to majority control over a period of time in the form of social movements—major types of minority group attempts to deal with their position of subordinate control?

6. *Major types of group relations:* What are the resultant group relations and their changing characteristics including majority–minority interaction as well as interaction among the six major types of minority (interminority) relations?

5

In all of the preceding, we are concerned with the foundation, evolution, major demographic, attitudinal, and institutional character-istics of minority groups, as well as with their changing reaction to the majority in the form of organized social movements. We shall relate these factors to an understanding of how these groups relate to each other. This represents an attempt to analyze minority groups sociologi-cally, that is, what major societal factors are behind them.

In examining the above dimensions we shall discuss a number of approaches implicit in the academic literature of today.

The physiological approach consists of assumptions regarding the physiological basis of minorities such as genetics, hormonal differences, the effects of age, assumed differences in levels of intelligence, and the assumed relationship between "body type" and social behavior.

The psychological approach focuses on assumed personality "types" and factors. Examples include Freudian theories of racism, sexual differences, childhood, deviance, and personality theories which account for ethnic and class differences, and deviant behavior.

The social-psychological approach includes reference group theo-ries, role, class consciousness, relative deprivation, and labeling of devi-ance, that is, assumptions concerning the operation of group factors on minority group relations.

The sociological approach stresses the importance of societal char-acteristics such as majority group values, the economic basis of a society, the effects of economic development, types of family structure, the development of "anomie," theories of stratification, and the extent to which particular minorities are assumed to differ physically, culturally, and economically from majority groups. We shall introduce and discuss all of these as they relate to particular minorities.

The above approaches consist of assumptions concerning minority group characteristics, (for example, females are more emotional than males)—such attitudes being part of the stereotyping process and sub-ject to high levels of bias; and attempts to understand, explain, or ac-count for minority group reactions and relations, such as relative deprivation theory. We shall discuss the first within the context of "the attitudinal dimension" of minority group relations and critically review the second when we abstract the major factors behind minority group relations in our analysis. In both cases, however, we shall be aware of the problems of "pseudo-scientific" stereotyping.

These dimensions and approaches will be applied to many minor-ity groups and the focus will be on those particular groups that are subject to most control in contemporary society. These are:

1. *Physiological criteria:* Nonwhite racial minorities (for example, blacks, Chicanos, Indians), women, young people, and the aged.
2. *Cultural criteria:* Non-Anglo-Saxon ethnic groups such as European immigrants (Italians, Germans, Greeks).
3. *Economic criteria:* Those without economic power such as the poor and the lower classes.
4. *Behavioral criteria:* Legal and social deviants such as criminals, sexual "perverts," and the mentally ill. and the mentally ill.

Each minority will be analyzed using the above dimensions and approaches in reference to the major characteristics of each majority group of relevance. We shall also concentrate on majority-minority group relations with respect to each type.

TERMINOLOGY

It is appropriate at this point to introduce some preliminary definitions of the major terms we shall use in this analysis. We shall define them in more detail in Chapter 4, but the following definitions will serve as guides in our introductory discussion:

Majority group: Any power elite that defines others as different and/or inferior on the basis of certain perceived characteristics and controls or treats them negatively (American whites, men, adults, WASPs, the "well-off," conformists).

Minority group: Any group that is defined by a power elite as different and/or inferior on the basis of certain perceived characteristics and is consequently treated in a negative fashion.

Physical minority: Any group that is defined by a power elite as different and/or inferior on the basis of assumed physiological characteristics and is subject to control and discrimination because of those characteristics (blacks, women, the young, and the aged).

Cultural minority: Any group that is defined by a power elite as different and/or inferior on the basis of assumed cultural characteristics and is consequently subject to control and discrimination (non-WASP minorities).

Economic minority: Any group that is defined by a power elite as different and/or inferior on the basis of assumed economic behavioral characteristics and is thereby subject to control and discrimination (the poor and the lower classes).

Behavioral minority: Any group that is defined by a power elite as different and/or inferior and so is subject to control and discrimination (criminals, homosexuals, and the mentally ill).

Minority group relations: Interaction (individual, group, or institutional) between groups defined by a power elite as different and/or inferior on the basis of certain perceived characteristics and subject to control and discrimination as a result, (black-Indian, female-aged, Italian-Jewish, Japanese-poor, poor-homosexual).

Majority-minority relations: Interaction (individual, group, or institutional) between any power elite that defines others as different and/or inferior on the basis of certain perceived characteristics, and subjects them to control and discrimination, (white-nonwhite, male-female, rich-poor, judge-criminal).

In these definitions a number of major emphases are evident: power elites define others as inferior on the basis of *perceived* characteristics, and subsequently *control* them and *discriminate* against them. According to this approach then, minority group relations are viewed primarily as a result of elite definitions of particular groups and the consequent levels of control and discrimination. Thus, minority groups are not simply a matter of numbers, they are "defined," "created," and "maintained" by particular power elites. It is such "processes" that we shall focus on in our analysis.

It should be emphasized that these relations are complicated by the extent to which any elite is able to mobilize substantial segments of the population to agree with them and help oppress particular minorities. In this manner, majority-minority cooperation reinforces the structure of domination-subordination. Sexual minorities, for example, may cooperate with racial minorities to aid in the suppression of economic, behavioral, cultural, and other racial minorities, just as particular racial minorities may work with racial majorities to protect their own interests through the exploitation of other subordinate racial groups. Minority group relations are multidimensional and complicated phenomena, requiring analysis on a number of different levels.

ANALYTICAL MODEL

We shall center attention on a number of factors and elements that have been outlined previously. Major *factors*—societal, group, and individual—influence the process by which groups are defined as minorities. Of relevance here are the approaches already profiled.

The major consequence of these factors is *minority group differentiation* or, the creation of minority groups in society, that consists of the historical, demographic, attitudinal, institutional, and social movement dimensions discussed previously as applied to the major types of minorities—physical, cultural, economic, and behavioral.

Such differentiation results in interaction among the groups defined as minorities—minority group relations—as well as majority-minority group relations. Relations within society are thus structured by power, definitions of particular groups as being inferior, consequent control and discrimination, and resultant elite and minority group interaction at the individual, group, and institutional level.

Finally, the dynamics of these relations result in changing relationships within the social system, providing feedback into the structure of minority group relations in the ongoing process of social change. We will be both dynamic and structural in focusing on the contributions of minority group relations to general social change.

Our analytical model thus consists of the major factors behind minority group differentiation, consequent minority group relations, and subsequent social change. The structure of this model is outlined in Figure 1.1.

PROCEDURE

In the chapters to follow, we shall apply this model by examining the sociological importance of minority groups—what they reveal about

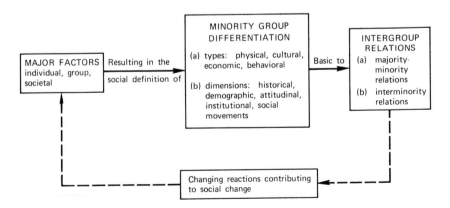

FIGURE 1.1 An Analytical Model of Minority Group Relations

society—as well as the problems involved in studying minority group relations.

Section Two of our analysis follows with a discussion of basic concepts and their definitions, a typology of major minorities and their characteristics, and a critical review of major approaches to minorities —physiological, psychological, social-psychological, and sociological.

Chapter 7 will present a preliminary synthesis of these approaches as we develop a general conceptual framework that accounts for the origin and emergence of minority groups and minority relations.

We shall apply this framework in Section Four by analyzing minority group differentiations and reactions within American society and, to a lesser extent, in other societies around the world. This part of the analysis will be summarized in order to examine minority group relations on the comparative level.

Section Five attempts to integrate the above in a general theory of minority group relations and deals with the practical implications of our theory and analysis with regard to the removal of prejudice and discrimination.

We begin with a preliminary discussion of the sociological importance of minority groups.

STUDY QUESTIONS

1. Select at least three major minority groups in contemporary society and:
   (a) Outline their historical development.
   (b) Describe their relations with each other.
   (c) Delineate their relations with majority elites.
   (d) Compare each minority with respect to these dimensions.
   (e) Draw some general conclusions regarding contemporary minority group relations.

2

Sociological Relevance

This chapter answers the question, "What is sociologically important about minority groups and minority group relations?" that is, "Why study them and what do they reveal about society?" It deals with ten major points ranging from minorities as the basis of a society's system of social organization to questions of social policy.

Minority groups raise a number of aspects and issues concerning the structure of society as follows:

The Issue of Universality

Minority groups raise the issue of the extent to which this type of differentiation is a constant, that is, whether minority groups have existed in all societies at various times, whether based on assumed physical, cultural, economic, or behavioral differences. It is important to determine the kinds of minorities or groups that appear to emerge in particular kinds of societies in order to deal with this problem in a practical way. Of central importance is the issue of whether minorities of whatever kind exist in all societies, (the problem of universal stratification). The degree and variety of minority group differentiation in all major societies, both past and present, are questions highlighted by the study of minority group relations.

The Visibility of Minority Groups

During the past several years minorities have increased dramatically in visibility, particularly women and children. The issue of minority group rights has moved to the forefront of the public scene, thereby highlighting the extent of discrimination and control in the social system. The study of minority groups reveals the extent and major types of discrimination in society. Attention moves from one group to another as particular minorities become more visible, and increased observation is given to the general social problem of minority group discrimination, contributing to greater awareness of the problem of social inequality and discrimination in society.

Minorities as the Basis of Social Organization

Insofar as minority groups are subject to particular forms of discrimination and are assigned limited political, social, and economic roles in society, they are basic to a society's system of social organization because these roles represent central elements in the institutional structure. For example, the extent to which blacks are defined as most suited to unskilled labor, women to homemaking, children to school attendance, senior citizens to residence in homes for the aged, Irish to police work, lower classes to vocational rather than academic education, and criminals to incarceration, the links between minority groups and a society's system of social organization remain strong and discriminatory. Then the extent to which roles are assigned on the basis of assumed physical, cultural, economic, and behavioral characteristics, indicates the degree to which minority group differentiation is central to the social structure of a particular society. Examination of such differentiation will highlight such bases accordingly, and will result in high levels of insight into major characteristics of the social structure.

Minorities as the Basis of Social Stratification

The amount of discriminatory role assignment in a society is closely related to the stratification system, that is, the extent to which minority group differentiation is the basis of this system. Thus, when minority group differentiation is high, stratification is based on the complex of majority-minority group power positions in the society. In America, for example, whites relating to nonwhites, men to women, parents to children, WASPs to non-WASPs, upper to lower classes, and conformists to deviants, represent important power relations in the stratification system. Examination of these relations reveals major characteristics of this system, such as power, domination, intergroup relations, and conflict. Minority group differentiation is a major type of stratification system and as such reveals significant aspects of the processes of unequal role assignment and reward.

Minorities as the Basis of Social Control

Assumed physical, cultural, economic, and behavioral inferiority obviously represent major bases of social control (that is, the foundation of behavior and control) as these groups are subjected to prejudice and discrimination by particular majority elites who believe in their own superiority. As a result, minorities of every kind are subject to political, social, and economic control throughout the social system by these elites. This discrimination is heavily legitimized in the general culture by the notion of assumed superiority-inferiority on all major dimensions. Thus, whites, males, parents, the middle-aged, WASPs, the rich, and conformists control (politically, socially, and economically) nonwhites, females, children, the aged, non-WASPs, the poor, and the deviant on the basis of their own assumed superiority. Minority groups thus reveal the basis and extent of general social control in a society.

Minorities as an Index of Basic Values

Rationales, such as arguments that reinforce assumed superiority-inferiority, highlight the types of values predominant in a society, particularly as defined by its majority group members. It would appear, for example, that high levels of minority group differentiation are more typical of cultures emphasizing individualism, materialism, economic development, WASP values, and high degrees of moralism and general ethnocentrism, which are the typical values of European colonial elites such as the United States. In these settings economic and material developments are heavily emphasized as prime motives in social relationships, resulting in high levels of differential role assignment, rationalized in terms of WASP ethnocentrism and pseudoscientific "findings." Societies are founded and developed by elites with particular values who in fact create minorities for their own economic interests or needs, and rationalize such discrimination in terms of their own value system as previously outlined.[1] Minority group differentiation thus reflects, and is a function of, elite majority values. Accordingly, the study of minorities reveals a great deal more of the characteristics of majority groups, particularly of their values, than of these subordinate groups themselves.

Minorities as an Index of Societal Development

Insofar as minority groups represent majority value systems they tend to be indicative of a society's foundation and type of economic development. As we shall see, societies founded on certain kinds of migration, in particular, the colonial type, and by elites with values emphasizing economic development in a capitalist direction (WASP elites), appear to create the highest numbers of minorities (variety of type) as they are concerned with economic development in the context of a highly exclusive and ethnocentric culture. This process is obviously a matter of degree rather than of type. Accordingly, the study of minorities in any society will highlight its foundation (type of elite: migrant-indigenous, WASP-non-WASP values, for example) and type of societal development (that is, level of industrial and capitalist economic development). In general, then, minorities and majority-minority relations reflect the society's historical foundation, majority group values, and types of ongoing economic development as groups may be created or decline in social significance. The study of minorities tends to reveal significant aspects of the social structure in both historical and contemporary contexts. As such, this field is both relevant and practical.

---

[1]For a very useful discussion of this process see L. Hartz, ed., *The Founding of New Societies. Studies in the History of the U.S., Latin America, South Africa, Canada, and Australia* (New York: Harcourt, Brace & World, 1964).

Minority Groups as the Basis of Interpersonal Relations

Minority group relations are obviously not restricted to the group level but define interpersonal relations as well. Individual members of a number of minority and/or majority groups interact with other individuals,[2] primarily on the basis of group membership and correlated levels of political, social, or economic power. Consequently, social relationships are clearly structured by majority-minority group factors. All interpersonal relations, then, are structured by these factors as they define social interaction in particular settings on the basis of the relative power of the individuals concerned. Thus, differing power levels exist when, for example, an upper-class white male interacts with a middle-class nonwhite female, a middle-class white WASP male with a lower-class white non-WASP female, a nonwhite upper-class male with a white lower-class male, and so on. Majority-minority factors clearly define social relationships and interaction to a significant degree. Such processes do not occur either in a vacuum or in a socially homogeneous environment. They are structured by the major dimensions of group differentiation in the larger society.

Minorities as the Basis of Social Dynamics and Change

Minority group relations are obviously not static phenomena as is evidenced by increased levels of reaction and consequent visibility. As minorities are subject to increasing levels of social and economic assimilation in conjunction with stable levels of discrimination, awareness of their disadvantaged and illegitimate positions in society increases. Accordingly, this results in the eventual emergence of organized social movements such as black power and women's liberation, which challenge and oppose majority group dominance. In response, the majority group may react conservatively, attempting to maintain dominance, or it may try to appease the minority in a fashion that does not threaten its own power position. Relations among minority groups themselves are dynamic. This results in changing reactions and relationships as these groups compete with one another for political, social, and eco-

[2]Such "interaction" is a complex process in that an individual may be a member of several minority groups simultaneously, as well as belong to a majority group, for example, a person might be a middle-class, white, female, non-Protestant, mentally ill patient.

nomic resources that the majority groups possess. Whatever the reactions, majority-minority as well as interminority relations are highly volatile, resulting in changing intergroup relations and thereby contributing to the general process of social change. Majority-minority group relations may therefore be viewed as a major source of social dynamics and change.

Minority Groups and Social Policy

Minority group differentiation may be seen as the major source of social problems in society. Racism, sexism, the economic deprivation of the aged, ethnic discrimination, crime, and mental illness are among its major consequences. Insofar as the reduction of minority group differentiation contributes to the possible solution of these problems, this topic is inherently related to questions of practical public policy. The sociological analysis of minority group relations is a highly relevant and practical process by definition; it is not simply a theoretical exercise. This work focuses on the analysis of these relations in order to deal with the real and practical problems they represent. Accordingly, minority group differentiation is basically a matter of political, social, and economic policy because it represents a major source of social problems. Minority group problems and social policy are closely interrelated.

CONCLUSIONS

In this discussion we have outlined the manner in which minority groups are created by elites under particular historical and cultural circumstances, primarily for economic and material purposes. As a consequence, minority group differentiation represents the basis of social organization, stratification, social control, underlying values, the foundation and development of a society, interpersonal relationships, social dynamics and change, and social policy. The universality of this creation process is a basic issue in the general understanding of society and social organization. Consequently, the study of minority groups is relevant to the general understanding of social organization, the dynamics of social change, and related matters of public policy. Minority group differentiation represents an index of a society's general level of differentiation and consequent social problems. An understanding of minority groups in particular results in an understanding of the basis and dynamics of social organization in general and related questions of social policy.

Minority groups are thus a consequence of general processes; they are highly significant as a result. Before examining them, however, we shall outline some of the theoretical and methodological problems involved in such an analysis.

STUDY QUESTIONS

1. Delineate all the minority and majority groups of which you are a member. Outline these memberships for another person you know, and:
   (a) Show how these factors define your relationship.
   (b) Show how these factors define your social interaction.
   (c) Describe how they operate at the group level in society.
   (d) Trace historically how these factors came to operate at the group level in this fashion.
   (e) State your conclusions about minority group relations from (a) through (d) above.

READINGS

DWORKIN, A. G., and R. J. DWORKIN (eds.), *The Minority Report. An Introduction to Racial, Ethnic, and Gender Relations.* New York: Praeger, 1976, Part 1.

FELLOWS, D. K., *A Mosaic of America's Ethnic Minorities.* New York: Wiley, 1972, Introduction.

GITTLER, J. B., (ed.), *Understanding Minority Groups.* New York: Wiley, 1956, I.

GORDON, M. M., *Assimilation in American Life, The Role of Race, Religion, and National Origin.* New York: Oxford University Press, 1964, Chapter 2.

GRIESSMAN, B. E., *Minorities, A Text with Readings in Intergroup Relations.* Hinsdale: Dryden, 1975, Chapter 1.

HOWARD, J. R., (ed.), *Awakening Minorities, American Indians, Mexican Americans, Puerto Ricans.* New Brunswick: Transaction, 1970, Introduction.

HUNT, C. I., and L. WALKER,, *Ethnic Dynamics, Patterns of Intergroup Relations in Various Societies.* Homewood: Dorsey, 1974, Chapter 1.

MAKIELSKI, S. J., Jr., *Beleagured Minorities, Cultural Policies in America.* San Francisco: Freeman, 1973, Part One.

MARDEN, C. F., and G. MEYER, *Minorities in American Society*. New York: Van Nostrand, (4th ed.) 1968, Chapters 1, 2.

MARTIN, J. G., and C. W. FRANKLIN, *Minority Group Relations*. Columbia: Merrill, 1973, Chapter 1.

NEWMAN, W. M. *American Pluralism. A study of Minority Groups and Social Theory*. New York: Harper, 1973, Chapter 1.

3

Problems
of
Bias and Method

Given the extent to which minority groups are part of the social system and subject to widespread prejudice, stereotyping, and discrimination, it is difficult to understand minority group relations in a nonbiased manner. Nonwhites, for example, are defined as incompetent, women as emotional, children as childish, the aged as senile, non-WASPs as clannish, the lower classes as dirty, and the deviants as unnatural or evil. These stereotypes, furthermore, are reinforced by particular disciplines such as psychiatry, child psychology, gerontology, ethnic studies, and criminology in the name of "science," thereby lending credence to these biased beliefs. As a result, it is extremely easy for the individual to believe that these characteristics are, in fact, "real."

Minority group differentiation and relations are complex and multidimensional phenomena. They operate in this atmosphere of bias and

19

stereotyping, making both majority and minority groups resistant to overt examination. Problems of method thus arise in the attempt to study and understand these relations. In this chapter we shall discuss these problems of attitude and method, as well as possible ways to minimize them, before analyzing these phenomena ourselves. We begin with attitudinal problems.

PROBLEMS OF ATTITUDE

Antiminority prejudice and stereotypes are part of society on a wide basis. They operate on the cultural level, within science, academia, and, obviously, within the individual. In this discussion we shall outline both the foundation and the extent of these attitudinal problems, beginning at the cultural level.

Cultural Bias

The bias against minorities exists most powerfully, perhaps, at the cultural level in a society wherein majority groups define minorities as their opposite, and therefore "legitimately" subject to control and exploitation. In America, WASP emphases on materialism, education, thrift, hard work, physical prowess, puritanism, moralism, "whiteness," the protestant ethic, and behavioral conformity represent the foundation of attitudes towards minorities insofar as these groups are defined as the opposite of, or lacking in these qualities. Such values represent the basis of a society which is racist, sexist, age oriented, ethnocentric, class based, and punitive. Minority group differentiation is based on the society's dominant value system and is very much part of the social structure as a result. This cultural bias makes it extremely difficult to analyze minority group relations in a nonbiased fashion.

Cultural bias is also basic to the society's institutional structure. Racist, sexist, age-oriented, ethnocentric, class-based, behavior-control norms, values, stereotypes, and forms of discrimination operate in the family, religion, education, economic system, politics, forces of law and order, the media, and scientific enterprise through the fundamental processes of socialization (learning), and social control. Minority group differentiation is basic to the society's institutional system both in structure (social control) and process (socialization—the perpetuation of negative stereotypes). This system is self-reinforcing and highly interrelated, maintaining notions of minority group differences, inferiority, and consequent "legitimate" discrimination in a stable and pervasive fashion throughout the social system. Institutionalized prejudice and discrimination make it extremely difficult for an individual to appreciate the widespread existence and exploitation of a variety of minorities in the society.

Scientific Bias

Cultural bias continues to be strongly reinforced by "scientific" notions of group differences based on physiological and cultural factors. Racial differences have been viewed as physiologically "real" by biologists, zoologists, geneticists, and Social Darwinists while the apparent cultural inferiority of nonwhites has been developed and supported by anthropologists and "learned" societies.[1] Such orientations, however, are not simply relics of the past. Contemporary versions include attempts to validate a genetic approach to racial differences in intelligence, the weakness of black culture and family structure, and to the ethnocentric notions of westernization, underdevelopment, and modernization.[2] Assumed physiological differences (for example, strength and intelligence characteristics) have also been applied to women, children, adolescents, and in particular, to deviants, while concepts such as the "culture of poverty" have been used in reference to the lower classes.[3] The "physical realty" of minority groups has been developed and reinforced by science.

Science has also contributed to the "reality" of minority groups by developing specialized subfields such as child psychology, the psychology of adolescence, gerontology, anthropology (reinforcing the split between traditional and modern, that is, the primitive and the civilized), ethnic studies, criminology, the sociology of deviant behavior, and even, minority group relations. To the extent that such specialties reinforce the view that these groups are different, they lead to the development of experts and specialized theories, and result in seg-

---

[1] For a useful discussion of this see M. Banton, *Race Relations* (New York: Basic Books, 1967), Chapter 2.

[2] See A. R. Jensen, "How Much Can We Boost IQ and Scholastic Achievement?" *Harvard Educational Review*, 39, (1969); W. Ryan, *Blaming the Victim* (New York: Pantheon, 1971); T. B. Bottomore, "Capitalism, Socialism and Development," in T. B. Bottomore, *Sociology as Social Criticism* (New York: William Morrow & Co., 1976), pp. 55–71.

[3] See J. S. Chafetz, *Masculine/Feminine or Human?* (Itasca: Peacock, 1974), Chapter 1; S. Firestone, *The Dialectic of Sea. The Case for Feminine Revolution* (New York: William Morrow, 1970), Chapter 4; H. J. Eysenck, *Crime and Personality* (Boston: Houghton Mifflin, 1964); O. Lewis, *The Children of Sanchez* (Hamondsworth: Penguin Books, 1961).

mented views of social problems in contrast to structural analyses of the minority group situation. They tend to reinforce and perpetuate the separate reality of each minority group and legitimize its continued existence as different and real.

Problems have also been caused by the major focus on attitudes toward specific minorities, ignoring the institutional structure behind discrimination. Until recently, for example, sociologists concentrated on racist attitudes,[4] psychologists focused on prejudiced personality types,[5] and psychoanalysts examined the sexual basis of personality structure.[6] Social scientists have also begun to explore implications of the "labeling" approach to deviance—the manner in which particular groups "create" deviance by defining or labeling particular forms of behavior as deviant.[7] These approaches are useful in highlighting the attitudes of majority group members toward minorities, particularly in the process of stereotyping, but they run the risk of ignoring the structural aspects of discrimination and may reinforce the psychological reality of these minorities by emphasizing assumed personality differences. Such an attitudinal approach tends to overlook the institutional structure of minority group differentiation—the *basis* of the problem as a whole.

Analyses of minority groups have changed markedly in emphasis beginning with the kind of physiological assumptions just described, moving to an attitudinal and psychological orientation, through an emphasis on group factors—the social-psychological viewpoint,[8] to a more recent structural or sociological emphasis.[9] These changing emphases have not resulted in any theoretical integration; rather, differing conceptualizations of minorities as physical groupings, personality types, group situations, or types of societies have emerged, with little attempt to analyze minority group differentiation as a whole. Such neglect, it may be claimed, has hampered the comprehensive understanding of minority group relations and has contributed instead to the reinforcement of their separate reality.

[4]For a summary see F. R. Westie, "Race and Ethnic Relations, in R. E. L. Faris, ed., *Handbook of Modern Sociology* (Chicago: Rand McNally, 1964).

[5]See G. W. Allport, *The Nature of Prejudice* (Cambridge: Addison-Wesley, 1958).

[6]For a discussion of this see B. Friedan, *The Feminine Mystique* (New York: Dell, 1964), Chapter 5.

[7]See H. S. Becker, *The Other Side: Perspectives on Deviance* (New York: Free Press, 1964).

[8]See I. D. Rinder, "Minority Orientations: An Approach to Intergroup Relations Theory through Social Psychology," *Phylon*, 26, (1965), 5–17.

[9]See P. L. van den Berghe, *Race and Racism* (New York: Wiley, 1967).

Science has made the study of minority group relations problematic in its physiological approach to these groups. The development of specialized subfields, emphasis upon an attitudinal type of analysis, and marked changes in orientation represents scientific bias and is a major problem in trying to understand this topic.

Academic Bias

Bias in the academic setting, particularly in the social sciences, also makes studying minority groups difficult. Many, if not most, courses on this topic have been taught by majority group members with resultant problems of individual bias. An obvious problem is the danger of an assimilationist, "blame-the-victim" orientation toward minorities (blaming minorities for their own deprived situation). Considering the extent of racial, sexual, cultural, and socioeconomic segregation in educational institutions, such teaching takes place in a relatively homogeneous environment and the learning opportunities are therefore strictly limited.

As pointed out earlier, academic materials on minorities are severely restricted in range and viewpoint. Coverage has generally been limited to racial and ethnic groups, most material is written by majority group members, many of whom have been elitist and assimilationist in orientation, while the concept "minority" has been applied primarily to those who have reacted to their own subordinate position, thereby ignoring the more passive groups. Defining minorities on the basis of group size rather than a lack of power has been a problem until recently, reflecting the general absence of a critical, conflict-oriented analysis of minority group exploitation.

In teaching, writing, and analysis, the field of minority group relations has been severely limited by academic bias, reflecting predominantly the viewpoint of majority group members. In order to counterbalance this problem, the perspective we shall adopt in this analysis is to identify with the position and orientation of minority group members as far as possible. Such an emphasis is important in guarding against perpetuating majority group bias within academia. While some may argue that this is simply another type of bias, it is clearly vital to present minority group relations from a nonelitist point of view in order to avoid the pitfalls of majority stereotypes and interests. Otherwise, the problems of academic bias are compounded, contributing further to elitist interests.

Subjective Bias

The most difficult problem in this area, perhaps, is individual, subjective bias. From the beginning of primary socialization in the family, an individual learns the "reality" and "validity" of sexual differences, racial inferiority, cultural pride, class-related values, and the moral wisdom of behavioral conformity. These norms are reinforced through sanctions (rewards and punishments), using a number of assumptions: physical, cultural, and behavioral inferiority attributed to minority groups and assumed negative consequences of a wide range of deviant behavior. This learning process is further reinforced in school and neighborhood settings, in the church, on the job, and in the media. The scapegoating function of prejudice and discrimination as these operate through the frustration-aggression process further reinforces and legitimates the "reality" of minority groups.[10] Minority group roles are also emphasized in varying group identities which come to the fore in situations of intergroup competition, tension, and conflict. The widespread existence of institutionalized minority group differentiation also supports the "reality" and "validity" of their existence.

Considering the general operation of these psychological, group, and institutional factors, it is extremely difficult for an individual to reject their validity and perceive such differentiations as exploitive, false, and as a function of elite-majority domination. Minority group discrimination and differences are so much part of the system, it is predictable that individuals will cling to their "reality" and "legitimacy." Subjective bias thus poses the greatest problem, perhaps, for readers attempting to understand minority group relations.

The study of minority group relations is beset with problems of cultural, scientific, academic, and subjective bias. The "reality" and "legitimacy" of minority group differentiation are reinforced by general cultural values, the institutional structure, scientific enterprise, academic settings, and individual processes such as socialization, scapegoating, and group identity. The individual needs to be aware of and break out of these social molds in order to analyze and understand this general form of differentiation, domination, and exploitation. It is with such a perspective that our analysis is concerned. Before discussing it, however, we shall discuss the methodological problems that are involved in the study of minority group relations.

[10]For a discussion of frustration-aggression as it applies to racism, see J. Dollard, *Caste and Class in a Southern Town* (Garden City: Doubleday, 1957).

PROBLEMS OF METHOD

The study of minority group relations is complicated not only by problems of bias, but with methodological difficulties as well. Problems with definition, and study of such groups abound, resulting in limited perspectives and levels of insight.

Problems of Definition

As we have already pointed out, many definitions of minorities are limited in their view of these groups because they are based on the premise of restricted size (that is, smaller than the majority) and on criteria such as race and/or ethnicity. Other approaches are broad, identifying minority group differentiation with ethnicity.[11] Earlier approaches, as we have indicated, defined minorities almost exclusively on the basis of assumed physiological differences. Consequently, conceptualization of minority group relations on the basis of *power* and discrimination is a comparatively recent approach.

Such limited, unclear, and physiologically-based definitions have obviously resulted in a number of problems: inconsistent conceptualizations, limited awareness of minorities, elitist views of minorities, and restricted insight into minority group relations. Clear and widely-based definitions are required to broaden the focus of the social sciences in this area and integrate diverse theoretical viewpoints.

Methodological Difficulties:

Minority group relations are obviously complex phenomena. They are multidimensional with a number of group types involved (physical, cultural, economic, and behavioral). Individuals may be members of several minority and majority groups simultaneously, while intergroup relations occur at a number of different levels—individual, group, and institutional. This topic is complex and multidimensional, resulting in methodological as well as conceptual problems which are aggravated by the limited material available. Difficulties with biased contexts, lack of historical, structural, and comparative material in the social sciences, and the general neglect of practical policy implications are some of the problems. What, for example, are the most appropriate empirical in-

[11]See E. K. Francis, *Interethnic Relations, An Essay in Sociological Theory* (New York: Elsevier, 1976).

dices of these relations and how does the researcher overcome group sensitivity, establish rapport, and deal with subjective bias on all levels of analysis? Such issues are crucial to the more accurate understanding of social differentiation throughout society and to the associated matters of public policy.

CONCLUSIONS

In this chapter we have outlined some of the major problems involved in the understanding of minority group relations: cultural, scientific, academic, subjective bias, problems of definition, and resultant methodological difficulties. Minority groups are so integral a part of the social system and represent such complex and multidimensional phenomena that it is extremely difficult to analyze minority group relations in a nonbiased and adequate fashion. The student needs to be aware of the difficulties with reference to himself before reading further.

In this work we shall attempt to deal effectively with at least some of these problems by taking a power-conflict approach to a wide range of types of minorities. We shall analyze minority group relations on a number of dimensions (historical, demographic, attitudinal, institutional, and social movement), and use a number of conceptual approaches (psychological, social-psychological, and sociological). All of these will be applied to the complexity and changing dynamics of majority-minority and interminority relations. In this manner we shall abstract major factors behind the structure and dynamics of minority group relations, and overcome some of the dangers of bias and method. We shall concentrate on minorities as groups singled out on the basis of overt distinguishing characteristics and subject to high levels of institutionalized discrimination and exploitation. This is a *specialized* definition of minorities, focusing on power relations and labeling. Thus, it will become obvious that poverty, deviance, sexual and age differences, and ethnic prejudice have existed for many centuries. However, this does not automatically imply specialized, institutionalized minority group status. Groups smaller in size than a society's majority have existed since time immemorial. However, large-scale, organized, institutionalized, and rationalized discrimination are fairly recent phenomena. Given the devastating effects of such prejudice and discrimination by power elites, it is particularly important to analyze these phenomena within the context of a critical, power-relations perspective, highlighting the major societal, institutional, and individual factors behind them. While other approaches have focused on particular sets of factors (that is, attitudes, reactions, and demographic variables), it is the social creation of minorities as a general process with which we are concerned so that we may highlight the foundations of the minority group problem and its possible solutions. Given the kinds of bias that have masked this general process, it would be very meaningful to attempt to overcome them by explicating the creation of minority groups in general without being hindered by limited definitions.

STUDY QUESTIONS

1. Select a minority group of which you are a member and another which does not apply to you. With respect to the "relations" between these groups, proceed to delineate:
   (a) Major problems of cultural, scientific, and academic bias.
   (b) Your own subjective problems in understanding them.
   (c) Specific definitional and methodological problems involved.
   (d) Specific steps you might take to overcome problems (a) through (c).
2. Discuss some of the major conclusions you draw from this analysis regarding general problems involved in the study of minority group relations.

READINGS

BLALOCK, H. M., JR., *Toward a Theory of Minority-Group Relations.* New York: Capricorn Books, 1970, Chapter 1.

FELLOWS, D. K., *A Mosaic of America's Ethnic Minorities.* New York: Wiley, 1972, Chapter 1.

GELFAND, D. E. and R. D. LEE (eds.), *Ethnic Conflicts and Power: A Cross-National Perspective.* New York: Wiley, 1973, Part 1.

GITTLER, J. B., (ed.), *Understanding Minority Groups.* New York: Wiley, 1956, Part VIII.

GRIESSMAN, B. E., *Minorities. A Text with Readings in Intergroup Relations.* Hinsdale: Dryden, 1975, Chapter 2.

MARDEN, C. R. and G. MEYER, *Minorities in American Society.* New York: Van Nostrand, (4th ed.), 1968, Chapter 2.

MARTIN, J. G., and C. W. FRANKLIN, *Minority Group Relations.* Columbus: Merrill, 1973, Chapter 1.

NEWMAN, W. M., *American Pluralism, A Study of Minority Groups and Social Theory.* New York: Harper, 1973, Chapter 2.

SCHERMERHORN, R. A., *Comparative Ethnic Relations: A Framework for Theory and Research.* New York: Random House, 1970, Appendix 2.

SUMMARY
OF
SECTION ONE

In this introductory discussion we have described minority groups as any group that is defined by an elite as different and/or inferior on the basis of certain perceived characteristics and is consequently treated in a negative fashion. Minority group relations, accordingly, may be viewed as the interaction (individual, group, or institutional) between such groups. Our emphasis, then, is on minorities as "defined," "created," and "maintained" by particular power elites on the basis of assumed physical, cultural, economic, and behavioral differences (that is, assumed differences and/or inferiority).

We saw minority groups raising the issues of universality and visibility as they revealed the extent of social differentiation (inequality) in society. We also indicated the degree to which they represent the basis of social organization, stratification, social control, cultural values, societal development, interpersonal relations, social dynamics and change, and social policy. We concluded that minority group differentiation is an index of a society's general level of differentiation and consequent social problems. Minorities are a basic part of the social structure. An understanding of them consequently results in an appreciation of the basis and dynamics of social organization and related policy questions.

Minority group relations are not easy to analyze. Attitudinal problems of cultural, scientific, academic, and subjective bias distort their image in society. Difficulties regarding definition and method also complicate any attempt to study them empirically. Since minorities are such an integral part of society, it is extremely difficult to define and analyze them in a nonbiased fashion.

Given the sociological importance of minority group relations as well as problems of bias and method, we shall attempt to apply a particular analytical model to their understanding. This consists of major factors—societal, group, and individual—which appear to define the process by which groups are defined as minorities. Major dimensions of the minority group differentiation which results—historical, demographic, attitudinal, institutional, and social movements —will then be analyzed with respect to a range of major types of minorities—physical, cultural, economic, and behavioral. Dynamics of the interaction among these groups as well as majority-minority relations will be examined, focusing on their contribution to social change (that is, the structure of intergroup relations) within society at large. We shall analyze the structure and dynamics of minority group relations on all major levels in society and refer to many of the major types of minorities. In so doing, greater insight into the social system and intergroup relations within it is anticipated, contributing to an understanding of social policy issues.

We proceed to apply this analytical model by defining our basic concepts, outlining major characteristics of the minorities we shall study, and discussing major approaches to them in the next section of our analysis.

Section Two

DEFINITIONS AND THEORIES

4

Concepts and Definitions

A major methodological problem discussed in Chapter 3 was the definition of concepts connected with minority group relations. We highlighted limitations of criteria (minorities based on group size), range (a focus on race and ethnicity), and the emphasis of earlier approaches on the "physiological reality" of minorities. Definitions thus illustrate problems of bias and method. We shall deal with some of these problems by analyzing recent definitions and developing our own. We shall focus specifically on the terms "minority group," "majority group," "physical minority," "cultural minority," "economic minority," "behavioral minority," "minority group relations," and "majority-minority relations." Our emphasis is upon the creation of (or the social definition of) social groups by elites (majorities) on the basis of certain perceived characteristics (that is, assumed physical, cultural, economic and behavioral differences) which become the foundation of exploitation and discrimination. We shall take a labeling-power view of minorities and their consequent relations.

Minority

What is a "minority"? The term has been popularly confused with groups which are smaller in size than the majority. According to this view, minorities consist of all groups in a society which are numerically smaller than the majority of the population. Such a definition is clearly limited on a number of accounts. Some societies contain elites controlling them that are much smaller than the majorities (for example, whites in Rhodesia and South Africa), while an individual may belong to several minority groups simultaneously (race, class, and ethnicity), making group size a relatively insignificant factor. Given the general unimportance of the size element, dimensions such as power and discrimination require discussion since minorities are primarily a product of these factors. The term is also complicated by those situations in which minorities are given the opportunity to assimilate economically, socially, and politically into the larger society (white ethnic groups) but believe in the viability of their own culture and choose not to assimilate. Group awareness and self-definitions of minorities themselves are a dimension of minority group status also. Minority group relations are influenced by the extent to which they are defined as different (physically, culturally, economically, and behaviorally) from majority elites. Assumed group characteristics are related to minorities as well. The dimensions of size, power, discrimination, group awareness, self-definition, and assumed group differences are all related to the minority group situation.

A number of writers have used these dimensions in their definition of minority. Schermerhorn, for example, has attempted to clarify the relationship between size and power as the basis of his approach. Minorities are low on both dimensions while majority groups are rated high on both.[1] Such an approach is useful but the relationship between these axes, by Schermerhorn's own admission, requires further definition and tends to become cumbersome as a result. However, it illustrates the need to relate size to power.

Several writers emphasize the salience of power differentials and discrimination in their definition of minority. Wirth refers to "collective

[1]R. A. Schermerhorn, *Comparative Ethnic Relations: A Framework for Theory and Research* (New York: Random House, 1970), pp. 12–17.

discrimination,"[2] Wagley and Harris emphasize the "low esteem" in which minorities are held by "dominant segments of the society,"[3] Blalock, Lieberson, and van den Berghe highlight the extent to which minorities lack resources and consequent power,[4] Dworkin and Dworkin view "differential power" and "differential . . . treatment" as basic qualities of minority groups,[5] Makielski outlines the extent to which minorities are subject to institutional control,[6] Marden and Meyer refer to the "imposed status" of minorities,[7] Martin and Franklin emphasize their "subordinate position in society,"[8] Newman discusses institutionalized discrimination,[9] while Simpson and Yinger claim that majority-minority situations are a question of power distribution rather than group size.[10] Differential power and discrimination are thus basic characteristics in the minority group situation.

An integral part of the minority group situation is its creation through processes of majority labeling and minority group awareness. One of the earliest definitions, for example, argues that minorities are groups "popularly" defined as such.[11] Wagley and Harris also view minorities as "self-conscious units,"[12] while Dworkin and Dworkin emphasize that these "salient groups" are identifiable on the basis of physical and other criteria and are aware of the "commonality of their fate."[13] Group awareness is thus basic to majority-minority relations. Makielski also underlines the importance of group awareness[14] while

[2]L. Wirth, "The Problem of Minority Groups," in R. Linton, ed., *The Science of Man in the World Crisis* (New York: Columbia University Press, 1945).

[3]C. Wagley and M. Harris, *Minorities in the New World* (New York: Columbia University Press, 1958).

[4]H. M. Blalock, Jr., "A Power Analysis of Racial Discrimination," *Social Forces*, 39 (1960), 53–59; S. Lieberson, "A Societal Theory of Race and Ethnic Relations," *American Sociological Review*, 26 (1961), pp. 902–10; P. L. van den Berghe, *Race and Racism* (New York: Wiley, 1967).

[5]A. G. Dworkin and R. J. Dworkin, eds., *The Minority Report. An Introduction to Racial, Ethnic, and Gender Relations* (New York: Praeger, 1976), p. 17.

[6]S. J. Makielski, Jr., *Beleagured Minorities. Cultural Politics in America* (San Francisco: Freeman, 1973), p. 11.

[7]C. F. Marden and G. Meyer, *Minorities in American Society*, 4th ed. (New York: Van Nostrand, 1973), p. 39.

[8]J. G. Martin and C. W. Franklin, *Minority Group Relations* (Columbus: Merrill, 1973), p. 39.

[9]W. M. Newman, *American Pluralism. A Study of Minority Groups and Social Theory* (New York: Harper & Row, 1973), p. 20.

[10]G. E. Simpson and J. M. Yinger, *Racial and Cultural Minorities: An Analysis of Prejudice and Discrimination*, 4th ed. (New York: Harper & Row, 1972), p. 11.

[11]D. Young, *American Minority Peoples* (New York: Harper, 1932).

[12]Wagley and Harris, *Minorities in the New World*.

[13]Dworkin and Dworkin, *The Minority Report*, pp. 17–23.

[14]Makielski, *Beleagured Minorities*, p. 25.

van den Berghe in his useful definition of the term "race" emphasizes that such groups define themselves and/or are defined by other groups as "different from other groups,"[15] thereby taking a labeling and self-definition approach. Accordingly, minority groups are subject to the process of majority labeling (that is, they are defined as different) and develop group awareness of their common situation (self-definition). Minorities and minority group relations are created through social labeling and self-definitions.

Another dimension is the extent of assumed minority group differences compared with majority elites. Newman, for example, highlights the extent to which a group differs from majority norms as a "measure of its social status."[16] Minorities tend to represent the perceived opposite of majority values, for instance, the nonwhites, the aged, Eastern European Catholics, the poor, and the mentally ill. The higher the perceived difference, the greater the consequent discrimination. In an analysis of American race relations, for example, this author has developed a model of a racial hierarchy based on a particular group's degree of physical similarity (the degree of whiteness), cultural similarity (the degree to which a group differs from the elite in terms of religion, language, values, and institutional structure) and objective similarity (the degree of demographic, economic, and occupational similarity to the elite—the minority's resources).[17] Consequently, the greater a minority's perceived dissimilarity compared with a majority group, the lower its status in the society. Perceived physical, cultural, economic, and behavioral majority-minority differences represent the basis of minority group differentiation.

We have delineated three major dimensions of minority group status: power and discrimination, social labeling and group awareness, and the extent of assumed group differences. We have also indicated that group size is not a satisfactory basis for classifying particular groups as minorities. Bringing these dimensions together, it is possible to define a *minority* as *any group that views itself and/or is defined by a majority power elite as different and/or inferior on the basis of assumed physical, cultural, economic, and/or behavioral characteristics and is subject to exploitation and discrimination.*[18] Minorities are *created* by majority elites, subjected to discrimination and exploitation for economic reasons, and develop their own group awareness as a result.

[15]van den Berghe, *Race and Racism,* p. 9.

[16]Newman, *American Pluralism,* p. 20.

[17]G. C. Kinloch, *The Dynamics of Race Relations, A Sociological Analysis* (New York: McGraw Hill, 1974), p. 171.

[18]This is based on my earlier definition in Kinloch, *The Dynamics of Race Relations,* p. 50.

Majority Group

It is popularly assumed that any society possesses only one majority group. References are made, for example, to the "silent majority," the "white majority," and "majority rights" in contrast to labels applied to minority groups. Any society, however, possesses a number of majorities—physical, cultural, economic, and behavioral—insofar as there are a number of groups which define others as different (that is, inferior) and possess the power to discriminate against them, that is, the labelers and discriminators. Major examples include whites, adults, parents, males, WASPs (white, Anglo-Saxon, Protestants), middle and upper classes, and agencies of social and/or legal control. These groups are all considered majorities because of their power to label particular groups and exploit them.

Once again, a number of dimensions are highlighted by various authors—group size, exploitation and discrimination, norm enforcement or labeling, and the definition of themselves as archetypes or exemplars (the view of themselves as "normal" and minorities as "abnormal"). The relationship between size and power is dealt with by Schermerhorn: majority groups are dominant with respect to both dimensions.[19] Elites are also dominant but only with respect to the power dimension. The analytical difference between majorities and elites highlights problems associated with the use of group size in defining minorities. Our approach concentrates primarily on the power dimension and views elites as power majorities.

The power superiority of majorities is also emphasized by a number of writers. Dworkin and Dworkin, for example, perceive "the dominant majority" as based on power resources with a resultant ability to discriminate against minorities;[20] others view majority institutions as "control institutions;"[21] while several analysts point to the superordinate power position of majority groups vis à vis the minorities they control and discriminate against.[22] The basic dimensions underlying majority-minority relations are power and discrimination.

A major function of majority groups, as Newman has indicated, is the enforcement of their own norms or mores.[23] Thus, questions of law and order and conformity—central issues of social control—are the

[19]Schermerhorn, *Comparative Ethnic Relations,* p. 13.

[20]Dworkin and Dworkin, *The Minority Report,* p. 20

[21]Makielski, *Beleagured Minorities,* p. 11.

[22]See, for example, Marden and Meyer, *Minorities in American Society,* p. 47; Martin and Franklin, *Minority Group Relations,* p. 40; Newman, *American Pluralism,* p. 21.

[23]Newman, *American Pluralism,* p. 21.

basic focus of majority groups whether referring to whites, males, adults, or the police. A basic dimension of majority-minority relations is the enforcement of majority norms within the context of power and discrimination. This enforcement applies even to personal relations within the family, as Firestone has pointed out,[24] since sexual, marital, and parent-child relationships are all based upon power. A central concern of majority groups, then, is *norm enforcement.*

Majority groups not only define minorities as different and inferior, they also, by implication, perceive themselves as normal and superior. Newman, for example, feels that majority groups represent most highly valued social traits.[25] In this manner, majorities define themselves as normal and superior—the *reference points* for their definition of minorities as abnormal and inferior. Thus, majority group ethnocentrism—belief in the superiority of one's own group characteristics—is the basis of the social creation of minorities and represents the core of the minority group "problem" in the strength and consistency of these belief systems.

In this discussion of majority groups we have emphasized a number of basic characteristics: exploitation and discrimination, norm enforcement or labeling, and the definition of self as archetype or exemplar. Bringing these together, it is possible to define *majority groups* as *any power group that defines itself as normal and superior and others as abnormal and inferior on the basis of certain perceived characteristics, and exploits or discriminates against them in consequence.* Our emphasis is upon the social creation of minorities based on perceived qualities by a power group that exploits and controls them.

We have defined minority and majority groups and proceed next to definitions of particular types of minorities—physical, cultural, economic, and behavioral.

Physical Minorities

Physical minorities are *groups defined as abnormal and inferior on the basis of assumed physiological characteristics such as race, sex, and age and are consequently subject to control and discrimination.* Racial beliefs refer to inherent physical characteristics—that is, color and physique—assumed to be closely related to intellectual and

---

[24]Firestone, *The Dialectic of Sex. The Case for Feminist Revolution* (New York: Bantam, 1971, Chapter 4.

[25]Newman, *American Pluralism,* p. 21.

behavioral characteristics.[26] Whites, for example, have tended to believe that nonwhites are physiologically inferior compared to themselves (that is, brain size, physique, and so on) with inferior intellectual, moral, and cultural capability as a result. The assumed relationship between physical, intellectual, and cultural characteristics is high and viewed as causal. These assumed characteristics become the basis of prejudice and severe forms of discrimination.

Sexual minorities, specifically women, have been subject to similar labeling. Given the natural reproductive difference between the sexes, the demands and limitations associated with reproduction, the dependency of children, and consequent dependency on males for resources,[27] women have been defined as essentially different from and inferior to males. Assumed differences in physique, intelligence, and personality as a consequence, result in a sexual division of labor in society—a sex class system.[28] In a similar manner to race, sexism is based on the assumed physiological characteristics of women and their relationship to physical, intellectual, and, in this case, personality factors and inferiority. Institutionalized control and discrimination result. Physiological differences become "translated" into assumed inferiority and discrimination as a result. Such labeling is not automatic. Some societies have been matriarchal with relatively equalitarian relationships between the sexes.

Another physiological dimension used to define groups is age. We are specifically concerned with children, adolescents, and the aged. Here the labeling process is similar. Physiological development (maturation) is assumed to be correlated with particular levels of physical, intellectual, and personality capability. With adulthood as the norm, groups which deviate to one side (that is, to children and adolescents) or the other (to the aged) are subject to labeling, control, and discrimination. Roles and groupings based on age emerge and become the foundation of discrimination. This too is not automatic. Societies exist where the aged are given high status and, as Firestone points out, childhood did not exist in the Middle Ages.[29] Margaret Mead has also indicated the extent to which adolescence is associated with western culture.[30] Roles and minority groups are created in specific social contexts.

Physical minorities are based on the assumed significance of physi-

[26]van den Berghe, *Race and Racism,* p. 9.
[27]Firestone, *The Dialectic of Sex,* pp. 8–9.
[28]Firestone, *The Dialectic of Sex,* Chapter 1.
[29]Firestone, *The Dialectic of Sex,* p. 86.
[30]M. Mead, *Coming of Age in Samoa* (New York: Morrow, 1928).

ological differences relating to color and physique, the reproductive function, and age which in turn are assumed to be correlated with inferior physiological, intellectual, personality, and cultural characteristics representing the basis of minority group roles and discrimination. While physical and cultural factors are obviously related, this type of minority is identified socially on the basis of assumed physiological characteristics. Cultural minorities, on the other hand, are defined primarily in terms of assumed cultural traits—their forms of political, economic, and social behavior, and tend to be labeled by elites from within the same race group.

Cultural Minorities

Assumed cultural differences and inferiority (way of life) represent the basis of cultural minorities, specifically ethnic groups. Since ethnic majorities, in particular WASPs, are highly ethnocentric in attitude, ethnic prejudice and discrimination continue to be social problems. *Cultural minorities*, then, are *groups defined by an elite as different and inferior on the basis of assumed cultural characteristics and are consequently subject to control and discrimination.*

Examples of severe cultural discrimination are well known: policies of genocide, tribal warfare and discrimination in Africa, and the extent to which discrimination continues to operate in American society—the ethnocentrism and anti-Semitism of WASPs, rejection of immigrant groups, and denigration of cultural groups which are not individualistic, materialistic, and capitalistic oriented. Traditions, customs, and ways of life which are different are variously defined as uncivilized, underdeveloped, weak, and/or inferior, and requiring civilization and development. In this manner, cultural ethnocentrism under conditions of intergroup competition and differential power becomes the basis of domination.[31]

It is important to emphasize that racial and ethnic minorities are interrelated. Cultural ethnocentrism reinforces racism while racial groups are subdifferentiated by culture. Thus in the United States whites who are similar in culture to the WASP elite (that is, the Scots, Swedes, Germans, Dutch, and Jews) have experienced relatively high levels of assimilation and socioeconomic success while others (for example, Southerners and Italians) have been less successful and have lower

[31]See D. L. Noel, "A Theory of the Origin of Ethnic Stratification," *Social Problems,* 16, no. 2 (1968), pp. 157–71.

assimilation and higher stereotyping.[32] Furthermore, certain physical features are associated with particular ethnic groups as the basis of the labeling process. In societies which are undifferentiated by race, ethnicity may represent the basis of discrimination and intergroup conflict (for example, Catholics and Protestants in Northern Ireland).

Minorities may be based on assumed cultural differences resulting in high levels of discrimination and conflict. Ethnic conflict may exist when racism is absent while racial groups may be subdifferentiated by cultural differences vis à vis the society's dominant elite. In all of this minority groups are created and discriminated against in reference to the power elite's definition of itself as being culturally superior.

Economic Minorities

Economic minorities reflect a society's economic system—its division of labor—as it relates to the processes of *role assignment* and *rewards*. Traditional societies tend to have economic systems which are not highly specialized and are more integrated with the society's kinship system. Property is relatively minimal and tends to be communal rather than individually owned. As a result, the society is relatively undifferentiated in property and role structure. As societies grow in size and begin to move from the horticultural and agrarian to the industrial, the division of labor increases as does private property.[33] Society becomes increasingly differentiated in its role structure and property distribution, resulting, according to Marx, in "ownership of the means of production" by a specific class—the bourgeoisie—with the proletarian class providing the labor supply for these capitalists.[34] In this manner new classes or economic-based minorities are created by changes in a society's economic system or mode of production. A socioeconomic hierarchy is created in which particular occupational roles are accorded varying levels of prestige and economic reward within the context of a capitalistic economic system in which material resources are subject to corporate elite control. Such a hierarchy tends to be relatively rigid and self-perpetuating, since the resources necessary to gain the educational qualifications required by higher status occupations are also differentially distributed. Stratification tends to be relatively stable and

---

[32]Kinloch, *The Dynamics of Race Relations,* p. 174.

[33]For more detailed discussion see G. Lenski, *Power and Privilege, A Theory of Social Stratification,* (New York: McGraw-Hill, 1966).

[34]K. Marx and F. Engels, *Manifesto of the Communist Party* (New York: International Publishers, 1932).

the poor, working classes, and unemployed are an integral part of contemporary industrial society. It can also be said that even the middle class is an economic minority because its economic resources and access to capital are severely restricted.

This socioeconomic hierarchy not only reflects differential "life chances"—a class's socioeconomic and material conditions[35] —but is also correlated with differences in "life style"—norms, status symbols, types of language, dress, behavior, aspiration, and so on. The class system possesses a subcultural dimension with associated forms of prejudice and stereotyping. As a result the lower classes are often considered dirty, naive, loud-mouthed, present rather than future-oriented, lazy, shiftless, and unreliable—therefore unsuitable for occupational roles other than unskilled labor. Residential segregation by income level along with differential community resources and institutions reinforce this negative stereotyping. The "economic suitability" of individuals for particular occupational roles, at least in broad terms, tends to reflect their class background, as related to their educational resources and class-based behavior.

Bringing this discussion together, it is possible to define *economic minorities* as *any group that is defined by an economic elite as different and inferior on the basis of assumed economic characteristics (that is, resources and behavior) and is consequently subject to control and discrimination.* We shall be concerned specifically with the lower classes, the poor, the unemployed, and also the manner in which class is related to other dimensions of minority group status. While economic and behavioral minorities obviously overlap, they are both identified on the basis of assumed behavioral characteristics. The former are defined primarily in terms of assumed occupational-economic behavior while the latter are viewed as deviant in their social behavior (crime, addiction, mental illness). *Type* of behavior is the important criterion in differentiating the two, with consequent differences in elite reaction and treatment.

Behavioral Minorities

We have referred to the fact that majority groups define themselves as normal and superior with respect to physiology, culture, and economic characteristics. Normality obviously refers to behavior as

---

[35]See *M. Weber: Essays in Sociology,* trans. H. H. Gerth and C. W. Mills, (New York: Oxford University Press, 1946), in particular his discussion of "Class, Status, Party."

well. Groups with the power to enforce particular norms automatically create deviance among those unwilling and/or unable to conform to them. Deviant subgroups are socially produced by the enforcement of particular majority group norms. In this manner, deviant minorities are an integral part of social order, reinforcing in-group conformity and contributing to the evolution of new norms as they challenge the relevance and legitimacy of the status quo. Particular kinds of deviance (for instance, larceny) reflect particular kinds of norms (such as materialism) as well as the society's "social control apparatus"[36] (that is, type of law enforcement agencies). The deviant label, furthermore, is conferred upon individuals and groups with the implication that they are morally inferior, second-rate citizens, and represent a threat to society.[37]

Deviance may be of two major types: *legal deviance* (crime, delinquency); and *social deviance* (sexual, mental illness, addiction). The first represents nonconformity to formal norms—rules which are defined as central to group welfare. Social deviance, on the other hand, consists of breaking group norms and customary behavior—norms which are defined as important, nevertheless, and some of which may eventually emerge as laws. We are dealing here with a continuum of formality and perceived priorities rather than categorical differences.

The creation of deviance is a distinctly political process. Elite interests, norms, and ideology operate in the political arena where they become translated into laws, which, in turn, are implemented by law enforcement agencies and reflect the political structure. Deviant minorities are thus produced within the context of majority group interests and politics.

Deviant behavior is highly correlated by majority groups with other dimensions of minority group status. Nonwhites are subject to higher levels of arrest and incarceration, juveniles are subject to legal limitations, women are presumed more likely to be sexually deviant, particular ethnic groups are assumed to be more crime oriented, and the lower classes and the poor possess few, if any, legal resources to combat legal prejudice and inequity. Behavioral minorities reflect the minority group structure of society.

Bringing the above points together, it is possible to define *behavioral minorities* as *any group that is defined by a power elite as different and inferior on the basis of assumed behavioral characteristics in reference to elite norms and is consequently subject to control and discrimination.*

[36]K. T. Erikson, *Wayward Puritans* (New York: Wiley, 1966), Chapter 1.

[37]R. A. Scott, "A Proposed Framework for Analyzing Deviance as a Property of Social Order," in R. A. Scott and J. D. Douglas, eds. *Theoretical Prospectus on Deviance* (New York: Basic Books, 1972), pp. 9–36.

Minority Group Relations

Members of minorities obviously daily interact with each other on an individual, group, or institutional level. These relations are complex phenomena given the range of minorities in contemporary society and the extent to which individuals belong to a number of minority and majority groups simultaneously. The multidimensionality of minority group relations has yet to be explored.

Within the context of this multifaceted majority-minority group hierarchy, minority group relations are influenced by competition for political, economic, and social resources controlled by elite majorities. Depending upon individual or group position in this hierarchy, and upon related access to these resources, minority group interaction may take a number of forms: passivity, competition, conflict, cooperation, accommodation, coalition, assimilation, and so on. These relations may be complicated by minority group role conflict (that is, conflicting demands made upon one by being a member of several groups simultaneously).

In general, *minority group relations* may be viewed as *the type of interaction (individual, group, or institutional) which occurs among groups defined by majority elites as different and inferior on the basis of assumed physical, cultural, economic, and behavioral characteristics and subject to control and discrimination as a result.*

Majority-Minority Relations

We have indicated the manner in which majorities relate to minority groups on the basis of control, exploitation, and discrimination since these minorities reflect the vested political, social, and economic interests of the majorities. A number of minority group reactions to this are possible: conformity, accommodation, acculturation, amalgamation, assimilation, integration, separatism, or nationalism.[38] Such relations, therefore, are dynamic and changing, and are complicated by the multidimensionality outlined before, representing ongoing cycles of majority control, minority reaction, and changing relations.

In view of these characteristics, it appears reasonable to define *majority-minority relations* as *the type of interaction (individual, group, or institutional) which occurs between power groups that define others as different and inferior on the basis of assumed physical, cul-*

[38]Dworkin and Dworkin, *The Minority Report,* Chapter 6; Marden and Meyer, *Minorities in American Society,* Chapter 2.

44

tural, economic, and behavioral characteristics and subjects them to control and discrimination.

CONCLUSIONS

In this chapter we have defined the basic concepts to be used in the analysis to follow. Majorities are power groups defining themselves as normal and superior, and others as abnormal and inferior on the basis of perceived physical, cultural, economic, and behavioral characteristics, and exploit or discriminate against these minorities. Minority groups are socially created by particular power elites who exploit and control them, consequent relations may be peaceful or conflict ridden, but are dynamic and constantly changing. Majority-minority as well as interminority relations represent intergroup relations within a power context in which physical, cultural, economic, and behavioral criteria are utilized as the basis of group differentiation. We shall attempt to analyze the major factors (societal, group, and individual) behind the processes of social labeling, and discrimination, and see the kinds of relationships which result. In the chapter to follow we shall examine major characteristics of these minorities—historical, demographic, attitudinal, and social movements—and develop a model of minority types. Chapter 6 will outline major approaches to understanding these groupings, while the final chapter in this section will summarize the major characteristics and assumptions delineated in this section of our discussion as a whole.

STUDY QUESTIONS

1. Using a dictionary, look up the major concepts defined in this chapter. Interrelate and compare them with the concept "minority" as we have defined it.
2. Compare physical definitions of the above minorities with the definitions developed in this chapter. What significant differences do you notice?
3. Outline a hierarchy of minorities (with reference to power) present in American society.
4. Interrelate this hierarchy with a hierarchy of relevant majority groups in this society.

5. Delineate the characteristics of majority-minority relations in such a hierarchy.

READINGS

BLALOCK, H. M., "A Power Analysis of Racial Discrimination," *Social Forces,* 39, 1960, pp. 53–59.

DWORKIN, A. G., and R. J. DWORKIN (eds.), *The Minority Report. An Introduction to Racial, Ethnic, and Gender Relations,* New York: Praeger, 1976, Chapters 1–6.

MAKIELSKI, S. J., Jr., *Beleaguered Minorities. Cultural Politics in America,* San Francisco: Freeman, 1973, Chapters 1–4.

MARDEN, C. F., and G. MEYER, *Minorities in American Society,* New York: Van Nostrand, (4th ed.), 1973, Chapters 1, 2.

MARTIN, J. G., and C. W. FRANKLIN, *Minority Group Relations,* Columbus: Merrill, 1973, Chapter 1.

NEWMAN, W. M., *American Pluralism. A Study of Minority Groups and Social Theory,* New York: Harper & Row, 1973, Chapters 1, 2.

SCHERMERHORN, R. A., *Comparative Ethnic Relations: A Framework for Theory and Research,* New York: Random House, 1970, Introduction.

SIMPSON, G. E., and M. J. YINGER, *Racial and Cultural Minorities: An Analysis of Prejudice and Discrimination,* (4th ed.), New York: Harper & Row, 1972, Chapter 1.

VAN DEN BERGHE, P. L., *Race and Racism,* New York: Wiley, 1967, Chapter 1.

WAGLEY, C., and M. HARRIS, *Minorities in the New World,* New York: Columbia University Press, 1958.

WIRTH, L., "The Problem of Minority Groups," in R. Linton (ed.), *The Science of Man in the World Crisis,* New York: Columbia University Press, 1945.

5

Major Types of Minorities

Having defined what minorities represent, we turn to outline major types of minorities and their characteristics. We shall be concerned with six aspects of minority group status:

1. The *historical circumstances* under which each type emerges.
2. *Demographic characteristics* of each such as size, economic, educational, occupational, and political resources.
3. Majority *attitudes* toward each type along with the latter's view of itself and reaction to the former.
4. The major dimensions of *institutionalized discrimination* against each with reference to processes such as social control, socialization, and economic/physical welfare.
5. The reaction of each minority to this control and exploitation in the form of *social movements*.
6. Major types of *group relations* and their changing characteristics including majority-minority interaction as well as relations

among the six major types of minorities (interminority relations).

We shall end our analysis with a typology of these characteristics and general conclusions regarding the "social creation" of particular types of minorities and their subsequent relationships. Using these six dimensions we shall examine the structure of minority group differentiation and relations prior to our analysis of particular societies.

RACIAL MINORITIES

Racial minorities have not always existed; they were created in the eighteenth and nineteenth centuries as specific, segregated, institutionalized groups for purposes of economic exploitation through three major processes: migration, subordination, and importation. As European colonial elites migrated to Africa, Asia, the Americas, and the Pacific, searching for natural resources and, eventually, cheap, unskilled labor to meet their expanding capitalistic needs, they subordinated indigenous populations, used them as labor supplies, and imported other groups for similar purposes. Given the emergence of biology, zoology, and Social Darwinism at this time, the exploitation of local and imported groups was rationalized on the basis of assumed physical, intellectual, and cultural superiority. In this manner "races" or groups based on assumed or perceived physiological inferiority emerged.[1] The general conditions under which they developed were extremely negative: race war, slavery, genocide, and lynching represent major examples. Colonialism, capitalist expansion, and Social Darwinism were basic elements behind the creation of racial minorities by migrant European elites, resulting in racial hierarchies and the "assumed validity" of racism to the present era. Accordingly, American blacks, Indians, Puerto Ricans, and Chicanos have all been created as racial minorities by white colonial migration, subordination, importation, and slavery within the context of capitalist economic exploitation. Racial minorities are produced for economic reasons and continue to represent the vested economic interests of racial elites, rationalized in terms of assumed racial superiority.

Demographically, racial minorities tend to be large, heterogenous, and subject to high levels of political, economic, and social deprivation. Numerically, they are often in the majority as exemplified by

[1]For fuller discussion of these processes see E. F. Frazier, *Race and Culture Contacts in the Modern World* (Boston: Beacon Press, 1965); G. C. Kinloch, *The Dynamics of Race Relations: A Sociological Analysis* (New York: McGraw-Hill, 1974).

typical colonial situations in Southern Africa and (preindependence) Asian societies. Insofar as colonial elites import a variety of racial groups for labor purposes, they may also be heterogeneous and contained within a racial (socioeconomic) hierarchy. This is characteristic of the American situation which contains a variety of racial minorities arranged in a hierarchy with a white-Oriental elite and subordinate Chicano, black, and Indian classes.[2] This kind of minority is normally subject to high levels of economic, political, and to a lesser extent, social discrimination. That is, there is a high correlation between race and economic resources, political power, and social status as dominant race groups strive to protect their vested economic interests inherent in the structure of institutionalized racism. Race tends to operate in a castelike manner, since characteristics based upon assumed physiological factors are highly visible and thereby subject to control. Accordingly, deprivation and discrimination based upon race tend to be most negative, widespread, and stable compared with other types. In general, racial minorities tend to be large, heterogeneous, and subject to high levels of control and exploitation. Race, particularly in colonial societies such as South Africa and the United States, represents the basis of each society's system of stratification and social organization.

Majority racial minority attitudes, based primarily on eighteenth and nineteenth century views produced by biology, zoology, genetics, and Social Darwinism,[3] view subordinate racial minorities as physiologically inferior with respect to physical capacity and condition, brain size, and level of intelligence. Such biological inferiority is linked to cultural inferiority (nonwhites are uncivilized) and behavioral deviance (racial minorities are assumed to be immoral, highly aggressive, and criminally oriented). These attitudes are reinforced by religious puritanism ("white is right") and notions such as manifest destiny (it is the destiny of the civilized to conquer and take over the uncivilized).[4] In heterogeneous societies a racial hierarchy is produced and based on the degree of perceived physical and cultural similarity-dissimilarity compared with the white elite. In America this is evident in a white-Oriental-black-Indian continuum from high to low racial status and economic power. Given the colonial context in which these attitudes operate (that is, a migrant racial elite which subordinates the indigenous population in order to take over natural resources and imports other race groups

---

[2]For further discussion of this hierarchy see Kinloch, *The Dynamics of Race Relations,* Chapter 13.

[3]For a useful discussion of this see M. Banton, *Race Relations* (New York: Basic Books, 1967), Chapter 2.

[4]For an American example of this see D. Brown, *Bury My Heart at Wounded Knee* (New York: Holt, Rinehart & Winston, 1970).

for labor purposes), majority racial orientations tend to be economically based and highly conservative because of their vested material interests in the racial status quo. In general majority racial attitudes represent the rationalization of economic and material exploitation of human beings in terms of assumed physiologically based intellectual, cultural, and behavioral inferiority, reinforced by the protestant ethic.[5]

Minority reaction to racial domination may take a number of forms: apparent acceptance of majority prejudice,[6] the self-denigration involved in this,[7] and gratitude to the majorite elite for its "civilizing" influence and the material benefits of modern society.[8] At the individual psychological level such reactions may involve "blindness to white suppression," self-hatred, and aggression against other minority members as the individual "identifies with his oppressor psychologically."[9] Racial minorities may incorporate majority stereotypes into their views of themselves, particularly at earlier stages of domination when they are subject to extremely high levels of control and economic dependence. Such attitudes, however, are far from static. They are influenced by changing demographic and economic situations. Accordingly, as racial minorities are increasingly assimilated into the majority economic system in the urban-industrial context, they move from a paternalistic to a competitive race relations situation with higher levels of racial tension and conflict as a result.[10] In this manner, intergroup relations become more competitive and threatening as the traditional racial caste system breaks down, and results in higher awareness of racism and its illegitimacy. Consequently, racial minorities begin to reject negative elite stereotypes, arguing for minority rights and equal opportunity as minority group nationalism evolves. Racial elites believe in their own physical and cultural superiority, rejecting integration as dangerous while minorities argue for physical and cultural equality and

[5]For a useful historical analysis of white racial attitudes in America see G. M. Fredrickson, *The Black Image in the White Mind* (New York: Harper & Row, 1971).

[6]I use the word "apparent" advisedly since minorities may appear to conform to majority stereotypes as a way of dealing with their oppression. Behind these "masks," however, they actively develop internal solidity and independence. For a useful example of this with respect to black Americans see J. W. Blassingame, *The Slave Community* (New York: Oxford University Press, 1972).

[7]For an example of this see D. P. Kunene, "African Vernacular Writing—An Essay in Self-Devaluation," *African Social Research,* 9 (1970), 639–59.

[8]G. C. Kinloch, "Changing Black Reaction to White Domination," *Rhodesian History,* 5 (1974), 67–78.

[9]An important example of this is contained in W. H. Grier, and P. M. Cobbs, *Black Rage* (New York: Bantam Books, 1968).

[10]For further discussion of this process see P. L. van den Berghe, *Race and Racism* (New York: Wiley, 1967), chapter I.

the need for integration in order to prevent racial strife.[11] Low interracial communication and high racial conflict result. Majority attitudes, furthermore, may become more nationalistic and racially conservative under these circumstances as they attempt to maximize and control their own vested economic interests.[12] Inevitably, race relations become more competitive and conflict-prone.

We turn to dimensions of institutionalized racism. Institutions represent sets of interlinked organizations developed to meet societal needs such as social control (political, military, and legal institutions), socialization (family, education, media, and religion), and economic-physical needs (economic, medical institutions, and the welfare system). Institutionalized racism represents the extent to which race is the foundation of each institution with respect to institutional access, resources, and stereotypes. In racist societies access to major institutions (politics, education, the economy) is clearly limited by race through segregation and discrimination. Resources (especially the economic) are controlled by the racial elite, and are reinforced by segregation (for example, the racial-community basis of school funding), while racist stereotypes are perpetuated through the media and educational system—institutions controlled by the racial elite. In this manner, the control and exploitation of racial minorities is rationalized (defended) through racist stereotypes within the context of institutionalized racism.[13]

Racial minorities are far from passive; they clearly react to the racial elites controlling them. These reactions consist initially of rebellions and racial wars as indigenous race groups (American Indians, Africans) resist the incursions of migrant colonials. Such violent incidents reinforce elite views of these minorities as savage and barbaric, and consequently, policies of severe control come into being. As colonial societies experience industrialization and urbanization, racial minorities are subject to differing levels of economic assimilation with a range of social movements as a result. Some groups emphasize the need for assimilation into the larger society, others fight for their own power base, the more radical groups argue for separation from the majority, while, as the latter demonstrates its unwillingness to de-institutionalize

[11]For an example of these "polar opposites," see G. C. Kinloch, "White and Black Definitions of the 'Race Problem' in Rhodesia: An Analysis of Underlying Rationales," unpublished M.S.

[12]For an example of this cycle see G. C. Kinloch, "Changing Intergroup Attitudes of Whites as Defined by the Press: The Process of Colonial Adaptation," *Zambezia*, 4, (1975–76), pp. 105–17.

[13]For more detailed discussion of institutionalized racism see Kinloch, *The Dynamics of Race Relations*, chapter 16.

racism, others develop their own type of nationalism.[14] Minority racial movements thus vary from moderate, to radical and assimilationist, to separatist in the wake of varying levels of economic assimilation. At all stages of race relations, however, even under slavery,[15] racial minorities organize against the devastating effects of racism. With economic development, these reactions simply become more varied and, in some cases, more radical.

Both majority-minority and interminority race relations are the interaction between race and the other dimensions of minority group differentiation. The first is closely tied to a society's predominant type of economy and the vested economic interests of the majority elite. van den Berghe, for example, distinguishes between "paternalistic" and "competitive" types of race relations in these terms: the former is characteristic of societies based on an agricultural economy, within which there is little mobility since race defines the society's division of labor. Race relations in this case exhibit a tightly integrated pattern since there is a high level of economic interdependence between the racial castes within the society at large. In contrast, the "competitive" type is most evident in societies based on an industrial urban economy with a high level of competition between the subordinate racial caste and dominant working class. In this situation economic development and a larger dominant elite have led to structural and economic fragmentation, resulting in structural strain and disequilibrium which in turn lead to racial hatred and terrorism. The dominant elite in the first type tends to be a small minority while in the second it is larger. Consequently, there is development of interdependence on nonracial lines and racial conflict and competition increase. Growth in the relative size of the dominant elite in conjunction with increased economic assimilation of the subordinate population thus results in economic differentiation, resultant intergroup competition, and eventually racial conflict.[16] Accordingly, with economic development race relations become more competitive and conflict prone. In the process racial minorities proceed through a number of stages in relation to the dominant majority: from apparent conformity and gratitude, rejection of discrimination, demands for equality and participation, to black nationalism. These stages reflect a society's economic frontiers as it becomes increasingly industrialized.[17]

The racial dimension is closely correlated with other types of mi-

[14]For a useful analysis of black social movements in America see R. Staples, *Introduction to Black Sociology* (New York: McGraw-Hill, 1976), chapter 10.

[15]Blassingame, *The Slave Community.*

[16]van den Berghe, *Race and Racism,* chapter I.

[17]See Kinloch, "Changing Black Reaction to White Domination."

norities. Racism has reinforced sexism through the sexual exploitation of minority group women, and is closely tied to age discrimination through the paternalistic treatment of racial minorities, defining them as "children." Racism reinforces ethnic prejudice as these groups adhere to the racist concept in the context of economic competition. It represents a caste element in stratification, and is highly correlated with deviance in the degree to which it defines the labeling, control, and punishment of "deviant behavior" (that is, the greater proportion of deviants is nonwhite). Racism is thus closely tied to the operation of other forms of prejudice and discrimination.

Specialized racial minorities were created in the eighteenth and nineteenth centuries through migration, subordination, and importation (extremely negative historical conditions). They are large in number and subject to high levels of deprivation, are defined as physically, culturally, and morally inferior, may partially internalize such views but eventually reject them. They are also subject to heavy levels of institutionalized racism, react to the majority through a range of social movements, and experience a number of other types of discrimination. Racial minorities are negatively created for economic purposes, defined as inferior in every way, and are subject to high levels of institutionalized control. With economic development, however, intergroup relations become more competitive and racial conflict ensues. Racism is a basic form of domination with extremely negative consequences.

SEXUAL MINORITIES

It is evident, given the child-bearing function, that a sexual division of labor has existed from the beginning of human society with women assigned family-related roles and men the economic and political functions. However, it can be argued that in traditional societies women were more integrated within the social structure both politically and economically with less sexual segregation and discrimination insofar as the family and society were closely related through the kinship system. In some societies women held important political and religious positions, reinforced by matrilineal descent. It would appear that sexism is more predominant in contemporary industrial society where the material needs of a highly specialized economy have resulted in the evolution of a segregated, specialized female role. Within the context of the nuclear family women are assigned the primary tasks of childrearing, satisfying the husband's emotional and physical needs, and running the household with little or no access to economic or political resources. Accordingly, women have been delegated a psychological role in society within the nuclear family. This role is reinforced by notions of physical, emotional, and intellectual differences with a cultural emphasis on eroticism and romance. In this manner sexist roles may be viewed as an outgrowth of economic development, particularly in industrialization, which led to institutional specialization, that is, the nuclear family. Those developments resulted in a highly specialized social structure in which women were assigned the family-psychological role and men the political and economic. Women became segregated from the larger social structure and put into the confines of the nuclear family with specialized roles, both psychological and physical, and little resources. Role specialization and segregation evolved as the family system responded to the changing needs of an increasingly specialized economic system. Given the patriarchal nature of western culture, it was perhaps inevitable that sexism would result with women subject to male domination and exploitation.[18] Once again it is clearly evident that economic factors are basic to the creation of minority groups.

Demographically, women are usually large in number (in some societies they are in fact the numerical majority), are heterogeneous in background since they are defined by factors such as race, ethnicity, social class, and deviance, and, like racial minorities, are subject to great degrees of economic and political deprivation.

Majority attitudes toward women tend to reflect the psychological role they have been assigned by males. They are assumed to be physically and intellectually inferior, more emotional and less psychologically controlled than men, and suited to a limited range of occupational roles as a result—roles which reflect an extension of their family functions such as secretaries, nurses, teachers, social workers. These notions are further reinforced by religious assumptions concerning moral inferiority and the origin of sin, hormonal research, and psychological assumptions regarding sexual differences in personality, which is borne out by Freud's work. Once again the minority is defined as possessing the majority's opposite physical, intellectual, and behavioral characteristics—the basis of majority viewpoints.

As with other minorities women may accept majority definitions of themselves, thereby participating in self-denigration, defining their major role as reflecting and reinforcing the male ego. In this manner a woman may deny herself an active self-concept, representing instead the "psychological feeder" of her husband's self and her children. The female self thus complements that of the male with few feelings of

---

[18]For an important discussion of this see S. Firestone, *The Dialectic of Sex* (New York: Bantam Books, 1971), chapter 4. See also M. K. Martin, and B. Voorhies, *Female of the Species* (New York: Columbia University Press, 1975).

independent self-worth, rewards, or resources. With increasing extra-familial activity, however, women have become increasingly dissatisfied with such negative self-concepts, searching instead for more active and positive definitions of their selves and for roles both within and outside the family system. Women's liberation in part then implies freedom from limiting, passive roles, and the development of more active and less family-bound pursuits in society at large.

Institutionalized sexism is as pervasive as its racial equivalent. Institutional access and resources in areas such as politics, the military, legal system, occupational structure, medicine, and credit continue to be controlled by the male elite while sexist stereotyping in education, religion, and the media continue to abound. In the context of a society whose predominant family type is patriarchal nuclear, sexism is implemented and reinforced at the most intimate levels as interpersonal relations are based primarily on the power dimension.[19] Women continue to be exploited and discriminated against at points throughout the social system, reinforced by cultural values that emphasize romance and eroticism.

Female social movements have also ranged from the assimilationist (trade unions) through the more separatist and moderate (suffrage movements) to radical (NOW). They have also met with ridicule and opposition, revealing a diversity of goals. In general, however, they represent varying reactions to particular types of discrimination and have become more vocal and radical in the wake of economic development and increasing participation in society at large. With such greater awareness of psychological, economic, and political deprivation have come more radical demands for the abolition of segregation, control, and discrimination on the basis of sex.[20]

Sexual relations have also tended to assume a paternalistic form with the male predominant and in control of all major political, economic, and psychological resources and the female in a dependent and essentially passive position, segregated within the confines of the nuclear family. The basis of sexual relations, however, is the vested psychological interests of dominant males. With economic change and greater participation of women in society at large, this traditional relationship has begun to change with contemporary notions of "open" marriage, nonsexist titles, self-written and renewable marriage contracts, the "househusband," and relations based on partnership rather than dominance. While the institutional significance of these trends is open to question, they indicate at least a partial shift away from traditional

[19]For more on "power relations" in the patriarchal nuclear family, see *The Dialectic of Sex*, chapter 7.

[20]For a useful discussion of American feminist movements, see *The Dialectic of Sex*, chapter 2.

patriarchal relations. Majority-minority relations in this area are thus subject to the dynamics of social change also.

Sex interacts with other types of discrimination in significant ways. Sex roles are emphasized in socialization among children and adolescents, chauvinism is continued throughout the life cycle, ethnic culture tends to support traditional female roles, poverty and welfare policies strengthen female dependence and vulnerability, while links between sexual status and deviance (prostitution, mental illness) are clear.

The segregated, dependent, and psychologically oriented, sexist roles assigned to women in contemporary society may be viewed as a function of role specialization produced by industrialization within the context of the patriarchal nuclear family system. Consequently, women are a large minority with few political or economic resources, are socially created as traditional society loses its structural homogeneity, and play a predominantly psychological role in contemporary society. This function is reinforced by their assumed physical, emotional, intellectual, and behavioral inferiority. They have reacted to this segregated, subordinate position through a variety of social movements, demanding greater resources and participation in the larger society. Finally, sexism overlaps significantly with other forms of minority group discrimination. In this manner, sexism represents an invidious form of discrimination, produced by economic change, and based on assumed physiologically-based inferiority. Another type of minority based on such assumptions is age-based discrimination.

AGE-BASED MINORITIES

A major type of minority based on assumed physiological differences is founded on age—children, adolescents, and the aged. As with sexism this form of discrimination may be attributed to the effects of economic development. In many traditional societies, status is positively correlated with age while children are highly integrated into the social structure and the adolescent role may not exist where adulthood is attained immediately upon puberty.[21] Traditional societies, with their low division of labor, are highly integrated and low in role specialization. Consequently, criteria such as sex and age are not used as the basis of rigid role assignment. With the onset of industrialization, however, role specialization occurs and age takes on significance in relation to the eco-

[21]The most famous study of the absence of adolescence in nonwestern society is Margaret Mead's research in Samoa. See M. Mead, *Coming of Age in Samoa* (New York: Morrow, 1928).

nomic system and occupational structure. Within the context of the nuclear family, role specialization and segregation evolve with respect to age in a fashion similar to sexual discrimination: Children, adolescents, and the aged are related to adults and parents on the basis of dependency, assigned an emotional-psychological function, possess little economic or political power, and are segregated into separate institutions such as schools and nursing homes. Such differentiation and discrimination are rationalized in terms of assumptions regarding physiological maturation and aging, restricted suitability for the labor market, and religious doctrines such as "original sin" which emphasize the need for strict discipline. In contrast to traditional culture where separate, age-based roles essentially do not exist, industrialization has led to a high level of role specialization, along with the nuclear family, within which severe segregation and control has emerged with respect to age. This results in the roles of "children," "adolescents," and the "aged,"—statuses assigned psychological functions with few economic or political resources, and reinforced by separate institutions. Minorities have been produced primarily for economic reasons. With respect to age, the specialized economic demands of an industrial system have resulted in segregation and control on the basis of assumed physiological differences in the life cycle, producing a highly differentiated role structure based on a "power psychology."[22]

With a modified birth-death ratio, particularly as it has stabilized, the size of age-based minorities has increased to the point where they represent a significant proportion of the population. Given the economic dependence of both young and old, their general level of deprivation is high. Legal restrictions and the power of the state also contribute to high levels of control, dependency, and institutionalization. As with racial and sexual minorities, these groups are large in number and greatly deprived.[23]

Majority attitudes toward children, adolescents, and the aged are highly formalized in scientific terms: pediatrics, adolescent medicine, geriatrics, and adolescent psychology all reinforce the social reality of age with assumed differences in physiology, personality, and intelligence. Members of these groups are thought of as immature, childish, emotional, unstable, and senile—qualities which ensure their control. Subgroup boundaries are further reinforced by specialized language, clothes, toys, media programming, and segregated institutions for all

[22]For an illuminating discussion of the social creation of childhood and its major characteristics, see Firestone, *The Dialectic of Sex,* chapter 4.

[23]For a demographic profile of children in America see D. Gottlieb, "Children in America: A Demographic Profile and Commentary," in D. Gottlieb, ed., *Children's Liberation* (Englewood Cliffs, N.J.: Prentice-Hall, 1973), pp. 7–22.

age levels. Age group members may accept these majority definitions, denigrating themselves, and remain highly dependent on parents and other adults. On the other hand, with awareness of their subordinate position they may develop their own subgroups or cliques. For adolescents this may involve deviant subgroups while the aged may become part of retirement communities, segregated in the confines of their own social structures. More radical groups include student movements developed in the 1960s and gang warfare. Moderate reaction among the aged includes the recent emphasis on "grey power" as well as legal resistance to forced retirement and discriminatory hiring practices. Reaction to age discrimination has become more visible and vocal. Nevertheless, contemporary society continues to highlight the negative aspects of aging and the importance of youth and virility. Such values make aging a traumatic experience with consequent psychological and economic insecurity and increasing conservatism as the old resist change and attempt to hold onto the past.

Institutionalized age discrimination is widespread and highly visible: This includes segregated educational institutions, controlled access to political and legal rights, compulsory military service, limited access to occupations, salary levels defined by "time-in-rank," specialized medical and psychological services by age, forced retirement policies, stereotypes in religion, and the media which emphasize the need to control and discipline the young because of their assumed potential for deviant behavior.

Age-related movements include student groups,[24] those concerned with child abuse, organizations of retired persons, and retirement communities. The extent to which age discrimination in hiring has become outlawed represents a significant advance. However, conservative reaction to some of these movements—students in particular —highlights the continued relevance of age discrimination and stereotyping in contemporary society.

Majority-minority age relations tend to be based on majority psychological needs, paternalism, dependence, and control with young and old alike treated as childish and immature while adults "know better." Children represent commodity items designed to reflect well on their parents and provide outlets for vicarious achievement. The aged, insofar as they participate in nuclear family activities, are expected to entertain their grandchildren and essentially play a passive role with little or no access to family policy, making them largely irrelevant to the family system.[25] While there has been some reduction in occupational discrim-

---

[24]S. M. Lipset, *Rebellion in the University* (Boston: Little Brown, 1971).

[25]For a useful analysis of the aged community see A. M. Rose, and W. A. Peterson (eds.), *Older People and their Social World* (Philadelphia: F. A. Davis, 1965).

ination and establishment of student rights, age remains a basic factor in role assignment and consequent power.

Age discrimination overlaps with other minority types in the reinforcement it receives from traditional ethnic culture, the economic dependence of poor children and the aged, age-specific types of deviance, agencies of control, and psychiatric diagnoses. Age discrimination is thus closely connected with other types of minority groups.

Age-based minorities may be attributed to the effects of industrialization and economic change, producing the nuclear family and segregated roles based on age. This has resulted in the creation of a large, dependent, controlled, and highly deprived minority defined as physically, emotionally, and intellectually different, rationalized through medicine and psychology. Acceptance of these labels results in self-denigration, dependence, self-doubt, and behavior which meets the psychological needs of adults. The institutional structure segregates people by age, controls their economic and political behavior, and defends their subordination. Majority-minority relations tend to be paternalistic and power based while age overlaps significantly with other types of minority. Age is a basic and pervasive source of discrimination in contemporary society and should be recognized as such.

We have examined minorities based on assumed physiological factors—racial, sexual, and age based. We shall now examine groups based upon assumed cultural inferiority, the ethnic minorities.

ETHNIC MINORITIES

Ethnic minorities, like racial groups, are produced primarily through the process of migration—either through the movement of a colonial elite which subordinates an indigenous population of the same race as itself (the Irish situation) or the voluntary migration of ethnic groups into a society to improve their economic situation (American Irish, Italians, Jews). In both cases, however, economic factors are paramount: In the former, the indigenous population's resources are taken over or severely controlled while it is subject to high levels of economic discrimination. In the latter situation ethnic groups settle in the society under limited historical circumstances and play particular occupational roles in the economic system. Segregated and subject to general discrimination, these ethnic groups tend to develop their own community institutions. Of crucial significance in their position are three major factors: (1) the *historical circumstances* under which they entered the society (positive or negative); (2) their degree of perceived *cultural similarity* to the dominant elite (in the American situation this is represented by degree of similarity to WASP culture). Perceived physical differences may also be a factor if ethnic groups vary in skin color; and (3) their *economic role* in the host society (low or high economic-occupational status and degree of economic resources). Groups which enter a society under negative historical circumstances are perceived as culturally different from the society's mainstream, and are assigned low economic status with few resources, tend to experience the most discrimination, remain highly segregated, and experience low levels of political, economic, and social assimilation into the larger society. Accordingly, ethnicity has most relevance in economically heterogeneous and competitive situations where cultural characteristics and economic status are highly correlated. Ethnic discrimination may be viewed as the cultural equivalent of racism since it reflects similar processes: migration, subordination, and importation for labor purposes. Perceived differences and the groups so created reflect vested economic interests.

Demographically, ethnic groups may vary widely: They may be large in size, particularly if they represent the indigenous population as in Ireland, or are contained within racial boundaries as in the United States, or they may be of medium size, relatively speaking. They are also heterogeneous with regard to political and economic resources, particularly in multiethnic situations where these minorities have tended to perform rather specific occupational functions, and produce a socioeconomic hierarchy. In general, however, ethnic minorities are typically of medium size with a variety of socioeconomic characteristics.

Majority attitudes tend to emphasize an ethnic minority's negative cultural characteristics. Given their economic function and potential economic threat, these characteristics are correlated with an assumed lack of intelligence and occupational skills, thereby rationalizing their subordinate economic position. They may also be viewed as violent and deviance-prone with low standards of moral conduct. These characteristics may also be identified with assumed physiological or racial factors as was the case with the American Irish.[26] Here the standard discrimination process is at work defining the minority as possessing the majority's opposite physical, intellectual, cultural, and behavioral characteristics.

Ethnic minorities may react by attempting assimilation into the larger economic, political, and social milieux or, as has happened in America recently, reject the legitimacy of ethnic discrimination and argue for the validity of their own culture or ethnic pride. Such ethnic

---

[26]For a discussion of this see R. E. Kennedy, Jr., "Irish Americans, A Successful Case of Pluralism," in A. G. Dworkin and R. J. Dworkin (eds.), *The Minority Report* (New York: Praeger, 1976), pp. 361–62.

nationalism, as with other types of minority reaction, tends to occur at later stages of a society's economic development when minorities possess more resources and greater awareness of the illegitimacy of discrimination. Thus, as economic independence increases so does minority nationalism.

The institutional dimensions of ethnic discrimination are highly visible: limited access to political power and legal resources, controlled economic opportunity, unequal educational facilities, media stereotypes concerning cultural characteristics, and "typical" occupational roles. In all of this majority ethnocentrism is evident as subordinate groups are negatively evaluated in order to rationalize elite monopolization of economic resources. Such prejudice is perpetuated throughout the cultural hierarchy as each group applies similar criteria to each other, thereby reinforcing a vicious cycle.

Ethnic movements include traditional community and professional organizations, links with majority political groups, recent emphases on ethnic power, and reflect the changing orientation of these minorities as they have developed independent, political, and economic resources. As dependence on the majority has lessened, ethnic nationalism has increased accordingly.

Majority-minority ethnic relations are based primarily on majority economic needs and reflect significant socioeconomic changes. In the early stages of migration, dependency tends to be high as is the desire for assimilation into the larger society. Desire for economic resources and social mobility thereby ensures conformity to majority control and their economic interests. However, economic development lessens such dependence, bringing with it greater awareness of the value of one's own culture as well as the negative characteristics of majority values. In the process majority conservatism and backlash may be felt. Nevertheless, changing ethnic relations are inevitable in the wake of economic change as these minorities achieve economic and political independence, and reinforce the validity of their own cultural backgrounds.

Ethnicity overlaps significantly with other dimensions of minority group status. It interacts with class in the predominant economic function of each ethnic group, with particular minorities assigned to low status occupations and with low economic resources as a result. Ethnicity is correlated with assumed types of social and criminal deviance through the media and general labeling process. Ethnicity is thus inherent in other forms of minority group differential as well.

Ethnic minorities are created through migration, subordination, and importation for economic purposes with assumed cultural characteristics used to legitimize economic exploitation. They may be large or medium in size and tend to be heterogeneous in socioeconomic characteristics. They are defined as culturally inferior with respect to physical, intellectual, and behavioral traits, thereby suited to limited occupational roles only. These groups, while economically dependent, may attempt assimilation but with greater resources will tend to develop cultural independence and nationalism. Majority-minority relations may thus exhibit dependence, attempted assimilation, and economic exploitation or independence, nationalism, and majority backlash as they are subjected to the dynamics of economic change. Finally, the ethnic dimension relates to poverty and deviant behavior through the labeling process. In general, in *racially homogeneous situations* assumed *cultural* rather than physical differences are used to legitimize economic exploitation with similar assumptions regarding physical, intellectual, and behavioral inferiority. The effects of economic change are similar also: increasing economic independence, minority nationalism, and intergroup conflict. Finally, economic factors are paramount in both types of minority situations, reflecting the *foundation* of minority group differentiation in general. This brings us to our fifth major type of minority—the "poor."

ECONOMIC MINORITIES

Defining "poverty" has never been a simple matter since it is always a relative state, compared with some individual or group definition of economic well-being. It is also evident that inequities in material resources have been present in all societies from the beginning of human existence. However, if poverty is defined as inadequate resources to meet basic human physical needs (that is, food, housing, and medical facilities) as well as low access to the occupational system through limited educational opportunity, the evolution of widespread economic minorities may be seen as a function of economic development, specifically *capitalism*. As feudalism (a land-based economy which at least dealt with an individual's physical needs even if in a limited fashion) declined and the processes of industrialization and urbanization occurred, the greater majority became subject to the demands of the capitalistic labor market with few resources of its own except labor. Accordingly, if we follow Marx, two major classes emerged in society: the bourgeoisie that owned the economic system or the means of production; and the proletariat that possessed nothing but had their labor for sale.[27]

[27]For further details on this see K. Marx, *Selected Writings in Sociology and Social Philosophy*, T. B. Bottomore (ed.) (New York: McGraw-Hill, 1964).

As *property*—the basis of the economic system—became monopolized in the hands of the former, an alienated (*separated* from the *means* of need fulfillment) class emerged with little access to property and highly dependent on the *labor market* for its living. Changing labor demands defined by a capitalist economy thus came to dominate economic relations in contemporary society and the individual's material welfare. Given this system's instability, its patterns of inflation and recession, high levels of unemployment, and the extent to which social services, such as medicine and education, become capitalist commodities governed by market factors, large numbers of people were subjected to high levels of economic and physical deprivation, resulting in the creation of economic minorities. Such deprivation is reinforced by other dimensions of discrimination—race, sex, age, and ethnicity. Furthermore, puritanical and individualistic ideologies prevalent in capitalistic societies blame deprived individuals for their own fate, arguing that if they were not so lazy, immoral, and drunken, they would automatically be able to obtain jobs and reduce their deprivation. The "usual" labeling process thus occurs: The poor are behaviorally inferior (that is, lazy, drunken, immoral, and extravagant) resulting inevitably in the notion that they are fit for unskilled and low paying positions only, since they are stupid.[28] Consequently, large economic minorities are created, subject to high levels of deprivation, provide cheap, unskilled labor for a capitalist economy, and are blamed for their own situation. Where capitalist wealth flourishes, so does economic deprivation. Furthermore, while the middle classes are not subject to such high degrees of deprivation, they are influenced by an unstable labor market, are controlled and exploited by the credit system, have little political power, and low access to capital resources. Alienation thus applies to them since they are a minority also.[29] Their own moralism and normative homogeneity, furthermore, ensure their conformity.

Demographically, economic minorities tend to be large, highly deprived, and relatively homogeneous. Compared with other types of discrimination they also tend to be nonwhite, female, and non-WASP. Furthermore, if the definition of poverty is extended to include the middle classes, economic minorities may in fact represent numerical majorities. Economic discrimination and deprivation are a significant feature of capitalist society.

---

[28]For a useful discussion of such attitudes see J. R. Feagin, *Subordinating the Poor, Welfare and American Beliefs* (Englewood Cliffs, N.J.: Prentice-Hall, 1975).
   [29]For an excellent analysis of this see C. H. Anderson, *The Political Economy of Social Class* (Englewood Cliffs, N.J.: Prentice-Hall, 1974).

Majority attitudes, as we have pointed out, tend to highlight the behavioral inferiority of economic minorities within the context of protestant ethic moralism, individualism, and the Horatio Alger myth concerning social mobility. These behavioral traits are further tied to assumed personality characteristics (for example, high aggression, emotionalism) and intellectual inferiority, thereby rationalizing the assignment of such groups to unskilled occupations. Members of the middle class may also be labeled as consumer oriented and potential "credit risks" whose appetites require regulation. Once again, assumed behavioral (and intellectual) inferiority is basic to minority group differentiation.

The effects of such labeling may, of course, be self-fulfilling: Members of these minorities may aspire to low status occupations only, devalue higher education, maximize immediate economic gratification, and channel their aggression into socially acceptable channels (recreation). On the other hand, they may attempt to improve their economic situation through union activity, consumer groups, or other minority social movements of which they are members (race, sex, age, or ethnicity). Economic boycotts may also take place but with limited effects. Economic minorities are far from passive, however, and have reacted to changing economic conditions through unions in particular.

Institutionalized economic discrimination is highly visible: economic control of politics, the law, education, and medical facilities, control of hiring on the basis of qualifications and personality characteristics, control of individual economic behavior through welfare institutions, stereotypes in education and the media concerning behavioral and cultural inferiority, and the manner in which religion and recreation provide outlets for material frustration. Institutionalized racism, sexism, age-based discrimination, and ethnic prejudice further broaden economic control and exploitation. The problem of economic minorities is widespread throughout contemporary society.

Economic social movements include consumer protection organizations, welfare groups, radical political parties such as communism and socialism, and other minority social movements which focus on economic issues (for example, unions). The latter, in particular, have emerged in the wake of economic development.

Majority-minority relations are based upon the normative needs of the majority and may involve the conformity of the minority to the majority definitions. This conforms to the prejudice discrimination cycle by limiting aspirations, de-emphasizing education, maximizing immediate gratification, and channeling aggression. Another alternative is to attempt social mobility through training, higher education, and deferring material gratification to the posttraining stage. One option is to organize in opposition to economic discrimination, using legal and political channels or to attempt to develop a separate subcommunity on a cooperative basis (co-ops, cooperative communities). The extent to which their reaction has a significant impact on the class structure, however, is open to question. Elite vested economic interests in the status quo are extremely high as is their political power. Combined with the material dependence of the majority of society, relations tend to be conservative and heavily rationalized in moralistic terms. In this sense, economic dominance may be the ultimate basis of social domination.

Finally, class overlaps significantly with other dimensions of minority group status and is highly correlated with behavioral minorities to the degree that the poor are more readily identified as deviant, possess few resources to combat legal oppression and social control agencies, or re-enter society successfully after institutionalization. The extent to which race, sex, age, and ethnicity are correlated with the economic system further indicates the extent of material control and exploitation throughout society.

Economic minorities have been created in the shift from feudalism to capitalism, making the majority of society a labor resource dependent upon the labor market with little or no access to the economic system or means of production. Large numbers of people are subject to high levels of economic and physical deprivation, reinforced by other types of minority discrimination and puritanical ideologies. Accordingly, the poor are defined as behaviorally inferior and assigned to unskilled work roles. These labels may be self-fulfilling with minority group members conforming to majority economic needs. On the other hand they may react by joining unions, consumer groups, or minority social movements. However, institutionalized economic discrimination is extremely high, controlling these minorities politically and economically, rationalized through stereotypes concerning their inferior culture. Majority-minority relations may involve conformity or reaction while poverty interacts significantly with major types of minority discrimination. Thus, economic development has resulted in political domination, economic exploitation, and socioeconomic ethnocentrism, despite notions of the "great society." Economic minorities, in fact, may be the most enduring of all with very conservative reactions to attempted change.

BEHAVIORAL MINORITIES

Deviant behavior, perceived nonconformity to social norms, has obviously existed from the beginning of human society. However, the extent to which it is institutionalized, controlled, and subject to specialized social control agencies is relatively unique to contemporary society. As unemployment and poverty increased with the evolution of capitalism, and as large numbers of individuals were brought together in the urban context, the threat they posed to a capitalist, materialist elite was great. Furthermore, the development of science and medicine encouraged the search for a physiological basis to deviant behavior. Given the moralistic and puritanical characteristics of capitalist culture, the need to isolate, control, and punish deviance possessed a religious fervor which has scarcely declined, using these "negative examples" to reinforce in-group conformity. In the context of a materialist, moralistic, and scientific culture with high rates of poverty and unemployment, the tendency to identify, institutionalize, and punish deviance is extremely high, producing a number of behavioral minorities. Accordingly, deviance is *created* and is a function of particular norms, economic situations, and power structures. When the church was dominant in European society, heresy was a major form of deviance whereas under capitalism two forms of deviance are most visible: property crimes, and unacceptable behavior such as homosexuality, assault, rape, addiction, and mental illness, that is, *material* and *moral* deviance. Behavioral minorities are created by specific power groups under particular socioeconomic conditions. Given the extent to which materialism, moralism, and science or rationality predominate in capitalist society, material and moral deviance is seriously labeled, punished severely, and subjected to institutionalization and medical-scientific forms of treatment. Furthermore, in societies which are heterogeneous and lack social cohesion, the perceived need to maintain law and order and punish deviants in order to protect social cohesion is extremely important.[30] Deviance is perceived as threatening social order and accordingly requires severe punishment. It also questions the legitimacy of norms and poses alternatives to need fulfillment, thereby challenging the symbolic status quo.[31] Reactions to these challenges are very conservative. Laws, furthermore, are far from universal; instead they reflect the vested economic interests of those in power, rationalized in ideological terms, making the law ultimately "political" in nature. Social control agencies are heavily subject to these political considerations to a far greater extent than the supposed rehabilitative needs of their clients. Finally, deviance is clearly defined by other types of minority criteria, in particular by race, age, and class, reinforcing

[30]Seibel, H. D., "Social Deviance in Comparative Perspective," in R. A. Scott and J. D. Douglas (eds.), *Theoretical Perspectives on Deviance* (New York: Basic Books, 1972), pp. 251–81.

[31]For a useful discussion of this see R. A. Scott, "A Proposed Framework for Analyzing Deviance as a Property of Social Order," in Scott and Douglas, *Theoretical Perspectives on Deviance*, pp. 9–36.

further the control of these groups with reference to behavioral control. Behavioral minorities are thus created, punished, and institutionalized to a significant degree in contemporary society, reflecting the vested material and normative interests of society's political elite. In this manner, materialism, moralism, and science represent a potent recipe for domination in contemporary society, despite mythical notions of humanism and democracy.

Demographically, behavioral minorities tend to be surprisingly large and clearly reflect other dimensions of minority group status, that is, they tend to be predominantly nonwhite, young (in the case of delinquents), and poor. They also lack the resources to challenge the power of law enforcement agencies and to rehabilitate themselves after incarceration. Furthermore, sentencing and punishment tend to be harsher when an offender is a member of these minorities. Such double punishment further reinforces control and domination throughout the social system.

Majority attitudes toward behavioral minorities are such that their deviant activities is viewed as a result of a number of factors: physiological inferiority (for example, genetic or chromosomatic deficiencies applied to criminals), personality problems (uncontrolled appetite and emotions), or cultural inferiority (the "wrong" kind of values, inadequate socialization). Given vested moral and material interests, these attitudes tend to be widespread and stable. Furthermore, they are heavily rationalized in medical and scientific terms in the search for the criminal or deviant "type."

Minority group members may respond to these views by accepting them and attempting to "reform," withdraw into the confines of their deviant subcultures and develop segregated life styles, or attack this discriminatory system, particularly in the courts, and fight for their legal rights. Once again, with economic change the third type of reaction has increased as deviants have attacked the illegality of discrimination on assumed behavioral grounds.

Institutionalized discrimination against behavioral minorities is widespread: political exclusion, legal oppression, job discrimination, medical and "scientific" control, religious prejudice, and media stereotypes make deviance entertaining, but socially threatening and illegitimate. Minority group discrimination in general reinforces these factors.

Minority social movements include groups such as "Gay Liberation" and organizations fighting for the legal rights of prisoners and mental patients (such as the American Civil Liberties Union). These groups are fighting primarily for the removal of legal oppression of deviants and restoring their individual rights in face of a general process which is dehumanizing and destroys the right to individual freedom, initiative, and responsibility. Such movements are attempting to restore the deviants' legal rights.

Majority-minority relations are heavily influenced by the former's vested material and (especially) moral interests, resulting in highly conservative reactions. Deviance is defined primarily as a moral threat to the status quo with society "breaking down" if it is not controlled. Furthermore, offenders are viewed as unreliable and untrustworthy, requiring continuous monitoring. As pointed out, deviants may accept these labels and attempt to "reform" through conformity and self-denigration, develop their own subcultures, or organize to obtain their legal rights. The last is viewed as particularly threatening by the majority and significant material and legal resources are required to accomplish such change.

Finally, deviance is highly correlated with other types of minority group status: Deviants are primarily nonwhite, young (in certain cases), and poor. They are the opposite of those with material and moral power in the society. Behavioral control is widespread throughout the society accordingly.

Behavioral deviants are dependent upon unemployment, poverty, and urbanization within the context of evolving capitalism. These minorities are created by moralistic and materialistic elites using medicine and science to rationalize their segregation and control. They represent a significant proportion of society, possess few resources, and are defined by other major dimensions of minority group status. Their behavioral inferiority is "explaineᵈ" in terms of physiological, personality, and cultural factors. They may react by attempting reform, developing subcultures, or fighting for their legal rights. Institutionalized discrimination is widespread throughout society while majority-minority relations are clearly defined by the former's moral and material interests. Behavioral minorities are a signficant aspect of contemporary society and suffer high levels of discrimination.

Having completed our descriptive portrait of these six major types of minorities, we draw some general conclusions.

CONCLUSIONS

In this chapter we have outlined major aspects of six types of minorities: the historical, demographic, attitudinal, institutional, reaction, and relational characteristics of racial, sexual, age-based, cultural, economic, and behavioral minorities. These qualities are summarized in Figure 5.1. From this chart it is possible to draw a number of relevant conclusions:

TYPE OF MINORITY

CHARACTERISTICS	Racial	Sexual	Age based	Cultural	Economic	Behavioral
1. Historical:	migration, subordination, importation, for labor	sexual division of labor, industrialization, nuclear family, segregated roles	industrialization, nuclear family, segregated roles	migration, subordination, importation, for labor	decline of feudalism, industrialization, unemployment	increased materialism, unemployment, industrialization
2. Demographic:	large numbers, heterogeneous, high deprivation	large numbers, heterogeneous, high dependence	large numbers, heterogeneous, high dependence	medium numbers, heterogeneous, economic roles	large numbers, heterogeneous, labor market	large numbers, reflect minorities, high deprivation
3. Attitudinal: (a) Majority	physiological, intellectual, cultural, behavioral inferiority	physiological, intellectual, behavioral inferiority	physiological, intellectual, behavioral inferiority	cultural, intellectual, behavioral inferiority	behavioral, intellectual, physiological inferiority	behavioral, physiological, cultural inferiority
(b) Minority	self-denigration, rejection, nationalism	self-denigration, rejection, activism	self-denigration, rejection, organization	assimilationist, rejection, nationalism	dependence, rejection, organization	reform, rejection, organization
4. Institutional:	low access, resources, high stereotyping	low access, resources, high stereotyping	controlled access, resources, high stereotyping	low access, resources, high stereotyping	low access, resources, high stereotyping	low access, resources, high stereotyping
5. Social Movements:	rebellions, assimilationist separatist nationalist	unions, suffrage groups radicalism	family organizations, student movements, aged organizations	community organizations, political groups, ethnic power	unions, consumer organizations, radical politics	liberation groups, legal organizations, criminal groups
6. Relational: (a) Majority-Minority	majority economic interests	majority psychological interests	majority psychological interests	majority economic interests	majority normative interests	majority normative interests
(b) Interminority						
racial	*	exploitive	paternalism	racism	racial caste	high nonwhites
sexual		*	patriarchal	traditionalism	control women	types deviance
age based			*	traditionalism	high dependence	age specific types
cultural				*	economic roles	types deviance
economic					*	high number of poor
behavioral						*

FIGURE 5.1   Characteristics of Major Types of Minorities

1. Minorities are created through two major processes: (1) *migration* with consequent subordination and importation; and, (2) *economic development,* specifically industrial capitalism and the role specialization it demands. As a consequence of these processes, minority groups are *created* to meet elite (or majority) *economic needs.* These groups tend to be *large* (they may represent the society's numerical majority), *heterogeneous,* possess *few resources,* and *overlap* to the extent the major criteria of discrimination are highly correlated. Majority group members view them as physically, intellectually, culturally, and behaviorally *inferior,* possessing the exact *opposite* of their own qualities. Minorities, in turn, may accept these views, denigrate themselves and attempt to become *acceptable* to the majority, develop their own *segregated subcultures,* or fight against discrimination and for their *legal rights.* The *institutionalized domination* they are attacking consists of limited access to institutions, resource deprivation, and the reinforcement of negative majority stereotypes. Minority group social movements consist of groups organized on the basis of the types of minority reaction just described, ranging from the *assimilationist* through the *separatist* to the *nationalist* and radical. These groups are concerned with *political, economic,* and *social rights*—the *opposite* of institutionalized discrimination. Finally, *majority-minority relations* are *conservative* and control-minded, reflecting the *majority's economic, physiological,* and *moral interests*—orientations minorities may accept or resist, while *interminority* relations reflect the *high intercorrelation* of major types of minority group domination. In short, minorities are subordinate groups created through migration and economic development in reference to elite economic and psychological needs, rationalized in terms of assumed physical, intellectual, cultural, and behavioral inferiority, and subject to widespread institutionalized discrimination. Consequent relations depend on minority reaction to this process as influenced by economic change and the intercorrelation of types of minority group differentiation.

2. Various types of minorities are produced by different processes: Racial and cultural minorities are caused by migration, subordination, and importation; while sexual, age-based, economic, and behavioral minorities are produced more by the material demands of economic development, specifically industrial capitalism. Since the former are based upon broader processes, they tend to provide the societal context in which the other types operate.

3. Each minority has distinguishing characteristics: Racial minorities are based on assumed color-related characteristics, sexual or assumed biological differences, age based on the concept "maturation," cultural on assumed cultural differences and inferiority, economic on

assumed behavioral deficiencies, and behavioral on assumed deviance. Minorities are thus based on assumed physical, cultural, economic, and behavioral inferiority.

Given their differences in origin and scope, a minority group hierarchy may be seen to exist with race at the peak, ethnicity operating within racial boundaries, class differences next, and within each class division, the effects of sex, age, and deviance. This hierarchy is summarized in Figure 5.2. Within such a structure, the various types of minorities, especially the racial, cultural, and economic, are influenced by economic development, becoming more organized and radical in orientation, while they also compete with each other and majority groups for economic resources. In this manner, minority group relations are both hierarchial and competitive. We turn next to examine the underlying *assumptions* on which minority groups are based—physiological, psychological, social psychological, and sociological.

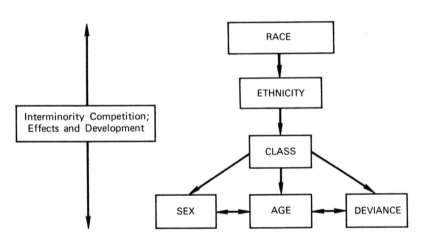

FIGURE 5.2   The Minority Group Hierarchy

STUDY QUESTIONS

1. Select a specific example of each type of minority in your own community. Compare each with respect to:

(a) The historical circumstances behind their evolution.

(b) Their demographic characteristics (that is, population size, socioeconomic characteristics).

(c) Majority attitudes towards these as well as their views of themselves.

(d) Major forms of institutionalized discrimination.

(e) Major types of minority social movements.

(f) Major types of intergroup relations as a result.

2. From your analysis what do you conclude regarding:

(a) The general processes by which minorities are created?

(b) Similarities among the major types with respect to the dimensions we have outlined?

(c) Specific characteristics of the major types of minorities?

READINGS

ANDERSON, C. H., *The Political Economy of Social Class*, Englewood Cliffs, N.J.: Prentice-Hall, 1974.

DWORKIN, A. G., and Dworkin, R. J. (eds.), *The Minority Report. An Introduction to Racial, Ethnic, and Gender Relations*, New York: Praeger, 1976, pp. 127–130.

FEAGIN, J. R., *Subordinating the Poor, Welfare and American Beliefs*, Englewood Cliffs, N.J.: Prentice-Hall, 1975.

FELLOWS, D. K., *A Mosaic of America's Ethnic Minorities*, New York: Wiley, 1972.

FIRESTONE, S., *The Dialectic of Sex*, New York: Bantam, 1971.

GITTLER, J. B. (ed.), *Understanding Minority Groups*, New York: Wiley, 1956, VIII.

GOTTLIEB, D. (ed.), *Children's Liberation*, Englewood Cliffs, N. J.: Prentice-Hall, 1973.

KUROKAWA, M. (ed.), *Minority Responses*, New York: Random House, 1970.

MAKIELSKI, S. J., JR., *Beleagured Minorities, Cultural Politics in America*, San Francisco, Freeman, 1973.

NEWMAN, W. M., *American Pluralism. A Study of Minority Groups and Social Theory*, New York: Harper & Row, 1973.

PERRUCCI, R., *Circle of Madness, On Being Insane and Institutionalized in America*, Englewood Cliffs, N.J.: Prentice-Hall, 1974, Chapters 1, 2.

ROSE, A. M., and W. A. PETERSON (eds.), *Older People and Their Social World*, Philadelphia: F. A. Davis, 1965.

VAN DEN BERGHE, P. L., *Race and Racism*, New York: Wiley, 1967, Chapters I, VI.

6

Assumptions Regarding Minorities

In our approach to minorities we have stressed the manner in which these groups are *socially created* on the basis of certain *assumed* qualities attributed to group members, primarily for *economic* or material *purposes.* These orientations are given scientific and religious respectability in the society at large. Since these assumptions are central to the creation of minorities and subsequent intergroup relations, it is important to analyze their characteristics and how they operate. In this chapter we shall examine major types of assumptions behind minority groups—physiological, psychological, social-psychological, and sociological.

MAJOR TYPES OF ASSUMPTIONS

Assumptions regarding minorities differ in a number of ways. Group members may be defined as *different* from majority group members (women and children) or *inferior* when compared with them (nonwhites, non-WASPs, the poor, and deviants). The two types are closely connected and differences may become defined as inferior qualities, particularly as economic competition evolves. These qualities may be characterized as inherent or *internal* (genetic, age-related color-founded, personality-based) or *external* and structural (cultural inferiority, role-based, or socially created).

This internal external axis is reflected in four major types of minority group assumptions:

1. Physiological assumptions: These define group differences and inferiority as physiologically based, for example, hormones, IQ, brain size, genetics, blood, body types, different drives, aging, stages of sexual maturation, and biological drives.
2. Psychological assumptions: According to these, minority group members possess different and/or inferior personality traits, for example, high levels of aggression, emotionalism and irrationality, immature behavioral traits, bad tempers, desire for immediate need-gratification, low self-control, and immature levels of personality development. Many of these assumptions are based directly on the idea that these traits are physiologically defined, representing an extension of the first approach.
3. Social-psychological assumptions: In contrast to the physiological and psychological assumptions, which focus on assumed internal factors, both social-psychological and sociological approaches to minorities emphasize the relevance of external factors such as norms, roles, culture, and social structure. The former view minorities as a function of norms and segregated roles, created by the society's dominant majorities: racial, sexual, age-based, ethnic, economic, and deviant *roles* are defined as created by society, resulting in minority group segregation, dependency, and exploitation, with specialized subcultures and identities. This does not imply, however, that prejudice or ethnocentrism is absent in such a perspective; minority group culture may still be viewed as deficient in some respect, as we shall see. The social-psychological perspective, however, represents an advance in social awareness since it perceives minorities as a function of *social* rather than purely *internal* factors.
4. Sociological assumptions: The sociological perspective on minorities stresses societal factors behind their creation, for example, migration, subordination, importation, the effects of capitalism, industrialization, urbanization, WASP values, materialism, and puritanism. All these are the societal factors behind the development of minority roles and subcultures in

the context of economic exploitation, based on assumed physiological and psychological characteristics. As the social sciences developed awareness of the structural basis of social problems in general and minority groups in particular, understanding of these groups shifted to the analysis of major structural factors behind their social creation.

The above four types reflect the contribution of specific sciences (biology, zoology, psychology, social psychology, and sociology) to the creation of minorities along with the reinforcing effects of religious doctrines (predestination), philosophical views (Social Darwinism and the "survival of the fittest"), and cultural values (in particular, WASP culture). Minorities are created in specific societal contexts through the physical and social sciences, religion, philosophy, and general cultural values, partly because of vested economic interests, moving from physiological assumptions to the more psychological, and then to the sociological.

Given the central importance of these assumptions in the creation process, we examine each in turn as they relate to the six types of minorities outlined, beginning with physiological assumptions.

PHYSIOLOGICAL ASSUMPTIONS

The physiological approach to minorities, particularly of the racial kind, drew its inspiration primarily from eighteenth and nineteenth century biology and zoology with the beginning of science and classification of the human species into distinct subdivisions. Further developments such as genetics and Social Darwinism with its concept, "survival of the fittest," reinforced the notion of an inherent physiological basis to social groupings. Given the capitalistic and colonial social context in which these ideas emerged, they were used to justify the assumed superiority of Caucasian, middle and upper class WASPs.[1] Such ideas were given further impetus by religious doctrines such as predestination, the "chosen race," and assumed differences between Christians and heathens.

The above ideas were applied primarily to racial, ethnic, and economic minorities: Nonwhites, non-WASPs, and the poor have been, and continue to be, viewed as physiologically different and inferior, having weaker intellects and constitutions generally, and representing lower orders of evolution. These "differences" were linked with assumed cultural inferiority, thereby rationalizing segregation, racial purity, and

[1]For a useful discussion of early ideas of "race," see M. Banton, *Race Relations* (New York: Basic Books, 1967), chapter 2.

the economic exploitation of racial, ethnic, and economic minorities who are forced to "earn" equality through conformity to majority culture and its economic needs. Science thus contributed heavily to physiological definitions of minorities. Later developments in medicine, hormonal research, genetics, and criminology extended this orientation to other groups. Women were defined as hormonally different with physical, intellectual, and emotional reactions assumed to differ from those of the male, intelligence became linked with "chronological age" through the "intelligence quotient," puberty became associated with particular types of emotional reactions as did aging, and deviant behavior was (and still is) accounted for in terms of body type, genetic deficiencies, and chromosomatic structure. Accordingly, physiological assumptions regarding sexual, age-based, and behavioral minorities evolved through medicine and science, reinforced within the context of a male-dominated, patriarchal, and puritan culture. All major minorities in contemporary society have been "given" physiological "reality" by the attribution of a biological foundation such as genes, hormones, chromosomes, brain size, and body type influenced by the processes of maturation and biological evolution.

Examining each minority type in turn, a common process emerges: Physiological assumptions concerning race originated primarily in eighteenth century biology and nineteenth century zoology in the scientific search for human origins and classification of the species into subdivisions or races.[2] These groups became viewed as differing stages of human evolution, with the Caucasian race defined as superior. Racial differences then became tied to culture with nonwhites viewed as essentially "uncivilized." These prejudiced assumptions were heavily reinforced by Social Darwinism with its emphasis on "survival of the fittest" and the emergence of genetics which provided the inheritance aspect of racial differences. Cultural values contained in imperial and colonial societies, particularly in those of the WASP type, further supported the physiological perspective of race. Finally, controversy over a possible genetic basis to racial differences in intelligence has continued in contemporary society.[3] The physiological definition of racial minorities thus originated with the development of biology, zoology, and genetics, reinforced by Social Darwinism and WASP culture—the philosophical and cultural contexts of colonialism. Assumed physiological differences were used to rationalize economic domination and ex-

[2]See Banton's discussion of Blumenbach, Buffon, Cuvier, Prichard, Knox, Morton, and Nott in Banton, *ibid.*, chapter 2.

[3]An example of this is contained in A. R. Jensen, "How Much Can We Boost I.Q. and Scholastic Achievement?" *Harvard Educational Review*, 39, (1969). Related discussion and rebuttal are presented later in the same volume.

ploitation as they operated within the processes of migration, subordination, and importation. Linked to cultural ethnocentrism, racism became an invidious and "scientific" argument for the legitimacy of segregation, domination, and exploitation. Since nonwhites were viewed as a lower order of the human species with inferior bodies, brains, and cultures, their negative fates were determined for the future.

Women, burdened with the reproductive function, have been portrayed as different with unique societal roles, concentrating on childrearing and family-related activities. As previously stated, it appears that in traditional societies women were less segregated from the larger society. With role specialization and segregation, however, along with the application of biology and medicine to the sexes, assumed sexual differences have taken a physiological form: Male and female are assumed to differ in hormones, chromosomes, internal organs, and instincts with correlated variation in traits such as self-control, fear, anxiety, aggression, competition, aspiration, and types of thought.[4] Sexual differences became physiologically based, thereby rationalizing their specialized and segregated role in society with little economic or political power. Once again, science, within the context of particular cultural values, has established an assumed physiological basis to societal roles.

A similar process has occurred with respect to age-based minorities. Biology and medicine have established a close connection between maturation and assumed body growth, hormonal development, intellectual growth, and emotional self-control.[5] These growth charts represent an underlying model: Physiological growth (that is, body size, hormonal development, and so on) results in significant developments with regard to coordination, strength, intelligence, emotional development, and self-control. Such assumptions obviously rationalize the segregation and control of the young, adolescent, and aged, maintaining their minority position in contemporary society. These notions are further reinforced by puritanical child-rearing practices. Once again science and medicine have succeeded in providing a physiological rationale for minority roles in contemporary society.

Ethnic minorities have been subject to physiological assumptions in a similar fashion to racial groups: They have been defined as inferior races with poor blood, variations in skin color, uncivilized cultures and

[4]For discussions of this see J. S. Chafetz, *Masculine, Feminine, or Human?* (Itasca: Peacock, 1974), chapter 1; see also J. Freeman, "Growing Up Girlish," *Transaction,* 8, 1970, pp. 36–43; E. Maccoby, ed., *The Development of Sex Differences* (Palo Alto, University of Stanford, 1966).

[5]For an example see D. Rogers, *The Psychology of Adolescence,* 2nd ed., (New York: Appleton-Century-Crofts, 1972), chapters 2–7.

behavior, high aggression, and low intelligence.[6] As is well known, in Nazi Germany "science" was applied to such assumptions in an attempt to produce a "pure race" and destroy the inferior. Such an example is extreme, but it serves to illustrate again the application of science to prejudice and domination where physiological differences are assumed to exist. Less formal assumptions involve the correlation of color differences and body characteristics with cultural inferiority, that is, the social labeling process.

The poor and lower classes have also been viewed as inherently inferior: Social Darwinists such as Sumner and Ward applied the "survival of the fittest" notion to the poor and deviant who are unfit and represent a lower order of human evolution.[7] The extreme form of this viewpoint argues for noninterference in the evolutionary process since nature will take care of the situation by weeding out the unfit.[8] In this manner the poor are regarded as generally unfit for the demands of modern society, and studies documenting their low nutrition, poor physical condition, lack of intellectual performance, and high level of social problems reinforce the view that they are deficient physically, mentally, and emotionally—the standard majority definition of minorities. Once again, science, philosophy, and religion have combined to reinforce a physiological definition of a minority group, thereby rationalizing the status quo, particularly by economic exploitation.

The contribution of medicine to a physiological view of behavioral minorities is well known: Deviants are assumed to be victims of physical addiction, particular body type characteristics, deficient chromosomes or genes, and represent lower levels of human evolution.[9] Consequent treatment is severe: electric shock, chemotherapy, and lobotomy, to name a few. Deviants continue to be viewed as physiologically deficient in some manner, with consequent physiological, intellectual, emotional problems, and require "scientific" solutions as a result. Within the context of a puritanical culture, such solutions tend to be severe and highly authoritarian.

Science, medicine, and religion combined to create a physiological definition of minority groups. Genetic, hormonal, chromosomatic, age-based, body type, and brain size differences have been applied to all major minorities with the assumption that they are intimately con-

[6]E. H. Hale, *Letters on Irish Emigration* (Boston: Phillips, Sampson, 1852).

[7]See M. R. Davie, ed., *William Graham Sumner* (New York: Crowell, 1963); I. Gerver, ed., *Lester Frank Ward* (New York: Crowell, 1963).

[8]Davie, ed., *William Graham Sumner.*

[9]The classic example is Lombroso who argued for the notion of the "born criminal," see G. Lombroso-Ferrero, *Criminal Man* (Montclair, Patterson-Smith, 1911). An "intelligence approach" is also taken by P. Tappan, *Crime, Justice, and Correction* (New York: McGraw-Hill, 1960).

nected with different and inferior emotional, intellectual, cultural, and behavioral traits thereby legitimizing the processes of segregation, control, and exploitation. In this manner physiological factors have been tied to the psychological, producing categorical views of groups which are inherently different both physiologically and psychologically from the majority.

PSYCHOLOGICAL ASSUMPTIONS

Physiological inferiority is closely correlated with assumed psychological inferiority: Nonwhites are sexually aggressive, women irrational, adolescents immature, non-WASPs dumb, the poor are lazy, and the deviant lack self-control—all the opposite characteristics of the WASP personality model. Again, these labels have been given "scientific credence" through IQ tests, Freudian models of personality development based on sex and age, child psychology, adolescent psychology, gerontology, the use of science for ethnic domination, achievement motivation tests, and personality profiles. Medicine and psychology have reinforced the notion of minority personality "types." Minorities are assumed to be significantly different in emotions, intelligence, and behavior, that is, they are emotional rather than rational, lack intelligence, and are behaviorally deviant with high levels of aggression. We examine such assumptions as they relate to each type.

Beginning with racial minorities, nonwhites have been labeled as high in aggression, some of which is transformed into self-hatred, while white intelligence tests have long been used to demonstrate that these minorities are low in academic achievement and, within the school setting, represent the majority of behavioral problems.[10] In the colonial situation these groups have been defined as nonacademic and nontechnological in orientation, rationalizing their assignment to unskilled occupational roles.[11] Finally, in the popular culture, blacks have been and continue to be defined as sexually aggressive, posing a threat to white "purity."[12] In this manner assumed physiological factors are correlated with negative emotional, intellectual, and behavioral characteristics.

Freudian psychoanalytic theory has, perhaps, been most responsible for a portrait of the "female personality" as inherently different from the male based on biological factors. Concepts such as "castration

---

[10]D. P. Moynihan, *The Negro Family: The Case for National Action* (Washington, D.C.: U.S. Dept. of Labor, 1965); W. H. Grier, and P. M. Cobbs, *Black Rage* (New York: Basic Books, 1968).

[11]"The Department of Interior Views the Indian," in P. Jacobs, and S. Landau, eds., *To Serve the Devil*, Vol. 1 (New York: Vintage, 1971), pp. 69–72

[12]C. C. Hernton, *Sex and Racism in America* (Garden City: Doubleday, 1965).

anxiety," "penis envy," "low female superego," and the "Electra complex" portray women at the mercy of their psychology and biology, designed to live within the context of their subordinate sexual position in the family.[13] Such a deterministic view of women's personalities rationalizes, once again, their segregated, subordinate position and predominantly psychological function in the nuclear family. Assumed connections between hormones, menstruation, and irrational, emotional behavior in females lend further credence to this viewpoint.[14] Finally, religious beliefs concerning the origin of sin and potential immorality of women reinforce a predominantly negative image of the "female personality."

Freudian personality theory has also been applied to children and adolescents: Concepts such as the "Oedipus complex" and stages of personality development (for example, "oral," "anal," and "genital" stages) strongly reinforce the assumed relationship between age and personality. The psychology of adolescence also links physiological development with assumed personality traits such as immaturity, emotional instability, storm and stress, confusion, and sexual experimentation.[15] Portraits of the aged personality as neurotic, withdrawn, and based on a fear of death also contribute to the assumed relationship between age and personality.[16] Once again, minorities are assumed to be inferior in emotion, intelligence, and behavior based on assumed physiological factors, in this case maturation.

Ethnic groups, in particular the non-WASP, are assumed to be different and inferior in temperament, behavior, and ability attributable to their non-American "blood." As with racial groups, they are often assumed to be more emotional, aggressive, deviant, and less intelligent than cultural majorities.[17] Such labels are reinforced by media stereotypes, ethnic segregation which persists for historical and demographic reasons, and the extent to which ethnicity and the occupational structure remain associated.

Social class and personality are also assumed to be related: The lower classes are lazy, irresponsible, lack aspiration, are low in intellectual achievement, devalue education, desire immediate gratification of desires, are highly aggressive, immoral, emotional, deviance oriented,

[13]See discussion by B. Friedan, *The Feminine Mystique* (New York: Dell, 1964), chapter 5; S. Firestone, *The Dialectic of Sex* (New York: Bantam, 1971), chapter 3.

[14]Chafetz, *Masculine, Feminine, or Human?* pp. 23–27.

[15]Rogers, *The Psychology of Adolescence,* chapter 4.

[16]A. M. Rose, "Mental Health of Normal Older Persons," in A. M. Rose, and W. A. Peterson, eds., *Older People and Their Social World* (Philadelphia: F. A. Davis, 1965), pp. 193–200.

[17]E. S. Bogardus, *Immigration and Race Attitudes* (Boston: Heath, 1928).

and more subject to mental illness.[18] The poor are viewed as psychologically deprived, lacking in emotional control, intelligence, and rational behavior, thus their subordinate position is rationalized.

Behavioral minorities are also subject to psychological stereotyping: They lack self-control, are highly aggressive, lack proper socialization, are low in intelligence, desire immediate gratification, are insecure, have inferiority complexes, are unable to control their ids, hate their parents, and are highly frustrated because of deprived childhood backgrounds.[19] A common theme runs through this portrait: Because of physiological factors, deviants lack adequate control of their emotions. This produces highly aggressive and inappropriate behavior— behavior which results in their severe control and subordination. As with other minorities, deviants are defined as inferior in self-control, intelligence, and behavior, rationalizing their control and subordination in the context of a materialist and puritanical culture.

Freudian personality theory, intelligence tests, adolescent psychology, studies of values and lifestyles, popular stereotying, medicine and psychiatry have all contributed to the psychological labeling of minority group personalities as deficient in *emotional control, intelligence,* and *civilized behavior,* possessing qualities assumed to be the opposite of majority group members, namely, high aggression, impulse rather than intelligence, and deviant behavior. As can be seen from our analysis, this psychological portrait is applied to all major types of minorities from the racial to the behavioral, revealing a basic process in majority labeling of minority personality types.

Physiological and Psychological Assumptions Summarized

The physiological and psychological labeling of minority groups reveals a common process: Within the context of migration, subordination, and importation, science, medicine, and religion combined to create a view of minorities as physiologically inferior while psychology, psychiatry, and popular stereotypes produced a negative model of the minority personality based on these factors. *Physical factors* included genetic, hormonal, chromosomatic, age-based, body type, and brain size differences. *Psychological factors,* on the other hand, consist of

[18]J. R. Feagin, *Subordinating the Poor* (Englewood Cliffs, N. J.: Prentice-Hall, 1975), p. 30.

[19]For a discussion see H. J. Eysenck, *Crime and Personality* (Boston: Houghton Mifflin, 1964).

emotional, intellectual, and behavioral factors. Bringing these together, three types of labeling are evident:

1. Differences in genes, hormones, chromosomes, age, and body type are assumed to be correlated with a lack of *emotional control.*
2. Age and other physiological factors such as small brain size are related to *intellectual deficiencies.*
3. Age differences and physiological limitations are correlated with *behavioral deviance.*

In this manner inherent physiological factors are assumed to be correlated with emotional, intellectual, and behavioral inferiority among minorities, rationalizing their control, domination, and exploitation. Assumed physiological and psychological inferiority thus serve majority economic interests for purposes of economic exploitation. This process is summarized in Figure 6.1. We turn now to social-psychological and sociological assumptions concerning these groups.

PHYSIOLOGICAL FACTORS	ASSOCIATED PSYCHOLOGICAL FACTORS
1. age, body type, chromosomes, genes, hormones	1. high aggression, lack of emotional control
2. age, brain size	2. low intellectual ability, lack of rationality
3. age, body type	3. lack of culture and civilized behavior

FIGURE 6.1   The Relationship Between Physiological and Psychological Assumptions Concerning Minorities

SOCIAL-PSYCHOLOGICAL ASSUMPTIONS

Thus far little mention of the social sciences in the labeling process has been made; however, they were certainly not free of prejudice. Early American sociology, as Frazier indicates, emphasized the Negro's inferior social heredity and low potential for assimilation, rejecting miscegenation. Early sociological writings by Ward, Sumner, Giddings, and

Cooley also highlighted racial conflict, the importance of mores, consciousness of kind, racial caste, and intellectual differences.[20] An establishment-oriented, ethnocentric view of minorities and social problems in general has also been typical of "mainstream" sociology, anthropology, criminology, and economics. Acceptance of assumed minority physiological and psychological inferiority is evident, particularly in the past. While it is no longer fashionable to express such viewpoints, it is clear that they still exist if only in modified form.[21]

Nevertheless, the social sciences have provided a breakthrough in the understanding of minorities by highlighting the *social context* in which these groups are *created* and *interact*, that is, they have revealed that minorities are socially created and represent *roles, subcultures,* and *separate institutional systems* produced by majority elites. At the social psychological or group level, minorities are viewed as separate subgroups or *roles* imposed and created by the larger society. Such a view is not necessarily prejudice free; these groups, for example, may still be defined as deviant or culturally deficient. However, this perspective sees minorities as an outgrowth of the social system rather than as inherent physiological or psychological factors. In this manner the level of analysis shifts from the physical and individual to group and social factors in which minority roles and subgroups have been created by majority elites through labeling individuals as physically and/or psychologically different and/or inferior. This conceptual shift is significant for two major reasons: It emphasizes the *social creation process* (minorities have no inherent reality); and it analyzes *social* rather than physical or psychological factors in this process as they affect both minority and majority group members.

This kind of analysis has been extensively applied to racial minorities: "Race" is viewed as the basis of individual and group identity, represents a sense of group position in reference to economic factors, and is the foundation of a racial socioeconomic status hierarchy produced by a society's racial elite.[22] A *racial status system* is thereby produced for economic reasons through migration, subordination, and importation, with assumed racial differences (physical and psychological) as its foundation, providing individual and group identity and operating through segregated institutional systems.

A similar kind of analysis has been applied to sexual minorities:

[20]See E. F. Frazier, "Sociological Theory and Race Relations," *American Sociological Review,* 12 (1947), pp. 265–71.

[21]The controversy over a genetic-racial basis of intelligence is one example (see Jensen, "How Much Can We Boost I.Q. and Scholastic Achievement?"); the Moynihan debate over the black family is another (Moynihan, *The Negro Family*).

[22]For a discussion of these approaches see G. C. Kinloch, *The Dynamics of Race Relations, A Sociological Analysis* (New York: McGraw-Hill, 1974), chapters 8, 13.

Based on biological limitations, the lengthy dependence of children, and the reproductive function, a set of sex roles has become institutionalized in contemporary society and used as the basis of a sexual division of labor, reinforced through socialization, the patriarchal nuclear family, and a male-dominated technological culture.[23] This perspective was greatly facilitated by Margaret Mead's comparative anthropological work on sex roles in which she demonstrated that they are societally rather than physiologically defined.[24] As with race, sex represents the basis of roles, the status system, and the institutional structure, which results in segregated, subordinate minorities in society, and is based on the labeling of these individuals by majority group members.

It is also evident that a similar process applies to age: According to Ariès, the childhood role did not exist until the fifteenth century when, with the evolution of the bourgeoisie and beginnings of the modern family, role specialization occurred and age became an important factor. The segregated, dependent status of the child evolved, creating high levels of economic and physical dependence.[25] Specific aspects of culture such as toys, language, and clothes emerged along with segregated institutions such as schools. Similar developments with respect to adolescents and the aged occurred also, with similar consequences.[26] As with the other minorities, majority labeling on the basis of assumed physical and personality differences resulted in the creation of minority roles and institutions.

Ethnic minorities may be viewed from a similar perspective: Through migration and WASP labeling, each minority's economic role in the society, its social segregation, ethnic roles, subcultures, and institutions were created, and were reinforced by cultural prejudice and discrimination. Ethnicity, accordingly, became the basis of identity, social status, and intergroup relations as it became *institutionalized.*[27]

Since the poor have been subject to similar physical and psychological labeling, separate roles, subcultures, and institutions have been created for them also, resulting in high levels of deprivation and dependency: Class becomes the basis of identity, social status, and intergroup

[23]Firestone, *The Dialectic of Sex*, chapters 1, 4, 6, 9; for a summary of sex role research see A. R. Hochschild, "A Review of Sex Role Research,"

[24]M. Mead, *Sex and Temperament in Three Primitive Societies* (New York: Dell, 1969), first published 1935.

[25]P. Ariès, *Centuries of Childhood. A Social History of Family Life*, trans. R. Baldick (New York: Knopf, 1962).

[26]Rogers, *The Psychology of Adolescence;* eds. Rose and Peterson, "Mental Health of Normal Older Persons."

[27]F. Barth, ed., *Ethnic Groups and Boundaries* (London: Allen, 1969), pp. 9–38.

relations with negative consequences. Money operates in social organizations and group relations also.[28]

The "labeling perspective" has been most extensively applied to behavioral minorities: A deviant is created through societal reaction to norm violations with major focus on the twin processes of majority labeling and majority response to it.[29] Deviance is created through majority implementation of its own norms, resulting in minority roles and institutions. Deviants may respond by developing their own identities and subcultures. Such identities may conform to the deviant role assigned to them producing secondary deviance.[30] Deviant subcultures may also be reinforced through recruitment of new members (differential association theory) while these recruits learn their deviant roles through socialization. Once again, the process is similar to the creation of other minorities: Individuals, whether criminals, perverts, or mentally ill, are defined as physically and/or psychologically deficient and assigned specialized roles and segregated institutions. They, in turn, may respond by cultivating different identities and subcultures. In this manner minorities are created, institutionalized, and controlled.

To summarize, the social-psychological approach to minorities focuses on the *labeling process:* individuals are defined as physiologically and psychologically different and/or inferior with respect to assumed racial, sexual, age-based, cultural, economic, and behavioral factors and are assigned unique roles and separate institutional systems, producing minority subcultures and separate identities. In this manner the criteria of minority group differentiation become the basis of roles, the status system, and institutional structure, that is, the social organization in general. In contrast to physiological and psychological assumptions, this approach views minorities as a function of the social labeling process, that is, they are artificially produced for economic reasons. It is the societal context of this process that brings us to the sociological type of analysis.

SOCIOLOGICAL ASSUMPTIONS

Contemporary sociological discussions of minorities focus on the question, "What are the major *societal factors* or characteristics behind the *social creation* of minorities?" Sociological analyses attempt to abstract

[28]R. Sennett, and J. Cobb, *The Hidden Injuries of Class* (New York: Knopf, 1973).

[29]For a summary see N. J. Davis, *Sociological Constructions of Deviance* (Dubuque: W. C. Brown, 1975), chapter 7.

[30]See T. J. Scheff, *Being Mentally Ill* (Chicago: Aldine, 1966.)

the major structural factors in society behind the institutionalization of minority roles and subcultures, based on assumed physical and psychological inferiority. These discussions tend to focus on two major sets of factors already outlined: migration, subordination, and importation of groups for economic exploitation purposes; and, the effects of economic development, specifically industrialization. Accordingly, minorities are created in response to migration and economic development as societies change demographically, moving from the traditional and agricultural to the contemporary and industrial, reflecting the changing basis and distribution of material goods. Minorities reflect the changing basis of a society's economic system and its power structure.

Racial minorities, as we have pointed out, are primarily created by migration, subordination, and the importation processes which were part of general colonialism. As capitalism produced colonial migrations in the context of eighteenth and nineteenth century science and political ideologies, racial minorities were produced to meet the colonial need for unskilled labor. Sociological discussions focus on the major characteristics of societies which are highly racist, the conditions of intergroup contact, and changing race relations. These studies tend to portray racist elites as migrant, usually WASP in culture, primarily concerned with economic exploitation. Initial racial contact tends to be negative and conflict ridden, setting a negative precedent for relations which follow. As industrialization and urbanization proceed, changing economic conditions, particularly the elite economic interests and minority resource levels, race relations move through a number of changing ecological frontiers, from the "paternalistic" to the "competitive" and conflict oriented.[31] In general, racial minorities are created by migrant WASP elites for capitalistic purposes. Contact is negative and race relations become increasingly competitive and conflict oriented. Consequently, a racial hierarchy is produced based upon the historical context of migration, perceived physical and cultural characteristics, and economic resources.[32] "Race" becomes institutionalized as the basis of political, economic, and social relations.

Sexual minorities are viewed more as a result of economic development: Unique biological characteristics of the female have resulted in a sexual division of labor which, with economic change, resulted in the patriarchal nuclear family based on a "power psychology," sexism,

[31]For a summary of this literature, see Kinloch, *The Dynamics of Race Relations*, chapter 9.

[32]Kinloch, *The Dynamics of Race Relations*, chapter 13.

and male dominated culture.[33] As a major consequence, women have little or no political and economic power, primarily offering psychological support for males. Economic specialization is viewed as transforming a sexual division of labor into sexism and sexual domination in response to the role specialization demands produced by industrialization. Sexist roles and labeling are thus a function of demographic-economic change.

Similar processes are assumed to apply to the evolution of age-based minorities: With economic change and evolution of the bourgeoisie, the extended family (extended kinship system) began to decline as institutional specialization emerged. Children became separated from the wider society within the boundaries of the family and became subject to segregation, dependence, and separate institutions.[34] These processes have been extended to the notion of "adolescence" in contemporary society. Role specialization and the decline of the extended family also resulted in the segregation, dependence, and institutionalization of the aged.[35] Consequently, age discrimination is also viewed as a characteristic of economic development and role specialization, based upon assumed physical and psychological inferiority. Production of a highly specialized family form has resulted in dependence, segregation, and institutionalization based upon age.

Ethnic minorities, on the other hand, are assumed to be an outgrowth of intergroup contact under conditions of competition, differential power, and ethnocentrism.[36] When migration occurs in situations which are not defined in racial terms, cultural minorities are produced in response to vested economic interests and an ethnic hierarchy develops in a similar manner to racial structures, subject to changing ecological frontiers too. As with racial minorities, the processes of migration, subordination, and importation apply also, as do particular elite characteristics (size, types of values) and the effects of economic change.[37]

[33]See Firestone, *The Dialectic of Sex;* Friedan, *The Feminine Mystique;* Chafetz, *Masculine, Feminine, or Human?* for examples of this approach. Firestone is, perhaps, the most theoretically developed of the three. See also R. Collins, "A Conflict Theory of Sexual Stratification," *Social Problems,* 19 (1971), pp. 3–20 and M. K. Martin, and B. Voorhies, *Female of the Species* (New York: Columbia University Press, 1975).

[34]See Firestone, *The Dialectic of Sex,* chapter 4.

[35]See, for example, "Institutionalization, Interaction, and Self-Conception in Aging," in Rose and Peterson, eds., "Mental Health of Normal Older Persons," pp. 245–58.

[36]See D. L. Noel, "A Theory of the Origin of Ethnic Stratification," *Social Problems,* 16 (1968), pp. 157–71.

[37]E. K. Francis, *Interethnic Relations. An Essay in Sociological Theory* (New York: Elsevier, 1976).

Economic minorities are also assumed to represent outcomes of economic development: As a society grows in size and its economic system moves toward materialism as its foundation along with a specialized division of labor, high levels of economic monopoly and differentiation occur, resulting in the production of subordinate and deprived economic groups.[38] Such deprivation is rationalized through cultural values such as moralism and individualism, and is based upon assumed physiological and psychological deficiencies. As capitalism evolves and property becomes the basis of the economic system, resource monopoly emerges as the basis of the class system, producing poverty and the working class. While material deprivation has obviously occurred throughout human history, the creation of economic classes is viewed primarily as a function of specific types of economic development, namely, industrial capitalism.

Behavioral minorities are also viewed as a creation of economic factors: The shift from feudalism to capitalism produced unemployment and groups without material resources. Links between materialistic-moralistic values, science, medicine, politics, and the law are seen as resulting in the institutionalization of "deviant" minorities while societies which are socially heterogeneous are extremely punitive as they attempt to maximize social cohesion through various mechanisms of social control.[39] Accordingly, as capitalistic societies become more materialistic and socially heterogeneous, behavioral deviance is subject to increasing levels of identification, control, institutionalization, and punishment. Behavioral minorities mirror or reflect moral, structural, and economic characteristics of the society in which they are created.[40]

The sociological approach to minorities views them primarily as a result of two major processes: Migration, subordination, and importation for economic exploitation, and the effects of economic development, specifically industrialization. Racial and cultural minorities are seen as products of various types of migration while sexual, age-based, economic, and behavioral minorities are the products of economic development. In all of this an underlying theme is evident: Economic change, specifically the shift from feudalism to capitalism, resulted in *economic migration* (producing racial and ethnic minorities) and *economic specialization* creating social groups based on assumed sexual,

---

[38]K. Marx, *Selected Writings in Sociology and Social Philosophy*, T. B. Bottomore, ed. (New York: McGraw-Hill, 1964; G. Lenski, *Power and Privilege. A Theory of Social Stratification* (New York: McGraw-Hill, 1966).

[39]See, for example, M. Foucault, *Madness and Civilization* (New York: Vintage, 1973); H. D. Seibel, "Social Deviance in Comparative Perspective," in R. A. Scott and J. D. Douglas, eds., *Theoretical Perspectives on Deviance* (New York: Basic Books, 1972), pp. 251–81.

[40]K. T. Erikson, *Wayward Puritans; A Study in the Sociology of Deviance* (New York: Wiley, 1966).

age-related, economic, and behavioral characteristics. In this manner sociological analyses delineate the *societal context* (particularly the economic) in which the social creation of minorities occurs. In Chapter 3 we emphasized that we were taking a power-relations approach to minority group relations in order to overcome problems of limited definitions, restricted perspectives, and academic bias. Considered in the context of sociological assumptions highlighting the societal factors of migration and economic specialization, it should be apparent that our perspective attempts to bring these approaches together in an effort to understand the creation and interaction of minority groups generally. Far from being unusual, it is situated *within* the sociological tradition.

Social Psychological and Sociological Assumptions Summarized

In contrast to physiological and psychological assumptions, the above two approaches focus on the social context of minority relations: Social psychological analyses focus on the social labeling process in which individuals are defined as physiologically and psychologically different and/or inferior and are assigned unique roles and separate institutions, producing minority subcultures and separate identities. The sociological, on the other hand, sees certain demographic developments producing economic migrations, and economic specialization producing major factors behind the labeling process. It is obvious that the two approaches are closely connected: Economic migration and specialization result in social labeling and the creation of unique roles, institutions, subcultures, and identities—the basis of minority relations. The former is more closely tied to the production of racial and cultural

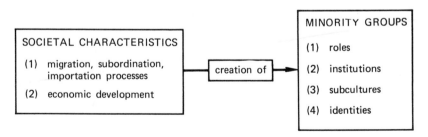

FIGURE 6.2   The Relationship Between Sociological and Social Psychological Assumptions Concerning Minorities

minorities, while economic specialization appears correlated with the creation of sexual, age-based, economic, and behavioral groups. Such a process is summarized in Figure 6.2.

CONCLUSIONS

In this chapter we have attempted to delineate major assumptions underlying the creation of minority groups. These involved ideas concerning the physiological characteristics of group members, their personalities, minority group roles, subcultures and institutions, and the social contexts in which these factors operate. In the first instance science, medicine, and religion combined to create a physiological definition of minorities; in the second, Freudian personality theory, intelligence tests, adolescent psychology, studies of values and lifestyles, popular stereotyping, medicine, and psychiatry contributed to the labeling of minority group personalities as deficient in emotional control, intelligence, and civilized behavior. The social psychological approach, on the other hand, views minorities as *a result of this physiological-psychological labeling process,* producing minority roles, institutions, subcultures, and identities; while sociological analyses explicate characteristics of the societal context in which this process occurs, specifically economic migration and specialization. It is possible to synthesize these four types of assumptions to highlight the *general process* by which minorities are created: *Economic migration and specialization result in the creation of minority roles, institutions, subcultures, and identities based upon assumed physiological and psychological differences and/or inferiority, representing the assumed opposite of majority characteristics and reinforced by science, medicine, religion, psychology, and psychiatry.* Minority groups are created for economic reasons, are rationalized by scientific and cultural ideologies, and represent the basis of interpersonal relations, the institutional structure, and stratification. The major characteristics of this process are summarized in Figure 6.3.

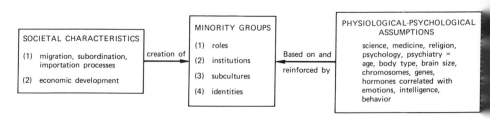

FIGURE 6.3 Major Factors Involved in the Social Creation of Minorities

STUDY QUESTIONS

1. Outline some popular assumptions concerning the physiology and personalities of children and the aged. What attitudinal similarities do you notice?
2. Delineate some popular notions concerning the "adolescent personality." What do they have in common with attitudes toward children?
3. What are some common stereotypes regarding "criminals." How do they relate to our discussion in this chapter?
4. Outline the structural dimensions of institutionalized sexism. What do they reveal about society?
5. Compare racial with economic minorities. What do you conclude?

READINGS

Aries, P., *Centuries of Childhood, A Social History of Family Life* (trans. R. Baldick), New York: Knopf, 1962.

Banton, M., *Race Relations*, New York: Basic Books, 1967.

Bremner, R. H., *From the Depths*, New York: New York University Press, 1966.

Chafetz, J. S., *Masculine/Feminine or Human?* Itasca: Peacock, 1974.

Collins, R., "A Conflict Theory of Sexual Stratification," *Social Problems*, 19, 1971, pp. 3–21.

Davis, N. J. *Social Contructions of Deviance*, Dubuque: W. C. Brown, 1975.

Dworkin, A. G., and R. J. Dworkin (eds.), *The Minority Report, An Introduction to Racial, Ethnic, and Gender Relations*, New York: Praeger, 1976.

Erikson, K. T., *Wayward Puritans: A Study in the Sociology of Deviance*, New York: Wiley, 1966.

Feagin, J. R., *Subordinating the Poor, Welfare and American Beliefs*, Englewood Cliffs, N.J.: Prentice Hall, 1975.

Firestone, S., *The Dialectic of Sex, The Case for Feminist Revolution*, New York: Bantam, 1971.

Foucault, M., *Madness and Civilization*, New York: Vintage, 1973.

Frazier, E. F., "Sociological Theory and Race Relations," *American Sociological Review*, 12, 1947, pp. 265–71.

Fredrickson, G. M., *The Black Image in the White Mind*, New York: Harper & Row, 1971.

Friedan, B., *The Feminine Mystique*, New York: Dell, 1964.

Gosset, T. P., *Race: The History of an Idea in America*, Dallas: Southern Methodist University Press, 1963.

Jordan, W. P., *White over Black: American Attitudes toward the Negro, 1550–1812*, Chapel Hill: University of North Carolina Press, 1968.

Kinloch, G. C., *The Dynamics of Race Relations, A Sociological Analysis,* New York: McGraw-Hill, 1974.

Lenski, G., *Power and Privilege, A Theory of Social Stratification,* New York: McGraw-Hill, 1966.

Martin, M. K., and B. Voorhies, *Female of the Species,* New York: Columbia University Press, 1975.

Noel, D. L., "A Theory of the Origin of Ethnic Stratification," *Social Problems,* 16, 1968, pp. 157–71.

Rothman, D. J., *The Discovery of the Asylum,* Boston: Little Brown, 1971.

Scott, R. A., and J. D. Douglas (eds.), *Theoretical Perspectives on Deviance,* New York: Basic Books, 1972.

SUMMARY
OF
SECTION TWO

In this section of our discussion we have dealt with three topics: basic concepts and definitions, major types of minorities, and assumptions concerning them. We reached the following conclusions:

Majorities are power groups which define themselves as "normal" and superior and others as "abnormal" and inferior on the basis of perceived physical, cultural, economic, and behavioral characteristics. Minority groups are socially created by particular power elites who exploit and control them. Consequent relations may be peaceful or conflict-ridden but are dynamic and constantly changing. Both majority-minority and interminority relations represent intergroup relations within a power context in which physical, cultural, economic, and behavioral criteria are used as the basis of group differentiation.

Minorities are created through two major processes: migration with consequent subordination and importation, and economic development, specifically industrial capitalism and the role specialization it demands. Racial and cultural minorities are an outgrowth of the former, while sexual, age-based, economic, and behavioral minorities are produced more by the latter. In general, however, minorities are large, heterogeneous, they overlap, are defined as possessing the majority's opposite characteristics, and are subject to institutionalized domination, and control-oriented policies. In heterogeneous societies, furthermore, a minority group hierarchy may exist with race at the peak, ethnicity operating within racial boundaries, class differences next, and within each class division, the effects of sex, age, and deviance last.

We focused on the major assumptions underlying the creation of minority groups—physiological, psychological, social-psychological, and sociological. In the first instance science, medicine, and religion combined to create a physiological definition of minorities. In the second, Freudian personality theory, intelligence tests, adolescent psychology, studies of values and lifestyles, popular stereotyping, medicine, and psychiatry all contributed to the psychological labeling of minority group personalities as being deficient in emotional control, intelligence, and civilized behavior. The social-psychological approach, on the other hand, views minorities as a function of this physiological-psychological labeling process, producing minority roles, institutions, subcultures, and identities. Sociological analyses highlight characteristics of the societal context in which this process occurs, specifically in economic migration and specialization. Bringing these sets of assumptions together we concluded that economic migration and specialization result in the creation of minority roles, institutions, subcultures, and identities based upon assumed physiological and psychological differences and/or inferiority, and represent the assumed opposite of majority characteristics, reinforced by science, medicine, religion, psychology, and psychiatry.

From these definitions and theories it is possible to view *minorities as groups socially created by power elites, on the basis of perceived physical, cultural, economic, and behavioral characteristics, for economic reasons and as a result of economic migration and specialization. The creation of these groups is rationalized in scientific, medical, and religious terms, produces minority roles, institutions, subcultures, and identities, and forms a minority hierarchy in society.* Furthermore, there appear to be three broad types of minority:

1. Those created through *migration, subordination,* and *importation,* that is, *racial* and *ethnic* minorities. Their function in society is primarily *economic,* with prejudice focusing on their lack of *intelligence,* rationalizing their subordinate economic and occupational position. These groups represent the foundation of the minority group hierarchy.

2. Minorities are created through *economic specialization* (particularly within the context of the nuclear family), or the *sexual* and *age-based* groups. Their function is primarily *psychological* and they are viewed as highly *emotional,* thereby rationalizing their segregation and political economic deprivation.

3. Minorities are produced through *economic differentiation,* that is, the *economic* and *behavioral minorities.* They are viewed as *behaviorally deficient* (lacking in civilized behavior), and so their subordinate economic position and level of institutionalized control are rationalized.

In general, then, three major types of minorities appear to exist, produced through migration, economic specialization, and economic differentiation. They perform *economic, psychological,* and *normative functions* in society, and are rationalized in *intellectual, emotional,* and *behavioral terms,* producing a hierarchy defined by the *economic type.*

Having defined the major elements in our approach to minorities, we now integrate them into a preliminary conceptual framework.

Section Three

A GENERAL CONCEPTUAL FRAMEWORK

7

Origin and Emergence of Minority Group Relations

Our discussion so far has included consideration of a number of concepts, characteristics of a range of minority types, and major assumptions underlying processes by which they are socially created. In this chapter we shall bring these factors together in a general conceptual framework before applying them to specific minorities, both in the United States and other parts of the world. We shall focus on major factors behind minority groups, relationships among these elements, characteristics of the minority group hierarchy, stages of minority group relations and the feedback they provide, and we shall develop a general framework which interrelates these factors.

MAJOR FACTORS

We have delineated three major types of factors involved in minority group relations: societal, group, and individual. The first of these consists of two elements both of which are economic in nature—migration, and economic development, specifically industrialization. The former consists of the migration of colonial elites who were concerned with material resources and a supply of cheap, unskilled labor to be used for capital gain. As a consequence the indigenous population was subordinated, its natural resources appropriated, and an attempt made to use it for labor purposes. Outside groups may also have been imported for specific economic roles, creating a racial hierarchy for material reasons, as already indicated. More voluntary migration may also have been involved, as exemplified in the case of European immigrants to the United States who emigrated to improve their economic conditions, resulting in the creation of ethnic minorities located within the racial hierarchy. The two types of minority, however, are closely correlated since colonial migration may produce involuntary ethnic groups as evident in the Irish situation. Tribal migrations in more traditional societies may have similar effects. Migration for economic purposes is thus a major societal factor in the creation of racial and ethnic groups.

Economic development may have two major effects: increased economic differentiation as economic systems become more materially based and subject to control and monopolization, resulting in economic and behavioral minorities; and, increased role specialization in response to the highly specialized role requirements of an industrial urban economy. Operating through the nuclear family, this has produced sexual and age-based minorities which are subject to segregation and dependency. In the first instance economic development has resulted in elitism and control of the economic system as society has moved from communal to private property and from feudalism to capitalism, increasing economic differentiation and deprivation generally. Furthermore, the legal system is designed to defend this elitism while the response to increasing social heterogeneity is highly punitive. The second process may be viewed as an "adaptive" societal reaction to society's increasing population size within the context of an economic system which is becoming increasingly specialized, resulting in *institutional specialization.* The family structure thus evolves from the extended toward the nuclear, segregating the aged in the process, while the need to prepare offspring for future occupational roles reinforces their segregation and control, creating the need for mothers, and producing *sexual minorities.* Accordingly, economic development may be viewed as contributing to the creation of sexual, age-based, economic, and behavioral minorities, while migration has produced racial and ethnic domination. In general, it appears that as a society increases in size so do its economic needs. This may result in economic specialization and differentiation as well as various population migrations for economic purposes. Major consequences of these processes include the creation of minority groups based upon assumed physical, cultural, economic, and behavioral characteristics. As society has expanded, moving from the traditional through the feudal to the capitalist, groupings have been created, reflecting expansion of, and reaction to, changing economic needs. Major societal factors in minority group relations are thus demographic and economic.

We also outlined basic *group factors* involved in this creation or "labeling" process: *roles, institutions,* and *subcultures,* subject to *segregation, control,* and *exploitation.* Roles represent majority labeling of the minority individual's assumed physiological and psychological characteristics and the person's assigned subordinate political, economic, and social position in society as a consequence. Institutions consist of sets of interlinked groups and organizations designed to meet majority political, economic, and social needs. Institutional access, resources, and stereotypes of minorities are controlled by majority elites to ensure vested interests and exploitation of the former. As a consequence of this segregation and control, minorities tend to develop their own subcultures as they adapt to their subordinate position in society. At the group level, then, minority roles, institutions, and subcultures are created, subject to majority segregation, control, and exploitation. The structural consequences of migration and economic development involve the formation of separate minority social structures in order to maximize the subordinate functions they are designed to serve, whether economic, psychological, or normative, and ensure the maintenance of majority group interests. Accordingly, varying types of structural arrangements are institutionalized (economic, psychological, and normative) to meet these differing functions, arranged in a minority group hierarchy. These functions tend to define the nature of majority-minority relations since they represent different kinds of vested interests.

At the individual level, these "structures" operate primarily through the process of socialization in which a person absorbs majority labeling in terms of assumed physiological and psychological inferiorities, resulting in minority group identities. Through controlled institutions such as education and the media, individuals learn their assigned minority roles in society with associated forms of expected behavior. Variations in individual status in the hierarchy will, of course, influence their self-concepts and identities, with an attempt to maximize higher status roles. In this regard, racial and ethnic factors may override psychological and normative-type roles since they serve economic functions primarily. Nevertheless, all dimensions of minority group status operate at the individual level through socialization and minority group identities.

To summarize, minority group relations consist of three major sets of factors: the *societal* (migration, economic development), *group* factors (roles, institutions, and subcultures subject to segregation, control, and exploitation), and the *individual* (socialization, identity). We shall examine how these elements are interrelated.

INTERRELATIONSHIPS

A number of relationships are evident in the factors we have just outlined: In general it appears that minority group differentiation is an outgrowth of migration, economic differentiation and specialization. Minority roles, institutions, and subcultures perpetuated through socialization and individual identity are produced by migration and economic development as a society develops demographically and in its division of labor. More specifically, migration, both external and voluntary, results in the creation of racial and ethnic minorities, serving economic functions. Economic differentiation, on the other hand, produces economic and behavioral minorities which serve normative functions, reinforcing majority ideologies. Economic specialization, operating particularly through the evolving nuclear family, results in the creation of sexual and age-based minorities serving psychological functions. It appears, then, that as society has increased in size, division of labor, and a materialistic type of economy in the shift from feudalism to capitalism, economic migrations, differentiation, and specialization occur. This results in the creation of racial, cultural, economic, behavioral, sexual, and age-based minorities which serve economic, normative, and psychological functions and become the basis of social organization through segregation, institutionalization, and socialization. A minority group hierarchy is created, representing a complex system of segregation, control, and exploitation. According to this perspective, *minority groups represent forms of social differentiation produced by demographic and economic change, serve the economic needs of majority groups, and are based upon assumed physiological and psychological inferiority.* In this manner minorities result from, and serve economic interests. The majorities rationalize the formation of these groups in terms of assumed inferiority that is reinforced through science and religion, and operates at individual, group, and societal levels of social organization. Consequently, social structure is complex and multidimensional, representing a hierarchal system of domination, control, and exploitation, the characteristics of which we discuss next.

THE MINORITY GROUP HIERARCHY

Depending upon a society's history of migration and economic development, a number of hierarchy types are possible: those based primarily upon migration—the typical *colonial* situation such as South Africa and Northern Ireland; situations in which *economic factors* are paramount (Great Britain); and, societies which represent a *combination* of both migration and economic development, the prime example being the United States. Such differences result in varying types of hierarchy: the *racial-ethnic, economic,* and the *racial-ethnic-economic.* In each case there is a majority-minority hierarchy based on the major societal factors involved. Where an individual stands with respect to each criterion (that is, whether he is a member of the majority or minority) defines his position in the hierarchy. Furthermore, the relative importance of each type of criterion in the hierarchy influences that position also. The operation of these criteria is further defined by a community's particular economic and ecological characteristics, (minority group relations at the local level reflect the community's past history, or types of migration), demographic make-up (population characteristics), as well as level and type of economic development.

In the typical colonial situation a simple hierarchy exists with race and/or ethnicity as its foundation, resulting in a castelike structure. While differentiation is based on other kinds of criteria, it is very limited and does not significantly alter the caste system. Economic-type hierarchies are also relatively homogeneous and limited by class boundaries. As they are subject to significant economic development, however, the influence of sexual, age-linked, and behavioral factors increases although class remains significant. The most complex hierarchies, on the other hand, are those produced in societies based upon both migration and significant levels of economic development. Here, as we have pointed out, all major types of minorities may exist, arranged in a hierarchy based on race and/or ethnicity and class, further differentiated by sex, age, and behavior. This appears so in America where a highly complex hierarchy exists in which a person's status with respect to at least six criteria locates him in the social structure and intergroup relations. Whether an individual is white or nonwhite, WASP or non-WASP, economically viable or poor, male or female, an adult or child, a conformist or deviate, defines his/her general position in society. It is the *combination* or *profile* of the *majority-minority status* with respect to these factors and how they operate at the *local level* that locates the person in society and within intergroup relations. Furthermore, we have attempted to show that different criteria represent differing *societal functions,* the economic, normative, and psychological. Particular combinations of status will maximize particular types of *resources* as related to these functions within the hierarchy. In earlier chapters we indicated the extent to which minority group criteria interact and overlap: Resource advantages become cumulative the more an individual is a member of minority groups at the higher levels of the hierarchy, particularly those with economic and normative functions. In this manner the hierarchy is highly structured and based on a *power hierarchy.*

To summarize, minority group hierarchies reflect particular combinations of migration and economic development on both societal and community levels, are defined by underlying economic functions, represent a combination of economic, normative, and psychological functions in the most complex societies, and operate at the individual level through a person's majority-minority membership profile. Resource advantages are cumulative when an individual is a member of majority groups at upper levels of the hierarchy.

In general, then, minority group hierarchies reflect societal and community characteristics, are economically based, represent varying resources and functions, define an individual's specific social status, and offer cumulative advantages at the upper levels. Such structures are also not static but proceed through a number of stages as we shall attempt to outline next.

STAGES OF MINORITY GROUP RELATIONS

Stages of minority group relations represent specific demographic economic situations, that is, population characteristics, migrations, and types of economic development. Variations in these situations occur at both societal and community levels. We have outlined three types of situations: (1) those minority situations which are primarily a function of migration, creating racial and ethnic problems (Northern Ireland); (2) situations in which economic differentiation and/or specialization are paramount creating sexual, age-based, economic, and behavioral minorities (Western Europe); and, (3) societies representing combinations of migration and economic development (United States, Canada). Accordingly, stages of minority group relations may be viewed as various combinations of demographic and economic factors. Beginning with the former, significant population growth may (or may not) occur. If it does take place, economic development may (or may not) be the outcome, starting with differentiation and resulting eventually (perhaps) in specialization. A major consequence of economic development may (or may not) be (colonial) migration producing significant racial and/or cultural minorities. Should economic development and migration combine—the racial-ethnic-economic type—the most complex form of minority group hierarchy may evolve as in the case of the United States. We thus have several major possibilities: demographic change without economic development, demographic growth with economic development, demographic growth, economic development, and migration, and a combination of all three, resulting in a complex hierarchy with economic specialization. Such a typology is broad and simplified but points to some of the ways in which demographic and economic factors operate in minority group relations. It is possible, for example, that any particular society or community may proceed through some or all of these combinations with varying outcomes while further demographic and/or economic changes in each type (but the last in particular) may modify the hierarchy, causing various minorities to reject their subordinate status and organize against discrimination, modifying the hierarchy's shape in an ongoing fashion and providing significant feedback into the social system. In this manner minority group hierarchies reflect demographic and economic factors and are significantly modified by them in an ongoing fashion, leading to constant change, modification, and feedback.

So far we have attempted to delineate major factors involved in minority group relations, their interrelationships, characteristics of minority group hierarchies, and stages in minority group relations. We next synthesize them in the form of a general conceptual framework.

A GENERAL CONCEPTUAL FRAMEWORK

We have stated that as a society increases in size so do its economic needs, resulting in economic differentiation and specialization as well as in various population migrations. These produce minority groups based upon assumed physical, cultural, economic, and behavioral characteristics. Specific stages in these processes may be delineated as follows:

1. As a society increases in the *size* of its *population* so do its *economic needs.*

2. Increased economic needs may result in an increase in the society's *division of labor,* that is, increased role specialization.

3. This may shift the basis of the economic system from communal to *private property,* particularly as the society moves from feudalism toward capitalism.

4. Private property, as it becomes subject to control and monopolization, may result in *economic differentiation,* producing *economic* and the beginnings of *behavioral minorities.* Consequently roles, institutions, and subcultures are developed through segregation, control, and exploitation, operating in socialization and individual identities, based upon assumed physiological and psychological inferiority.

5. A major demographic consequence of this differentiation may be *colonial migration* for capitalist economic purposes, with associated processes of *subordination* and *importation. Racial* and/or *cultural minorities* may be produced as a result, reinforced by science and religion.

6. Economic differentiation and migration may result in *economic specialization,* producing the nuclear family and associated *sexual* and *age-based minorities.*

7. The combination of economic differentiation, migration, and economic specialization may result in a *complex minority hierarchy* based on race, ethnicity, class, sex, age, and behavior, reinforced by science, medicine, psychology, and religion, and serving economic, normative, and psychological functions. This hierarchy reflects societal and community characteristics, is economically based, represents varying resources and functions, defines an individual's specific social status, and offers cumulative advantages at the upper levels.

8. Finally, *further demographic and/or economic developments modify* this hierarchy and provide *feedback* into the social system.

This framework is summarized in Figure 7.1. A number of points at this stage require emphasis. This framework is broad and preliminary only. Specific minority group situations represent particular combinations of these factors, and the framework as a whole is based on the *general proposition* that *minority groups are a consequence of demographic growth, migration, and economic development, and are based upon assumed physical, cultural, economic, and behavioral characteristics.*

We turn now to some of the framework's major implications.

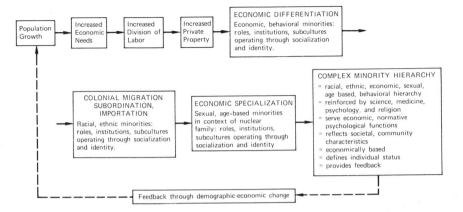

FIGURE 7.1 A Conceptual Framework of Major Factors Defining Minority
Group Relations

MAJOR IMPLICATIONS

This approach to minority group relations implies a number of major
conclusions:

1. Minority group relations are primarily an outgrowth of demographic and economic factors.
2. Economic development, far from representing functional societal evolution, leads in fact to the emergence of various types of domination and exploitation.
3. As we have attempted to show, different types of economic development are related to the evolution of different types of minority: Differentiation produces economic and behavioral minorities while specialization appears correlated with sexual and age-based types.
4. Migration (for economic purposes) on the other hand, appears to produce the most basic and negative forms of domination —the racial and ethnic—since they serve economic functions primarily.
5. According to this approach, science, medicine, and religion, far from liberating human beings from domination, rationalize their segregation, control, and exploitation. This implies that science requires careful scrutiny for evidence of its "legitimizing" role in contemporary society.
6. The links between specific societal characteristics and types of minority group relations appear high and require further

examination as we shall carry out in Chapter 12 of our analysis.

7. The structure of minority domination/exploitation operates at all levels of the social system—individual, group, and societal —defining *all* human relations as well as the individual's definition of himself.

8. As minority groups evolve, the societal functions they serve increase, moving from the economic, to the normative, to the psychological. In this manner domination becomes more institutionalized with economic change.

9. Such a framework provides a focus for detailed examination of the relationship between demographic economic development and changing minority group relations as well as the comparative, cross-cultural analysis of these structures.

CONCLUSIONS

In this chapter we have developed a general conceptual framework used to analyze minority group relations by linking major societal, group, and individual factors to the processes by which minority groups are created and the hierarchies within which they interact. We concluded that these groups are a function of demographic growth, migration, and economic development, and are based upon assumed physical, cultural, economic, and behavioral characteristics. In the next major section of our discussion we shall attempt to apply this framework to minority group relations both in the United States and other societies, moving toward a general theory of these relations and its practical implications on a number of levels.

STUDY QUESTIONS

1. Using the conceptual framework developed in this chapter, attempt to account for:
   (a) The economic position of the British working class.
   (b) The segregated position of American children.
   (c) The legal oppression of American behavioral minorities.
   (d) Cultural prejudice in the United States.
   (e) The subordinate political position of American women.

Section Four

AN ANALYSIS OF MINORITY GROUP RELATIONS

8

Physically Defined Minorities in the United States

Having completed a preliminary conceptual framework, we shall apply that perspective to an understanding of minority group relations in the United States and other parts of the world. We shall deal with physical, cultural, economic, and behavioral minorities in American society, focusing on their historical, demographic, attitudinal, institutional, social movement, and relational characteristics in the context of the analytical framework we have just developed. In Chapter 12, on the other hand, we shall carry out a comparative analysis of major types of minority with reference to general variables such as migration and economic development at the societal level of analysis. We begin with an analysis of racial, sexual, and age-based minorities in the United States, outlining the general characteristics of the society first.

THE GENERAL CHARACTERISTICS OF
AMERICAN SOCIETY

America possesses all the major characteristics of a highly differentiated society: Its social structure consists of a complex hierarchy of all types of minorities, it has been subject to all major kinds of migration, subordination, and importation, while economic differentiation and specialization have occurred at very high levels. Founded by a migrant, WASP, colonial elite, it has experienced high exploitation and domination for economic purposes, resulting in a complex social structure clearly defined by all major minority criteria, heavily rationalized in scientific and moral terms. This is a *highly developed colonial-type society* with a large number of minorities as a result. Racial minorities have been created through colonial white migration, the subordination of Indians, and importation of a wide variety of other racial groups for economic-labor purposes, in some cases as slaves. Sexual and age-based domination, on the other hand, have evolved through high rates of industrialization and urbanization while cultural minorities have emerged primarily through European migration but under conditions of economic exploitation and control. Processes such as industrialization, depression, inflation, and recession have also produced economic minorities where subordinate status is reinforced by the economic exploitation of other minorities, integrating the social hierarchy further. Finally, these economic developments have contributed to the development of behavioral minorities subject to high levels of institutionalization and control. In general, this society may be ranked high in terms of the three major processes we have delineated as crucial to the creation of minorities: migration-subordination-importation, economic differentiation, and economic specialization. As a consequence, it is highly differentiated by minority group criteria as well as economic exploitation and control. More specifically, the major characteristics of minority group relations in the United States may be outlined as follows:

1. They have been created and are controlled by a *colonial, WASP majority* whose prime motives and cultural values emphasize materialism and economic exploitation.

2. These orientations have resulted in high levels of *migration, subordination,* and *importation* for economic purposes.

3. As a result of these processes, *economic differentiation* and *specialization* have been extremely high.

4. Within the context of this utilitarian, pragmatic culture, *science* and *religion* have been used to rationalize minority group domination and exploitation on the basis of assumed

physical and psychological inferiority—a labeling process which judges minorities as less "human" than majorities—a process of dehumanization.

5. A *complex hierarchy* has been produced based on race—a function of original colonial migration, ethnicity, and class, further differentiated by sex, age, and deviance. These elements in the hierarchy represent specific stages in societal development based on economic processes.

6. This hierarchy is *highly integrated* with upper level elements defining the operation of other dimensions, for example, race influences economic and behavioral discrimination, class mediates behavioral sanctions.

7. As previously indicated, this hierarchy defines an *individual's status in society* depending upon his majority-minority profile, that is, the closer he is to a white, male, adult, WASP, middle- or upper-class conformist, the more status he will tend to possess. Such status also tends to be *cumulative* the higher the person's rank is on this hierarchy, and results in *intergroup competition*. These status factors define *interaction* at both individual and group levels, that is, minority group relations.

8. This hierarchy also represents various *societal functions* with the economic defining the *normative* and *psychological*. This social structure serves a number of purposes in society and is *highly institutionalized* as a result.

9. The ranking is subject to *modification and change through economic development* which may result in the creation of further minorities, their radical reaction, and eventually perhaps, decline. Processes such as industrialization, urbanization, depression, and recession all influence the hierarchy in one way or another.

10. Nevertheless, the system remains basically *stable* in structure given the extent to which it is institutionalized and represents vested economic interests. Majority-minority relations thus tend to be *conservative* as the former attempt to maintain and maximize their material resources.

In general, American society represents a complex hierarchy of minority groups, produced and controlled by a colonial WASP elite attempting to maximize its economic interests. This structure is rationalized in scientific and religious terms, is highly integrated, defines status and interaction, serves a variety of societal functions, and is subject to economic change but remains basically stable. Far from being a "melting pot," this society is highly structured, hierarchical, and exploitive, founded to maximize material gain. We examine these characteristics in greater detail by focusing on each of the society's major minority groups.

Racial Minorities

Race is basic to the foundation of American society: The dominant political, economic, and social majority remains white while the socio-economic structure is heavily defined by the economic roles historically assigned to each race group through subordination and importation. Reinforced by segregation and institutionalized exploitation, race remains the foundation of the society's social system. America may thus be viewed as a colonial, racist-type society. Furthermore, race operates as the basis of the socioeconomic hierarchy, stereotyping, and cultural differences. Its influence throughout the society is extensive, reinforced by the instrumental values inherent in WASP culture.

The historical context in which American race relations originated and continue to operate is overwhelmingly negative and consists of race wars, slavery, lynching, colonial seizure, importation for labor purposes, and elite backlash to attempted social change.[1] Reinforced by WASP culture, religion, and science, racism serves an important *economic* function in the society in the manner nonwhite groups provide labor resources for a capitalist economy or, in the case of Indians, have been relegated to a segregated and essentially irrelevant societal role. Indians were subjugated through warfare for the sake of land. Blacks were subjected to slavery, the Japanese and Chinese were imported for labor purposes and suffered severe treatment including lynching, Mexicans continue to be exploited for unskilled labor, while Filipinos, Hawaiians, and Puerto Ricans have all been subjected to American colonial domination. Racial minorities in this society were created (for economic purposes) under extremely negative circumstances—conditions which continue to influence race relations.

The demography of "race" in American society reveals a large white majority (87.5 percent), blacks next (11.1 percent) with other groups much smaller (Indians 0.4 percent, Japanese 0.3 percent, Chinese 0.2 percent, Filipino 0.2 percent).[2] Blacks represent the largest minority with other races small but approximately equal in size at 0.2

[1]For a documented history of these circumstances see P. Jacobs and S. Landau, eds., *To Serve the Devil*, Vols. I, II, (New York: Vintage, 1971).

[2]Based on U.S. Bureau of the Census, *Statistical Abstract of the United States: 1974*, 95th ed., (Washington, D.C.: 1974), Tables 1, 16, 33.

percent to 0.4 percent of the total population. When the occupational characteristics of these groups is examined, a clear racial socioeconomic hierarchy is evident: Chinese, Japanese, and whites are more heavily concentrated in professional, managerial, sales, and clerical positions. Filipinos, those of Spanish origin, Indians, and blacks are more involved in skilled, semiskilled, and unskilled occupations.[3] Earlier work by Schmid and Nobbe confirms the existence of this Oriental-white-Filipino-black-Indian hierarchy in the 1960s.[4] Whites and Orientals thus clearly compose the upper ranks with other nonwhites in the lower levels. Income data, furthermore, indicate that Blacks are consistently paid less than whites at all levels of the occupational structure[5] while poverty statistics reveal that in contrast to whites, 9.0 percent of whom are below the "low income level," approximately 24 percent of Mexicans, 21 percent of those of Spanish origin, and 32 percent of Blacks (and others) fall below this level compared with a national rate of 12 percent.[6] Race is highly correlated with occupational status, income, and poverty. In general, the racial structure of this society reveals a large white majority, a white-Oriental socioeconomic elite, and a high correlation between nonwhite status, low income, and high levels of poverty. Race is clearly tied to the economic system with nonwhites being in discriminatory, subordinate positions.

Majority attitudes reflect this socioeconomic hierarchy and tend to be more negative the darker and more different the particular group. Blacks and Indians tend to be rejected the most, Mexicans to a lesser extent, while Orientals are more accepted.[7] Rationales used as the basis of this rejection are remarkably homogeneous: Nonwhites are assumed to be physically, intellectually, and behaviorally inferior to whites whether they are Black, Indian, Oriental or Chicano.[8] Once again the opposite or reverse definitional process is operating: Nonwhites are

[3]Based on U.S. Bureau of the Census, *1970 Census of Population, Subject Reports, Occupational Characteristics,* PC(2)-7A, (Washington, D.C.: 1971), Table 2.

[4]C. F. Schmid and C. E. Nobbe, "Socioeconomic Differentials among Nonwhite Races," *American Sociological Review* 30 (1965), pp. 909–21.

[5]Based on U.S. Bureau of the Census, *Statistical Abstract,* Table 571.

[6]*Statistical Abstract,* Tables 631, 642.

[7]See, for example, A. Campbell and H. Schuman, "White Beliefs about Negroes," in M. G. Goldschmid, ed., *Black Americans and White Racism* (New York: Holt, 1970); H. J. Ehrlich, "Stereotyping and Negro-Jewish Stereotypes," *Social Forces,* 41 (1963), pp. 171–76; J. D. Forbes, "Race and Color in Mexican-American Problems," *Journal of Human Relations,* 16, (1968), pp. 55–68; A. Pinkney, "Prejudice Toward Mexican and Negro Americans: A Comparison," *Phylon,* (1963).

[8]G. M. Fredrickson, *The Black Image in the White Mind* (New York: Harper & Row, 1971); Jacobs and Landau, eds., *To Serve the Devil.*

assumed to possess the opposite physiological, intellectual, and cultural characteristics of the white majority in order for the majority to rationalize the subordinate economic position of nonwhites.

Minority reaction has included warfare, slave rebellions, race riots, radicalism, nationalism, attempts to assimilate, self-denigration, as well as apparently high levels of social problems such as marginality, alienation, drug and alcohol addiction, and marital instability as means of coping with their subordinate status in this racist society.[9] Minority reaction has been far from static as these groups have resisted majority domination, attempted to assimilate, suffered further rejection, become nationalistic, or have tried to withdraw from the personal effects of discrimination. However, whatever the reaction, majority policy consistently maximizes control of these minorities in order to maintain economic dominance and defines minority orientations as barbaric, savage, a communistic threat, illegal, or pathologically deficient requiring legislation and control. These rationales, once again, serve to legitimize their domination.

Institutionalized racism represents those aspects of the social structure designed to maximize economic exploitation and political control on a racial basis, rationalized through negative physical, intellectual, and cultural stereotypes. This is achieved through control of institutional resources, access to major institutions, and negative stereotypes by the white majority. The first two are monopolized with respect to political, military, legal, and economic institutions in the society while racist stereotypes are perpetuated through the family, educational and religious institutions, and the media. Residential segregation further reinforces racial control. In this manner the racial hierarchy is an integral part of the society's institutional system, ensuring political, economic, and social domination of nonwhite groups by the white majority.[10]

[9]D. Brown, *Bury My Heart at Wounded Knee* (New York: Holt, Rinehart & Winston, 1970); W. E. DuBois, *Black Reconstruction* (New York: Harcourt Brace, 1935); T. Hayden, *Rebellion in Newark: Official Violence and Ghetto Response* (New York: Random House, 1967); L. Lomax, *The Negro Revolt* (New York: Harper, 1962); R. Staples, *Introduction to Black Sociology* (New York: McGraw-Hill, 1976); R. L. Derbyshire and E. B. Brody, "Marginality, Identity, and Behavior in the American Negro," *International Journal of Social Psychiatry*, 10 (1964), pp. 7–13; H. L. Kitano and S. Sue, "The Model Minorities," *Journal of Social Issues*, 29 (1973), pp. 1–9; J. C. Ball and M. P. Lau, "The Chinese Narcotic Addict in the U.S.," *Social Forces*, 45 (1966), pp. 68–72; P. Uhlenberg, "Marital Instability among Mexican Americans: Following the Pattern of Blacks," *Social Problems*, 20 (1972), pp. 49–56; E. P. Dozier, "Problem Drinking among American Indians: The Role of Sociocultural Deprivation," *Quarterly Journal of Studies on Alcohol*, 27 (1966), 72–87.

[10]For useful analyses of institutional racism in American society see Staples, *Introduction to Black Sociology*, pp. 34–45; T. F. Pettigrew, *Racially Separate or Together?* (New York: McGraw-Hill, 1971).

Social movements among subordinate racial minorities are a function of the society's stage of economic development. During the plantation era slave rebellions occurred, separatist movements emerged in the early 1900s (Pan Africanism), civil rights groups evolved later, while racial nationalism (black student groups, Afro-American movements) came to the forefront of American race relations in the 1960s—a period of economic development and change. With increased economic development and differentiation, radicalism and nationalism developed also. Increased social heterogeneity has resulted in the emergence of different kinds of racial movements, for example, moderate groups with religious leaders, radicals with intellectual leaders, and union groups. In general, racial social movements increase in number, become more varied and radical with economic development, and race relations thus become more dynamic.[11]

Majority-minority race relations are based primarily on the vested economic interests of the majority, rationalized in physical, intellectual, and cultural terms, reinforced by science and religion. Given this economic foundation, these relations are subject to the influence of economic change as the society moves from a "paternalistic" to a more "competitive" situation.[12] Intergroup relations become economically competitive, resulting in increased dynamism and racial conflict.[13] While these changes do occur, however, majority reaction tends to be highly conservative and "backlash" oriented in the attempt to maintain societal dominance. Racism may become more overt rather than less with increased antagonism, prejudice, and ethnocentrism as the elite struggles to maintain its power monopoly and vested economic interests. Consequently it can be said that while overt and expressed racism has declined somewhat in the general society, this does not imply a reduction in covert or institutional racism, particularly since the racial hierarchy has not disappeared significantly. Race relations tend to be economically based and dynamic but generally stable insofar as the hierarchy within which they operate has not changed greatly, that is, political, economic, and social power are retained by the white majority.

Finally, interminority relations are based upon the correlation between race and other major minorities as well as interracial competition for status and power within the larger racial hierarchy. Nonwhite

[11]For a useful discussion of major types of social movements with respect to Blacks, see Staples, *Introduction to Black Sociology*, chapter 10.

[12]See P. L. van den Berghe, *Race and Racism* (New York: Wiley, 1967), chapter 1.

[13]For a discussion of this notion see C. Bagley, "Race Relations and Theories of Status Consistency," *Race*, 11 (1970), pp. 267–89.

status is closely tied to sexual exploitation, paternalism, cultural prejudice, poverty, and deviance reflecting a synthesis of a variety of types of exploitation and discrimination. The multidimensionality of this structure makes interminority relations complex and competitive on a number of different levels within society, that is, it exacerbates perceived differences, competition, and resultant conflict. Interracial relations therefore, are highly complex, tense, and competitive—characteristics which increase with economic differentiation.

American racial minorities were created under extremely negative conditions, reveal a white-Oriental socioeconomic elite, and a high correlation between nonwhite status, low income, and poverty. They are viewed as physically, intellectually, and behaviorally inferior, have reacted to their subordinate status in a variety of ways, are subject to high levels of institutionalized racism, represent elite economic interests, and are strongly influenced by other types of minority group status. In short, race is a basic dimension of American social structure which has high levels of exploitation and discrimination.

Sexual Minorities

Another major type of minority based on assumed physiological factors is sexual, that is, American women. Although more visible in recent decades, sexual discrimination has been a basic factor in American society.

Female roles in this society have proceeded through a number of historical stages: the colonial, industrial, and familistic. During the colonial period, religion emphasized the relative equality between male and female with the latter significantly involved in community, social, and economic affairs, that is, family and community were closely integrated. With the onset of economic migration and industrialization, particularly in the early 1900s, sexual role segregation began but women still participated significantly in the labor force—a trend which increased with the war effort in the 1940s. Postwar developments, however, (the familistic period) brought the soldiers' return and injection into the labor force, the baby boom, the development of a consumer-type economy, and family psychology. This led to the evolution of familism, effectively segregating women into the home, made childbearing "scientific," marketed sex appeal, and highlighted the women's psychological function in family and society.[14] Economic development and specialization effectively removed the female from significant par-

---

[14]For useful discussions of these trends see M. P. Ryan, *Womanhood in America, From Colonial Times to the Present* (New York: New Viewpoints, 1975); J. S. Chafetz, *Masculine/Feminine or Human?* (Itasca: Peacock, 1974), chapter 6.

ticipation in the larger society and segregated her within the family, assigning her a psychological-sexual role, reinforced by a male dominated consumer-type culture.[15]

Demographically speaking, women represent a numerical majority in this society (51.3 percent).[16] However, they represent a minority of the labor force (38 percent,)[17] are heavily concentrated in sales and clerical-type occupations (41.8 percent) relative to men (14.3 percent),[18] and are consistently paid less at all levels of the occupational structure.[19] From this it is clear that they are a disadvantaged minority subject to significant levels of exploitation and discrimination.

Majority attitudes, once again, highlight the minority's assumed physical, intellectual, and behavioral inferiority. It has been found that American men view women as weak, domestic, sexually inexperienced, emotional, intuitive, coy, and vain, suited primarily to housewife and mother roles[20] —once again the *opposite* of assumed male characteristics.

Female response may take a number of forms: acceptance of these views and a segregated, subordinate role, self-denigration, and psychological dependence on the male in a passive, male-ego-reinforcing role.[21] There may be prejudice against other females,[22] bewilder-

[15]S. Firestone, *The Dialectic of Sex* (New York: Bantam, 1971), chapter 8; M. K. Martin and B. Voorhies, *Female of the Species* (New York: Columbia University Press, 1975).

[16]Based on U.S. Bureau of the Census, *Statistical Abstract of the U.S., 1974,* Table 27.

[17]*Statistical Abstract of the U.S.,* Table 543.

[18]*Statistical Abstract of the U.S.,* Table 568.

[19]*Statistical Abstract of the U.S.,* Table 571. See also W. T. Martin and D. L. Poston, "The Occupational Composition of White Females: Sexism, Racism, and Occupational Differentiation," *Social Forces,* 50 (1972), 349–55; L. E. Suter and H. P. Miller, "Income Differences between Men and Career Women," *American Journal of Sociology,* 78 (1973), 962–74; D. J. Trieman and K. Terrell, "Sex and the Process of Status Attainment: A Comparison of Working Women and Men," *American Sociological Review,* 40 (1975), 174–200; G. Williams, "A Research Note on Trends in Occupational Differentiation by Sex," *Social Problems,* 22 (1975), 543–47.

[20]See, for example, Chafetz, *Masculine/Feminine or Human?,* chapter 2; C. C. Naffziger and K. Naffziger, "Development of Sex Role Stereotypes," *The Family Coordinator,* 23 (1974), pp. 251–58; C. B. Flora, "The Passive Female: Her Comparative Image by Class and Culture in Women's Magazine Fiction," *Journal of Marriage and the Family,* 33 (1971), pp. 435–44. See also S. S. August, "Role Conception as a Predictor of Adult Female Roles," *Sociology and Social Research,* 50 (1966), 448–59; J. Freeman, "Origins of the Women's Movement," *American Journal of Sociology,* 78 (1973), 792; E. Haavio-Mannila, "Sex Differentiation in Role Expectations and Performance," *Journal of Marriage and the Family,* 29 (1967), 568–78; M. W. Osmond and P. Y. Martin, "Sex and Sexism: A Comparison of Male and Female Sex Role Attitudes," *Journal of Marriage and the Family,* 37 (1975), 744–58.

[21]For an excellent discussion of this see Firestone, *The Dialectic of Sex,* chapter 6.

[22]See, for example, P. Goldberg, "Are Women Prejudiced against Women?" *Transaction,* 5 (1968), pp. 28–30.

ment,[23] or rejection of these stereotypes and attempted equality. Accordingly, they may accept male prejudice or attempt to fight it. In either case, their situation is difficult and subject to high levels of resistance with accusations of lesbianism and "unfeminine" behavior.

Institutionalized sexism is evident in all sections of the society: political exclusion, legal discrimination, economic inequality, and negative stereotypes portrayed in the media, religion, and the family system[24] Sexual specialization in publishing and the consumer economy serves to reinforce assumed sexual differences also. Such differences are constantly visible and therefore real throughout the society, maximized by a capitalistic, consumer-oriented economy.

The reaction of American women has been far from static: A number of social movements have emerged at particular stages of female participation in the larger society. Early groups include female labor organizers, suffrage movements, temperance groups, trade union leagues, reformers, and recently, the more radical National Organization for Women (NOW).[25] These movements are dynamic and varied, representing the women's changing economic role in the society and have become more radical with economic development.[26]

Male-female relations are based on the vested psychological needs of the male, given the latter's specialized emotional role in contemporary society. Consequently, the security of the male ego is dependent upon the psychological reinforcement of the female within the context of what Firestone terms a "power psychology."[27] The female ego, in turn, is based upon male approval—the source of psychological power in sexual relations. As a result these relations are highly emotional, insecure, and subject to psychological bargaining for material resources. Love and romance tend to be euphemisms for male exploitation and domination of the female as she is assigned a psychological role in contemporary society. Given the extent to which ego identity and security are based upon this inequality, male reaction to female liberation tends to be conservative and prejudicial—an equivalent of white backlash in race relations. Significant modification of this power relationship as the female begins to participate more in the larger society may also affect its brittle balance resulting in severe levels of interpersonal conflict and divorce. The multidimensionality of the female role

[23]See B. Friedan, *The Feminine Mystique* (New York: Dell, 1963), chapter 1.

[24]J. F. Seggar and P. Wheeler, "World of Work on TV: Ethnic and Sex Representation in TV Drama," *Journal of Broadcasting*, 17 (1973), pp. 201–14.

[25]Firestone, *The Dialectic of Sex*, chapter 2.

[26]See M. B. McDowell, "The New Rhetoric of Woman Power," *Midwest Quarterly*, 12 (1971), pp. 187–98.

[27]Firestone, *The Dialectic of Sex*, chapter 6.

in the family (wife, mother, homemaker, career woman) subjects her to potentially high levels of role conflict (incompatible demands), straining and complicating the male-female relationship, placing her in a "no-win" situation. Generally, then, relationships between the sexes are complicated, potentially unstable, highly emotional, and psychologically oppressive.[28]

Interminority relations between the sexes are complex also: Female status is significantly correlated with racial exploitation, age discrimination, traditional ethnic roles, economic deprivation, and particular types of deviance such as mental illness and prostitution. Given the woman's restricted role and the extent to which these other dimensions of minority group status operate, female relations are bound to be competitive in the attempt to maximize nonpsychological resources. This may partially explain female prejudice against other women, as well as the uneven relationship between female and racial liberation groups.[29] Whatever the case, interfemale relations are complicated by other dimensions of minority group status, in particular by race, ethnicity, class, and the competitive nature of relationships within the minority group hierarchy as a whole.

Sexual minorities in America have been created through economic development and specialization. They represent a numerical majority which is underrepresented in the labor market and occupational system, tend to be underpaid and are defined as physically, intellectually, and behaviorally inferior. These minorities have reacted to their subordination by a variety of movements, and are subject to political exclusion, legal discrimination, economic inequality, represent a psychological resource for the male, and interact within the context of a competitive, multidimensional hierarchy. The lot of American females, while appearing more comfortable than previously, is thus far from easy, particularly since they are subject to psychological and institutional oppression.

Age-based Minorities

We turn to age-based minorities, focusing on children, adolescents, and the aged.

As has been indicated, America has historically proceeded through a number of distinct economic stages as the society has become

---

[28]For a useful discussion of this see Chafetz, *Masculine/Feminine or Human?* chapter 5.

[29]See Goldberg, "Are Women Prejudiced against Women?"

more specialized: the colonial, industrial urban, and contemporary consumption-oriented era. During this evolution it is also evident that a number of significant demographic developments have occurred, namely, increasing numbers of the young and the aged. In conjunction with a decline in the general significance of kinship and the extended family, along with increasing economic specialization, rising affluence, a more complex division of labor, and predominance of the nuclear type family structure, it is evident that these population changes have increased role assignment on the basis of age for economic purposes. Consequently, children, adolescents, and the aged have been increasingly segregated, withheld from the labor market, sent to war, educated for lengthier periods of time, and made economically dependent. Minorities have been created on the basis of age for assumed economic-demographic reasons. Thus, with economic specialization children have been increasingly removed from participation in the larger economic system (as with women), subjected to segregated educational institutions and a consumer economy which exploits them.[30] Adolescents have been subjected to similar processes and also to military service, lengthened periods of education, and consequent economic dependence.[31] The aged have become segregated from younger adults through the decline of the nuclear family and subjected to early "obsolescence," institutional segregation, and increasing economic dependence on the state.[32] Thus, demographic change coupled with economic specialization has resulted in removal from economic participation, segregated institutions, lengthy periods of education, and high levels of economic dependence among children, adolescents, and the aged.

Demographic characteristics of age-based minorities reveal that over 34 percent of the population is seventeen years of age or younger while almost 10 percent are sixty-five and over.[33] Furthermore, in 1973 the labor force consisted of only 3.3 percent of the latter age group while approximately 10 percent were nineteen or younger.[34] With

[30]P. B. Meyer, "The Exploitation of the American Growing Class" and G. B. Leonard, "How School Stunts Your Child," in D. Gottlieb, ed., *Children's Liberation* (Englewood Cliffs, N.J.: Prentice-Hall, 1973), pp. 35–52, 145–66.

[31]See E. Z. Friedenberg, "The Generation Gap," *Annals of the American Academy of Political and Social Science,* 382 (1969), pp. 32–42.

[32]See J. S. Francher, "American Values and the Disenfranchisement of the Aged," *Eastern Anthropologist,* 22 (1969), pp. 29–36; D. H. Fischer, *Growing Old in America* (New York: Oxford University Press).

[33]See U.S. Bureau of the Census, *Statistical Abstract of the U.S.: 1974,* Table 34.

[34]*Statistical Abstract of the U.S.,* Table 544.

regard to children, Gottlieb has indicated that seven million of them live in poverty, 300,000 are in institutions, only 5 percent receive adequate health care, and infant mortality is higher than in Japan and five other European countries. Illiteracy is also high while segregation is increasing through the proliferation of preschools.[35] Age-based minorities are large and subject to intense degrees of economic and social deprivation. Also, time trends reveal, for example, that while health care for the aged has improved, their economic resources have declined, thereby increasing the financial disparity between them and other occupational groups.[36] Age is an important source of minority group differentiation and discrimination.

Majority attitudes toward children, adolescents, and the aged tend to focus on the assumed effects of the aging process, that is, maturation and senility. As with other minorities these groups are viewed as physically, intellectually, and emotionally limited by age: Children are immature, adolescents are unstable, while the old are dependent and irrational.[37] There is also a "blame the child" complex (rejection of behavior as "childish"), an emphasis in education on proper socialization of the young,[38] a tendency to view children as extensions of the parental self, jealousy of the physical and sexual prowess of adolescents, and impatience with the psychological and economic dependence of the old, increasing the perceived need to institutionalize and remove them from the extended family. In a similar fashion to sexual minorities, these groups serve a psychological function in the society, reinforcing the ego needs of adults through the childrearing process, grandparent-grandchildren relationships, and parent-grandparent interaction. Given these psychological needs, assumed physical, intellectual, and emotional inferiority became the underlying rationale for exploitation and control.

Minority reaction to these attitudes consists of frustration, self-doubt, and the formation of subcultures. Children, subject to parental pressure, engage in deviant behavior.[39] Adolescents suffer marginality

[35]See D. Gottlieb, "Children in America: A Demographic Profile and Commentary," in D. Gottlieb, ed., *Children's Liberation*, pp. 7–22.

[36]E. B. Palmore and F. Whitington, "Trends in the Relative Status of the Aged," Paper presented at the Annual Meetings of the Southern Sociological Society, 1971.

[37]See, for example, Firestone, *The Dialectic of Sex*, pp. 91–104; D. Rogers, *The Psychology of Adolescence* (New York: Appleton-Century-Crofts, 2nd ed., 1972), chapter 1.

[38]See D. Gottlieb, ed., *Children's Liberation*, pp. 23–34, 125–44.

[39]L. I. Pearlin, M. R. Yarrow, and H. A. Scarr, "Unintended Effects of Parental Aspirations: The Case of Children's Cheating," *American Journal of Sociology*, 73 (1967), pp. 73–83.

and disillusionment, creating their own society,[40] while the aged participate in self-blame, self-preoccupation, and form their own subgroup
environments.[41] Adolescents also exhibit fear of adult roles, choosing to
"freak out" instead,[42] while the aged appear to become more insecure
and ideologically conservative as they attempt to hold on to the past in
a rapidly changing world.[43] The effects of age discrimination are devastating: lack of self-confidence, frustration, and segregation.

Dimensions of institutionalized age discrimination are highly visible: legal discrimination, economic dependence and exclusion, educational discrimination, military exploitation, family domination, and
religious control. Specialized language, media, "psychologies," recre-
ational equipment, and voluntary organizations based on age, reinforce
minority consciousness and age-group boundaries, particularly as they
define status characteristics and appropriate behavior.[44] Segregation,
legal control, institutional care, economic dependence, and specialized
material culture thus ensure age domination and exploitation.

Age-based social movements reveal increased concern with this
type of minority and have resulted in groups dealing with children's
needs[45] and the problem of child abuse, attempts to develop students'
rights in schools, increased legal and political rights for youth, and
"senior citizen" and retirement organizations with a recent emphasis
on "gray power." However, the extent to which these groups have
succeeded in significantly altering the social status of these minorities
is open to question. While these movements have increased with economic development along with greater awareness of individual rights,
children, adolescents, and the aged remain subject to segregation, control, and exploitation. The viability and visibility of these movements,

---

[40]B. Goodnight, "Toward a Sociological Theory of Adolescence in American Soci-
ety," *Proceedings of Southwestern Sociological Association,* 19 (1968), pp. 137–41; R. S.
Laufer, "Sources of Generational Consciousness and Conflict," *Annals of American
Academy of Political and Social Science,* 395 (1971), pp. 80–94; J. S. Coleman, *The
Adolescent Society* (New York: Free Press, 1971).

[41]See G. G. Brissett, *The Significance of Life-Goals in Aging Adjustment—a Pilot
Study* (Sacramento: California Mental Health Res., Monograph no. 9, 1967); E. Shanas,
"A Note on Restriction of Life Space: Attitudes of Age Cohorts," *Journal of Health and
Social Behavior,* 9 (1968), pp. 86–90; A. M. Rose, "Group Consciousness among the
Aging," in A. M. Rose and W. A. Peterson, eds., *Older People and their Social World*
(Philadelphia: F. A. Davis, 1965), pp. 19–36.

[42]See T. J. Cottle, "Parent and Child: The Hazards of Equality," in D. Gottlieb, ed.,
Children's Liberation.

[43]A. M. Rose, "Mental Health of Normal Older Persons," in A. M. Rose and W. A.
Peterson, eds., *Older People and their Social World,* pp. 193–200.

[44]See G. B. Leonard, "How School Stunts Your Child," in D. Gottlieb, ed., *Children's Liberation,* pp. 145–66; Firestone, *The Dialectic of Sex,* chapter 4.

[45]*Report to the President: White House Conference on Children* (Washington, D.C.:
U.S. Govt. Printing Office, 1970).

furthermore, are reduced by the greater urgency of other minority movements dealing with discrimination such as racism and sexism. Age-based social movements tend to be in the background rather than the forefront of national protest.

We have remarked on the psychological function of age-based minorities. Children represent sources of vicarious achievement and ego gratification while the aged are assigned a babysitting and surrogate parent role in the larger family. Consequently, majority-minority relations are highly emotional and power oriented as parents attempt to maximize these functions within the context of a "power psychology"[46] with an emphasis on normative conformity and status achievement for the sake of parental gratification. The aged are also assigned a passive role with an emphasis on their noninterference in the above relationships. Should they demand more active roles their presence is resented. Majority-minority relations based on age tend to be built on power and control, the ego needs of parents and adults, and are highly emotional, all of which is reinforced by the societal context of institutionalized discrimination. Furthermore, when problems arise in these relations, psychology, religion, or psychiatry are resorted to in an attempt to reassert balance and thereby dominance. The power and dominance of age are given further reinforcement and legitimacy in scientific and moral terms—an extremely powerful combination.[47]

Interminority relations, given the extent of age-based discrimination in society, are highly competitive and complicated by other dimensions of minority group relations: Problems of sibling rivalry are well known as is the extremely competitive nature of adolescent culture. The aged also have to compete for the attention of the young as well as their own offspring. Furthermore, the extent to which age discrimination is reinforced by racism, sexism, traditional ethnic roles, economic deprivation, and age-specific forms of deviance, complicates interminority relations also. Factors such as race, ethnicity, and class serve to further segregate and control individuals of particular ages. As a result, age relations tend to be competitive and hierarchical.

Age-based minorities in American society have been created through demographic change coupled with economic specialization, are large in number and subject to high levels of economic and social deprivation, are defined as physically, intellectually, and emotionally limited, have responded with frustration, self-doubt, and the formation

[46] An excellent discussion of this is contained in Firestone, *The Dialectic of Sex*, chapter 4.

[47] An excellent essay on this is J. Kovel, "Therapy in Late Capitalism," *Telos*, 30 (1976–77), pp. 73–92.

of subcultures. They are subject to high levels of institutionalized discrimination, represent a psychological function in society in relation to adult ego gratification, and interact with one another on a competitive and hierarchical basis. While not as visible as racism and sexism, age discrimination is equally widespread and invidious in its destructive influence.

Having examined several major types of American minorities based on assumed physiological characteristics we draw some general conclusions before examining other groups.

CONCLUSIONS

In this chapter we have emphasized the extent to which American society has experienced two major processes: *colonial migration* and *economic specialization.*

The former has resulted in the creation of a racial hierarchy which is highly correlated with socioeconomic power, negative stereotypes, institutionalized domination, and other dimensions of minority group status. Race is a basic dimension in American social structure, representing elite vested economic interests. Economic specialization, on the other hand, has produced other types of minority serving more psychological functions, namely, sexual and age-based minorities. As a result, sexual minorities have been created through economic development and specialization, are subject to institutionalized domination, negative physical, intellectual, and behavioral stereotypes, and represent a psychological resource for the male ego. Economic development has thus segregated the female within the boundaries of the nuclear family, and subjected her to extremely powerful forms of exploitation and control.

Economic specialization coupled with demographic growth, has produced age-based minorities which are large, highly deprived, subject to negative stereotypes, institutionalized segregation and domination, and also represent a psychological function in society in reference to adult ego gratification.

From this it is evident that the basic processes on which the society was founded and developed economically have resulted in the creation of economic and psychological minorities who serve elite-majority interests. These minorities, defined as physically, intellectually, and behaviorally different and/or inferior, are subjected to high levels of institutionalized domination and exploitation. Consequently, contrary to public ideology, both the historical foundation and development of this society have had extremely negative consequences for the population as a whole. This is a minority-ridden, exploitive society which is highly differentiated and prejudicial despite myths concerning Horatio Alger (that is, equality of opportunity) and the great "melting pot." Intergroup relations are highly competitive and hierarchical, serving economic and psychological interests. The major characteristics of these minorities based on assumed physiological characteristics are summarized in Figure 8.1.

TYPE OF MINORITY

CHARACTERISTICS	Racial	Sexual	Age based
1. Historical:	migration-subordination, importation for labor purposes	colonial, industrial, familistic economic stages	economic role assignment based on age, nuclear family segregation
2. Demographic:	white-Oriental elite, high correlation between nonwhite status and poverty	numerical majority, limited occupations and income	large numbers young and old, high economic and social deprivation
3. Attitudinal:			
(a) Majority	reflect racial socioeconomic hierarchy, opposite physical intellectual, cultural characteristics	assumed physical, intellectual, and behavioral inferiority	assumed physical, intellectual, and emotional limitations by age
(b) Minority	self-denigration, assimilation, nationalism, radicalism	self-denigration, dependence, bewilderment, attempted equality	frustration, self-doubt, subcultures
4. Institutional:	control access, resources, stereotypes in political, economic, social institutions	political exclusion, legal discrimination, economic inequality, negative stereotypes	legal discrimination, military exploitation, family domination, religious control
5. Social Movements:	rebellions, separatism, civil rights, nationalism radicalism	labor organizers, suffrage groups, reformers, N.O.W.	children's needs, youth rights, aged rights
6. Relational:			
(a) Majority-Minority	majority vested economic interests, paternalism to competition and conflict	make ego needs and female need for approval	ego-gratification surrogate parent roles
(b) Interminority			
racial	*	sexual exploitation	reinforces age discrimination
sexual	sexual exploitation	*	reinforces age discrimination
age based	paternalism	age discrimination	*
cultural	ethnocentrism	traditional roles	traditional roles
economic	poverty	economic deprivation	economic dependence
behavioral	high deviance	mental illness, prostitution	age-specific offenses

FIGURE 8.1. Characteristics of Physically Defined Minorities in the U.S.

STUDY QUESTIONS

1. Select three physically defined minority groups in your community (racial, sexual, and age based), and:
   (a) Delineate the major historical circumstances behind their evolution.
   (b) Outline their major demographic characteristics.
   (c) Describe majority and minority attitudes toward each other.
   (d) Outline the dimensions of institutionalized domination.
   (e) Describe the characteristics of majority-minority relations.
2. What conclusions do you draw regarding major differences and similarities among these three groups?

READINGS

MINORITY GROUP RELATIONS: GENERAL

BELL, DANIEL, "On Meritocracy and Equality," *Public Interest*, 29 (Fall, 1972), 29–68.

BLACK, D., *The Behavior of Law*. New York: Academic Press, 1976.

BLALOCK, H. M. JR., *Toward a Theory of Minority-Group Relations*. New York: Capricorn Books, 1970.

BONACICH, EDNA, "A Theory of Middleman Minorities," *American Sociological Review*, 38, no. 5 (October, 1973), 583–94.

BOTTOMORE, T. B., *Sociology as Social Criticism*. New York: Morrow, 1976.

COLEMAN, JAMES S., "Equality of Opportunity and Equality of Results," *Harvard Educational Review*, 43, no. 1 (February, 1973), 129–37.

DWORKIN, A. G., and R. J. DWORKIN, eds., *The Minority Report, An Introduction to Racial, Ethnic, and Gender Relations*. New York: Praeger, 1976.

EITZEN, D. STANLEY, "A Conflict Model for the Analysis of Majority-Minority Relations," *Kansas Journal of Sociology*, 8, no. 2 (Spring, 1967), 76–92.

ETZKOWITZ, HENRY, and GERALD M. SCHAFLANDER, "A Manifesto for Sociologists: Institution-Formation—A New Sociology," *Social Problems*, 15, no. 4 (Spring, 1968), 399–407.

GITTLER, J. B., ed., *Understanding Minority Groups*. New York: Wiley, 1956.

GORDON, M. M., *Assimilation in American Life*. New York: Oxford University Press, 1964.

GRIESSMAN, B. E., *Minorities, A Text with Readings in Intergroup Relations*, Hinsdale: Dryden, 1975.

HARTZ, L., ed., *The Founding of New Societies*. New York: Harcourt, Brace & World, 1964.

KOVEL, J., "Therapy in Late Capitalism," *Telos*, 30 (1976–77), pp. 73–92.

KUROKAWA, M., ed., *Minority Responses*. New York: Random House, 1970.

LASCH, CHRISTOPHER, *The New Radicalism in America, 1889–1963.* New York: Alfred A. Knopf, 1965.

MARDEN, C. F., and G. MEYER, *Minorities in American Society* (4th ed.), New York: Van Nostrand, 1968.

MARTIN, J. G., and C. W. FRANKLIN, *Minority Group Relations.* Columbus: Merrill, 1973.

MOSCOVICI, SERGE, and PATRICIA NEVE, "Studies on Polarization of Judgments: III. Majorities, Minorities and Social Judgments," *European Journal of Social Psychology,* 3, no. 4 (1973), 479–84.

NEWMAN, W. M., *American Pluralism, A Study of Minority Groups and Social Theory.* New York: Harper, 1973.

RINDER, I. D., "Minority Orientations: An Approach to Intergroup Relations Theory through Social Psychology," *Phylon,* 26, (1965), 5–17.

RYAN, W., *Blaming the Victim.* New York: Pantheon, 1971.

SCHERMERHORN, R. A., "Towards a General Theory of Minority Groups," *Phylon,* 25, (1964), 238–46.

SIMPSON, G. E., and J. M. YINGER, *Race and Cultural Minorities: An Analysis of Prejudice and Discrimination* (4th ed.), New York: Harper & Row, 1972.

U.S. Bureau of the Census, *Statistical Abstract of the United States: 1974* (95th ed.), Washington, D.C.: 1974.

WAGLEY, C., and M. HARRIS, *Minorities in the New World.* New York: Columbia University Press, 1958.

WHITE, TERRENCE H., "Minority Groups: Beyond Description," *Wisconsin Sociologist,* 6, no. 1 (Spring–Summer 1968), 25–33.

WIRTH, L., "The Problem of Minority Groups," in R. Linton, ed., *The Science of Man in the World Crisis.* New York: Columbia University Press, 1945.

YOUNG, D., *American Minority Peoples.* New York: Harper, 1932.

RACIAL MINORITIES: GENERAL

ALLPORT, G. W., *The Nature of Prejudice.* Cambridge, Addison-Wesley, 1958.

BAGLEY, C., "Race Relations and Theories of Status Consistency," *Race,* 11, (1970), 267–89.

BANTON, M., *Race Relations.* New York: Basic Books, 1967.

BLALOCK, H. M., JR., "A Power Analysis of Racial Discrimination," *Social Forces,* 39, (1960), 53–59.

BLASSINGAME, *The Slave Community.* New York: Oxford University Press, 1972.

BOGARDUS, E. S., *Immigration and Race Attitudes.* Boston: Heath, 1928.

COLBY, VERONICA, "Minority Group Residential Patterns in Milwaukee," *Wisconsin Social,* 2, no. 2 (Fall, 1963), 17–20.

DOLLARD, J., *Caste and Class in a Southern Town.* Garden City: Doubleday, 1957.

FOX, WILLIAM S., and JOHN R. FAINE, "Trends in White-Nonwhite Income Equality," *Sociology and Social Research,* 57, no. 3 (April, 1973), 288–99.

FRAZIER, E. F., "Sociological Theory and Race Relations," *American Sociological Review,* 12 (1947), 265–71.

———, *Race and Culture Contacts in the Modern World.* Boston: Beacon Press, 1965.

Furnivall, J. S., *Colonial Policy and Practice*. London: Cambridge University Press, 1948.

Gossett, Thomas F., *Race: The History of an Idea in America*. Dallas, Tex.: Southern Methodist University Press, 1963.

Hare, Nathan, "The Sociological Study of Racial Conflict," *Phylon*, 33, no. 1 (Spring, 1972), 27–31.

Heer, David M., "Inter-marriage and Racial Amalgamation in the United States," *Eugenics Quarterly*, 14, no. 2 (June, 1967), 112–20.

Henderson, Donald, "Minority Response and the Conflict Model," *Phylon*, 25, no. 1 (Spring, 1964), 18–26.

Howard, J. R., ed., *Awakening Minorities, American Indians, Mexican Americans, Puerto Ricans*. New Brunswick: Transaction, 1970.

Jacobs, P., and S. Landau, eds., *To Serve the Devil*, Vols. I, II, New York: Vintage, 1971.

Jensen, A. R., "How Much Can We Boost I.Q. and Scholastic Achievement?" *Harvard Educational Review*, 39 (1969).

Katz, D., and K. Braly, "Racial Stereotypes of One Hundred College Students," *Journal of Abnormal and Social Psychology* (1933), 280–90.

Katzman, M. T., "Discrimination, Sub-Culture, and Economic Performance of Minority Groups," *American Journal of Economics and Sociology*, 27, no. 4 (October 1968), 371–76.

Killian, L., *White Southerners*. New York: Random House, 1970.

Kinloch, G. C., *The Dynamics of Race Relations, A Sociological Analysis*. New York: McGraw-Hill, 1974.

———, "Changing Black Reactions to White Domination," *Rhodesian History*, 5 (1974), 67–78.

———, "Changing Intergroup Attitudes of Whites as Defined by the Press: The Process of Colonial Adaptation," *Zambezia*, 4 (1975–76), 105–17.

Lieberson, S., "A Societal Theory of Race and Ethnic Relations," *American Sociological Review*, 26 (1961), 902–10.

Masuoka, Jitsuichi, "Conflicting Role Obligations and Role Types: With Special Reference to Race Relations," *Japanese Sociological Review*, 11, no. 1 (July, 1960), 78–108.

Metzger, Paul L., "American Sociology and Black Assimilation: Conflicting Perspectives," *American Journal of Sociology*, 76, no. 4 (January 1971), 627–47.

Pettigrew, T. F., *Racially Separate or Together?* New York: McGraw-Hill, 1971.

Rex, John, "Race as a Social Category," *Journal of Biosocial Science*, Supplement 1, (July, 1969), 145–52.

Roucek, Joseph S., "The Power and Ideological Aspects of the Majority-Minority Relationships," *Sociologia Internationalis*, 3, no. 11 (1965), 97–120.

———, "Special Characteristics of the Problem of Racial Minorities in the U.S.A.," *Revista Internacional de Sociologia*, 23, no. 89 (1965), 37–54.

Schuman, Howard, and John Harding, "Prejudice and the Norm of Rationality," *Sociometry*, 27, no. 3 (September 1964), 353–71.

Teahan, John E., and James Hug, "Status Threat and White Backlash," *Journal of Human Relations*, 12, no. 2 (1970), 939–47.

Valentine, C. A., "Voluntary Ethnicity and Social Change: Classism, Racism, Marginality, Mobility, and Revolution with Special Reference to Afro-American and Other Third World Peoples," *The Journal of Ethnic Studies*, 3, no. 1. (Spring, 1975), 1–27.

VAN DEN BERGHE, P. L., *Race and Racism*. New York: Wiley, 1967.
WESTIE, F. R., "Race and Ethnic Relations," in *Handbook of Modern Sociology*, R. E. K. Faris, ed., Chicago: Rand McNally, 1964.

Black Americans

BABCHUK, NICHOLAS, and JOHN A. BALLWEG, "Black Family Structure and Primary Relations," *Phylon*, 33, no. 4 (Winter 1972), 334–47.
BRIMMER, ANDREW F., "The Black Revolution and the Economic Future of Negroes in the United States," *American Scholar*, 38, no. 4 (August 1969), 629–43.
BROOM, LEONARD, "Status Profiles of Racial and Ethnic Populations," *Social Science Quarterly*, 52, no. 2 (September 1971), 379–88.
CAMPBELL, A., and H. SCHUMAN, "White Beliefs about Negroes," in *Black Americans and White Racism*, M. G. Goldschmid, ed., New York: Holt, 1970.
CONANT, RALPH W., SHELDON LEVY, and RALPH LEWIS, "Mass Polarization: Negro and White Attitudes in the Pace of Integration," *American Behavioral Scientist*, 13, no. 2 (November–December 1969), 247–64.
COTHRAN, TILMAN C., "The Negro Protest against Segregation in the South," *Annals of the American Academy of Politics and Social Science*, 357 (January 1965), 65–72.
DERBYSHIRE, ROBERT L., and EUGENE B. BRODY, "Marginality, Identity and Behavior in the American Negro: A Functional Analysis," *International Journal of Social Psychiatry*, 10, no. 1 (Winter 1964), 7–13.
DU BOIS, W. E., *Black Reconstruction*. New York: Harcourt Brace, 1935.
FREDRICKSON, G. M., *The Black Image in the White Mind*. New York: Harper & Row, 1971.
GOSSETT, T. P., *Race: The History of an Idea in America*. Dallas: Southern Methodist University Press, 1963.
GRIER, W. H., and P. M. COBBS, *Black Rage*. New York: Bantam Books, 1968.
HAYDEN, T., *Rebellion in Newark: Official Violence and Ghetto Response*. New York: Random House, 1967.
HAYS, WILLIAM C., and CHARLES H. MINDEL, "Extended Kinship Relations in Black and White Families," *Journal of Marriage and the Family*, 35, no. 1 (February 1973), 51–57.
HUNTER, CHARLES A., "Self-Esteem and Minority Status," *Proceedings of the Southwestern Sociological Association*, 18 (March, 1967), 194–99.
JORDAN, W. P., *White over Black: American Attitudes toward the Negro 1550–1812*. Chapel Hill: University of North Carolina Press, 1968.
KRYSTALL, ERIC R., NEIL FRIEDMAN, GLENN HOWZE, and EDGAR C. EPPS, "Attitudes Toward Integration and Black Consciousness: Southern Negro High School Seniors and Their Mothers," *Phylon*, 31, no. 2 (Summer 1970), 104–13.
LEVY, SHELDON G., "Polarization in Racial Attitudes," *Public Opinion Quarterly*, 36, no. 2 (Summer 1972), 221–34.
LOMAX, L., *The Negro Revolt*. New York: Harper, 1962.
LOVRICH, NICHOLAS P., JR., "Differing Priorities in an Urban Electorate: Service Preferences Among Anglo, Black, and Mexican American Voters," *Social Science Quarterly*, 55, no. 3 (December 1974), 704–17.
MCPHERSON, J., *et al.*, *Blacks in America: Bibliographical Essays*. New York: Doubleday, 1971.

NELSEN, HART M., and LYNDA DICKSON, "Attitudes of Black Catholics and Prot-
    estants: Evidence for Religious Identity," *Sociological Analysis*, 33, no. 3
    (Fall, 1972), 152–65.
NESBITT, RITA, "Conflict and the Black Panther Party: A Social Psychological
    Interpretation," *Sociological Focus*, 5, no. 4 (Summer 1972), 105–19.
OLSEN, MARVIN E., "Social and Political Participation of Blacks," *American
    Sociological Review*, 35, no. 4 (August 1970), 682–97.
PAIGE, JEFFERY, "Changing Patterns of Anti-White Attitudes Among Blacks,"
    Journal of Social Issues, 26, no. 4 (August 1970), 69–86.
PINKNEY, A., "Prejudice toward Mexican and Negro Americans: A Compari-
    son," *Phylon*, (1963).
RELYEA, HAROLD C., " 'Black Power': The Genesis and Future of a Revolution,"
    Journal of Human Relations, 16, no. 4 (1968), 502–13.
RONDOT, P., "Les 'Black Muslims,' " *Etudes*, 319, no. 21 (December 1963),
    359–64.
ROSE, ARNOLD, ed., *Assuring Freedom to the Free: A Century of Emancipation
    in the U.S.A.* Detroit: Wayne State University Press, 1964.
ROSE, P. I., *They and We.* New York: Random House, 1964.
SHACK, WILLIAM A., "Black Muslims: A Nativistic Religious Movement Among
    Negro Americans," *Race*, 3, no. 1 (November 1961), 57–67.
SIEGEL, PAUL M., "On the Cost of Being a Negro," *Sociological Inquiry*, 35, no.
    1 (April, 1965), 41–57.
STAPLES, R., *Introduction to Black Sociology.* New York: McGraw-Hill, 1976.
WARREN, DONALD I., "Neighborhood Structure and Riot Behavior in Detroit:
    Some Exploratory Findings," *Social Problems*, 16, no. 4 (Spring, 1969),
    464–84.
WELLMAN, BARRY, "Social Identities in Black and White," *Sociological Inquiry*,
    41, no. 1 (Winter 1971), 57–66.
YELLOWITZ, IRWIN, "Black Militancy and Organized Labor: An Historical
    Parameter," *Midwest Quarterly*, 13, no. 2 (January 1972), 169–83.

Chinese Americans

BALL, JOHN C., and M. P. LAU, "The Chinese Narcotic Addict in the United
    States," *Social Forces*, 45, no. 1 (September 1966), 68–72.
FANG, STANLEY L., "Assimilation and Changing Social Roles of Chinese Ameri-
    cans," *Journal of Social Issues*, 29, no. 2 (1973), 115–27.
FUJIMOTO, TETSUYA, "Social Class and Crime: The Case of the Japanese Ameri-
    cans," *Issues in Criminology*, 10, no. 1 (Spring, 1975), 73–93.
LYMAN, S., *Chinese Americans.* New York: Random House, 1974.
YUAN, D. Y., "Chinatown and Beyond: The Chinese Population in Metropolitan
    New York," *Phylon*, 27, no. 4 (Winter 1966), 321–32.

Japanese Americans

BAKER, DONALD B., "Identity, Power, and Psychocultural Needs: White Re-
    sponses to Nonwhites," *The Journal of Ethnic Studies*, 1, no. 4 (Winter
    1974), 16–44.
BOYD, MONICA, "Oriental Immigration: The Experience of the Chinese, Japa-
    nese, and Filipino Population in the United States," *International Migra-
    tion Review*, 5, no. 1 (Spring, 1971), 48–61.

CAIN, LEONARD, D. JR., "Japanese-American Protestants: Acculturation and Assimilation," *Review of Religious Research.*, 3, (1962) 113–21.

FUJIMOTO, TETSUYA, "Social Class and Crime: The Case of the Japanese Americans," *Issues in Criminology*, 10, no. 1 (Spring, 1975), 73–93.

HERMAN, M., *Japanese in America*. Dobbs Ferry: Oceana, 1974.

KITANO, HARRY H. L., and STANLEY SUE, "The Model Minorities," *Journal of Social Issues*, 29, no. 2 (1973), 1–9.

American Indians

BROWN, D. *Bury My Heart at Wounded Knee*. New York: Holt, Rinehart & Winston, 1970.

DOZIER, EDWARD P., "Problem Drinking Among American Indians: The Role of Sociocultural Deprivation," *Quarterly Journal of Studies on Alcohol*, 27, no. 1 (March, 1966), 72–87.

Mexican Americans

ALVAREZ, RODOLFO, "The Psycho-Historical and Socioeconomic Development of the Chicano Community in the United States," *Social Science Quarterly*, 53, no. 4 (March, 1973), 920–42.

DWORKIN, ANTHONY GARY, "Stereotypes and Self-Images Held by Native-Born and Foreign-Born Mexican-Americans," *Sociology and Social Research*, 49, no. 2 (January 1965), 214–24.

FORBES, JACK D., "Race and Color in Mexican-American Problems" *Journal of Human Relations*, 16, no. 1 (1968), 55–68.

GREBLER, LEA, JOAN W. MOORE, and RALPH C. GUZMANN, *The Mexican-American People: The Nation's Second Largest Minority*. 1970.

HELLER, CELIA STOPNICKA, "Class as an Explanation of Ethnic Differences in Mobility Aspirations: The Case of Mexican Americans," *International MigraReview*, 2, no. 1 (Fall, 1967), 31–37.

McLENOU, DALE S., "The Origins of Mexican American Subordination in Texas," *Social Science Quarterly*, 53, no. 4 (March, 1973), 656–70.

MARRETT, CORA B., "The Brown Power Revolt: A True Social Movement," *Journal of Human Relations*, 19, no. 3 (1971), 356–66.

MARTINEZ, G. T., and J. EDWARDS, *Mexican Americans*. New York: Houghton Mifflin, 1973.

MOORE, JOAN W., "Colonialism: The Case of the Mexican Americans," *Social Problems*, 17, no. 4 (Spring, 1970), 463–72.

MOORE, J. and A. CUELLAR, *Mexican Americans*. Englewood Cliffs, N.J.: Prentice-Hall, 1970.

NEAL, JUSTIN, "Mexican American Achievement Hindered by Culture Conflict," *Sociology and Social Research*, 56, no. 4 (July, 1972), 471–79.

PENALOSA, FERNANDO, "Recent Changes Among the Chicanos," *Sociology and Social Research*, 55, no. 1 (October 1970), 47–52.

———, "The Changing Mexican-American in Southern California," *Sociology and Social Research*, 51, no. 4 (July, 1967), 405–17.

SAMORA, JULIAN, "The Educational Status of a Minority," *Theory into Practice*, 2, no. 3 (June, 1963), 144–50.

SOTOMAYOR, MARTA, "Mexican-American Interaction with Social Systems," *Social Casework*, 52, no. 5 (May, 1971), 316–22.

UHLENBERG, P., "Marital Instability Among Mexican Americans: Following the Pattern of Blacks," *Social Problems,* 20, no. 1 (Summer 1972), 49–56.
WHITEHEAD, CARLTON J., and ALBERT S. KING, "Differences in Managers' Attitudes Towards Mexican and Non-Mexican Americans in Organizational Authority Relations," *Social Science Quarterly,* 53, no. 4 (March, 1973), 760–71.

SEXUAL MINORITIES

ANGRIST, SHIRLEY, "Role Conception as a Predictor of Adult Female Roles," *Sociology and Social Research,* 50, no. 4 (July, 1966), 448–59.
BANNER, L. W., *Women in Modern America: A Brief History.* New York: Harcourt Brace, 1974.
BRUCE, VIRGINIA, "The Expression of Feminity in the Male," *Journal of Social Research,* 3, no. 2 (May, 1967), 129–40.
CHAFETZ, J. S., *Masculine/Feminine or Human?* Itasca: Peacock, 1974.
COLLINS, R., "A Conflict Theory of Sexual Stratification," *Social Problems,* 19, (1971,), 3–21.
FEATHERMAN, DAVID L., and ROBERT M. HAUSER, "Sexual Inequalities and Socioeconomic Achievement in the U.S., 1962–1973," *American Sociological Review,* 41, no. 3 (June, 1976), 462–83.
FIRESTONE, S., *The Dialectic of Sex, The Case for Feminist Revolution.* New York: Bantam, 1971.
FLORA, CORNELIA BUTLER, "The Passive Female: Her Comparative Image by Class and Culture in Women's Magazine Fiction," *Journal of Marriage and the Family,* 33, no. 3 (August 1971), 435–44.
FREEMAN, J., "Growing Up Girlish," *Trans Action,* 8 (1970), 36–43.
———, "The Origins of the Woman's Liberation Movement," *American Journal of Sociology,* 78, no. 4 (January 1973), 792–811.
———, "Political Organization in the Feminist Movement," *Acta Sociologica,* 18, nos. 2–3, (1975), 222–44.
FRIEDAN, B., *The Feminine Mystique.* New York: Dell, 1964.
GOLDBERG, PHILIP, "Are Women Prejudiced Against Women?" *Trans-Action,* 5, no. 5, (April, 1968), 28–30.
GORNICK, VIVIAN, and BARBARA K. MORAN, eds., *Woman in Sexist Society: Studies in Power and Powerlessness.* New York: Basic Books, 1971.
GOULD, C. C., and M. W. WARTOFSKY, eds., *Women and Philosophy: Toward a Theory of Liberation.* New York: Putnam, 1876.
GREER, G., *Female Eunuch.* New York: McGraw Hill, 1971.
HAAVIO-MANNILA, E., "Sex Differentiation in Role Expectations and Performance," *Journal of Marriage and the Family,* 29 (1967), 568–78.
HEIDE, WILMA SCOTT, "What's Wrong with Male-Dominated Society," *Impact of Science on Society,* 21, no. 1 (January-May, 1971), 55–62.
HERNTON, C. C., *Sex and Racism in America.* Garden City: Doubleday, 1965.
HOCHSCHILD, A. R., "A Review of Sex Role Research," *American Journal of Sociology* 78 (1973), 1011–29.
HOLTER, HARRIET, "Sex Roles and Social Change," *Acta Sociologica,* 14, nos. 1–2 (1971), 2–12.
JOHNSEN, KATHRYN P., "The Factors Associated with the Male's Tendency to

Negatively Stereotype the Female," *Sociological Focus,* 2, no. 3 (Spring, 1969), 21–36.

KLEEMAN, JAMES A., "The Establishment of Core Gender Identity in Normal Girls," *Archives of Sexual Behavior,* 1, no. 2 (1971), 103–29.

KLEIN, DORIE, "The Etiology of Female Crime: A Review of the Literature," *Issues in Criminology,* 8, no. 2 (Fall, 1973), 3–30.

LERNIR, GERDA, "Women's Rights and American Feminism," *American Scholar,* 40, no. 2 (April 1971), 235–48.

MCDOWELL, MARGARET B., "The New Rhetoric of Woman Power," *Midwest Quarterly,* 12, no. 2 (January 1971), 187–98.

MACCOBY, E., ed., *The Development of Sex Differences.* Palo Alto: University of Stanford Press, 1966.

MANDLE, JOAN, "Women's Liberation: Humanizing Rather than Polarizing," *The Annals of the American Academy of Political and Social Sciences,* 397, (Sept. 1971). 118–28.

MARTIN, M. K., and B. VOORHIES, *Female of the Species* New York: Columbia University Press, 1975.

MARTIN, W. T., and D. L. POSTON, "The Occupational Composition of White Females: Sexism, Racism, and Occupational Differentiation," *Social Forces,* 50 (1972), 349–55.

MASON, K. O., and L. BUMPASS, "U.S. Women's Sex Role Doctrology, 1970," *American Journal of Sociology,* 80 (1975), 1212–19.

MASON, K. O., J. L. CZAJKA, and S. ARBER, "Change in U.S. Women's Sex-Role Attitudes, 1964–1974," *American Sociological Review,* 41 (1976), 573–96.

MEAD, M., *Sex and Temperament in Three Primitive Societies.* New York: Dell, 1969.

MURDOCK, GEORGE P. and CATERINA PROVOST, "Factors in the Division of Labor by Sex: A Cross-Cultural Analysis," *Ethnology,* 12, no. 2 (April, 1973), 203–25.

NAFFZIGER, CLAUDEEN CLINE and KEN NAFFZIGER, "Development of Sex Role Stereotypes," *The Family Coordinator,* 23, no. 3 (July, 1974), 251–58.

OSMOND, M. W. and P. Y. MARTIN, "Sex and Sexism: A Comparison of Male and Female Sex Role Attitudes," *Journal of Marriage and the Family,* 37 (1975), 744–58.

PRATT, ANNIS, "Archetypal Approaches to the New Feminist Criticism," *Bucknell Review,* 21, no. 1 (Spring, 1971), 3–14.

ROSSI, A., ed., *Feminist Perspectives: From Adams to De Beauvoir.* New York: Columbia University Press, 1973.

RYAN, M. P., *Womanhood in America, From Colonial Times to the Present.* New York: New Viewpoints, 1975.

SEGGAR, JOHN F. and PENNY WHEELER, "World of Work on TV: Ethnic and Sex Representation in TV Drama," *Journal of Broadcasting,* 1973, 17, no. 2 (Spring, 1973), 201–14.

SHANLEY, MARY L. and VICTORIA SCHUCK, "In Search of Political Woman," *Social Science Quarterly,* 55, no. 3 (Dec., 1974), 632–44.

STOLL, C., *Female & Male: Socialization, Social Roles and Social Structure.* Dubuque: W. C. Brown, 1974.

SUTER, L. E., and H. P. MILLER, "Income Differences between Men and Career Women," *American Journal of Sociology,* 78 (1973), 962–74.

TRIEMAN, D. J., and K. TERRELL, "Sex and the Process of Status Attainment: A Comparison of Working Women and Men," *American Sociological Review*, 40 (1975), 174–200.

WILLIAMS, G., "A Research Note on Trends in Occupational Differentiation by Sex," *Social Problems*, 22 (1975), 543–47.

AGE-BASED MINORITIES

Children

ADAMS, PAUL, LELIA BERG, NAN ROBERT OLLENDORFF, *Children's Rights: Toward the Liberation of the Child*. London: Elek, 1971.

ARIÈS, P., *Centuries of Childhood, A Social History of Family Life*, trans. R. Baldick, New York: Knopf, 1962.

CHILMAN, CATHERINE S., "Economic and Social Deprivations: Its Effects on Children and Families in the United States—A Selected Bibliography," *Journal of Marriage and the Family*, 26, no. 4 (November 1964), 495–98.

COTTLE, T. J., "Parent and Child: The Hazards of Equality," in *Children's Liberation*, D. Gottlieb, ed., Englewood Cliffs, N.J.: Prentice-Hall, 1973, pp. 87–102.

ELKIND, D., *Children and Adolescents: Interpretive Essays on Jean Piaget*. New York: Oxford University Press, 1974.

GIL, DAVID G., "A Holistic Perspective on Child Abuse and Its Prevention" *Journal of Sociology and Social Welfare*, 2, no. 2 (Winter 1974), 110–25.

GOTTLIEB, D., ed., *Children's Liberation*. Englewood Cliffs, N.J.: Prentice-Hall, 1973.

———, "Children in America: A Demographic Profile and Commentary," in *Children's Liberation*, D. Gottlieb, ed., Englewood Cliffs, N.J.: Prentice-Hall, 1973, pp. 7–22.

GRAHAM, HILLARY, "Children Under the Law," *Harvard Educational Review*, 43, no. 4 (November 1973), 487–514.

KEITH-LUCAS, ALAN, "Child Welfare Services Today: An Overview and Some Questions, *Annals of the American Academy of Political and Social Science*, 355 (September 1964), 1–8.

LEONARD, G. B., "How School Stunts your Child," in *Children's Liberation*, D. Gottlieb, ed., Englewood Cliffs, N.J.: Prentice-Hall, 1973, pp. 145–66.

LORENCE, BOGNA W., "Parents and Children in Eighteenth-Century Europe," *History of Childhood Quarterly*, 2, no. 1 (Summer 1974), 1–30.

McCOY, NORMA, and EDWARD ZIGLER, "Social Reinforcer Effectiveness as a Function of the Relationship Between Child and Adult, *Journal of Personality and Social Psychology*, 1, no. 6 (1965), 602–12.

MEAD, M., and M. WOLFSTEIN, eds., *Childhood in Contemporary Cultures*. Chicago: University of Chicago Press, 1963.

MEYER, P. B., "The Exploitation of the American Growing Class," in *Children's Liberation*, D. Gottlieb, ed., Englewood Cliffs, N.J.: Prentice-Hall, 1973, pp. 35–52.

MULLER, J. F., *Children of Frankenstein: A Primer on Modern Technology and Human Values*. Bloomington: Indiana University Press, 1970.

PAPPENFORT, DONNELL M., ADELAIDE DINWOODIE, and DEE, MORGAN KILPATRICK, "Children in Institutions, 1966: A Research Note," *Social Service Review*, 42, no. 2 (June 1968), 252–60.

PEARLIN, LEONARD I., MARIAN RADKE YARROW, and HARRY A. SCARR, "Unintended Effects of Parental Aspirations: The Case of Children's Cheating," *American Journal of Sociology*, 73, no. 1 (July, 1967), 73–83.

ROTHMAN, SHEILA M., "Other People's Children: The Day Care Experience in America," *Public Interest*, 30 (Winter 1973), 11–27.

SHIPMAN, M., *Childhood: A Sociological Perspective*. New York: Humanities, 1972.

WHITING, B. B., and J. W. WHITING, *Children of Six Cultures*, Cambridge: Harvard University, 1974.

Adolescents

ALEXANDER, C. NORMAN, and ERNEST Q. CAMPBELL, "Peer Influences on Adolescent Drinking," *Quarterly Journal of Studies on Alcohol*, 28, no. 3 (September 1967), 444–54.

COLEMAN, J. S., *The Adolescent Society*. New York: Free Press, 1971.

FRIEDENBERG, EDGAR Z., "The Generation Gap," *Annals of the American Academy of Political and Social Science*, 382 (March, 1969), 32–42.

GOODNIGHT, BARBARA, "Toward a Sociological Theory of Adolescence in American Society," *Proceedings of the Southwestern Sociological Association*, 19 (1968), 137–41.

GOTTLIEB, DAVID, and ANNE LEINHARD HEINSOHN, "Sociology and Youth," *Sociological Quarterly*, 14, no. 2 (Spring, 1973), 249–70.

HAVIGHURST, R. J., and P. H. DRYER, eds., *Youth*. Chicago: University of Chicago Press, 1975.

HIMES, JOSEPH S., "Some Work-Related Cultural Deprivations of Lower-Class Negro Youths," *Journal of Marriage and the Family*, 26, no. 4 (November 1964), 447–49.

HOUGH, RICHARD L., "Parental Influence, Youth Contraculture, and Rural Adolescent Attitudes Toward Minority Groups," *Rural Sociology*, 34, no. 3 (September 1969). 383–86.

HURLOCK, E. B., *Adolescent Development*, (4th ed.). New York: McGraw-Hill, 1973.

LAUFER, ROBERT S., "Sources of Generational Consciousness and Conflict," *Annals of the American Academy of Political and Social Science*, 395, (May, 1971), 80–94.

LIPSET, S. M., *Rebellion in the University*. Boston: Little Brown, 1971.

MAHONEY, ANNE RANKIN, "The Effect of Labeling upon Youths in the Juvenile Justice System: A Review of the Evidence," *Law and Society Review*, 8, no. 4 (Summer 1974), 583–614.

MARANELL, GARY M., "An Examination of the Self and Group Attitudes of Adolescent Clique Members," *Kansas Journal of Sociology*, 1, no. 3 (Summer 1965), 123–30.

MEAD, M., *Coming of Age in Samoa*. New York: Morrow, 1928.

MILLER, D., Adolescence: *Psychology, Psychopathology, and Psychotherapy*. New York: Aronson, 1974.

MURDOCK, GRAHAM, and GUY PHELPS, "Youth Culture and the School Revisited," *British Journal of Sociology*, 23, no. 4 (December 1972) 478–82.

PEARSON, G. H., *Adolescence and the Conflict of Generations*. New York: Norton, 1958.

Petroni, Frank A., "Adolescent Liberalism—The Myth of a Generation Gap," *Adolescence*, 7, no. 26 (Summer 1972), 221–32.

Piccone, Paul, "Students' Protest, Class Structure, and Ideology," *Telos*, 2, no. 1 (Spring, 1969), 106–22.

Rivera, Ramon J., and James F. Short, Jr., "Significant Adults, Caretakers and Structure of Opportunity: An Exploratory Study," *Journal of Research in Crime and Delinquency*, 4, no. 1 (January 1967), 76–97.

Rogers, D., *Adolescence: A Psychological Perspective*. New York: Appleton-Century-Crofts, 1972, (2nd ed.)

Rush, Gary B., "The Radicalization of Middle-Class Youth," *International Social Science Journal*, 24, no. 2 (1972), 312-25.

Sebald, H., *Adolescence: A Sociological Analysis*. New York: Appleton-Century-Crofts, 1968.

Short, James F., Jr., "Youth, Gangs, and Society: Micro- and Macrosociological Processes," *The Sociological Quarterly*, 15, no. 1 (Winter 1974), 3–19.

Templin, Lawrence, "The Pathology of Youth," *Journal of Human Relations*, 16, no. 1 (1968), 113–27.

Troll, Lillian E., " 'Generation Gap' in Later Life: An Introductory Discussion and some Preliminary Findings," *Sociological Focus*, 5 (1971), 18–28.

van Manen, Gloria Count, "Father Role and Adolescent Socialization," *Adolescence*, 3, no. 10 (Summer 1968), 139–52.

Wells, J. Gipson, "A Selected Bibliography on the Sociology of Adolescence," *Sociological Symposium*, 7 (Spring, 1971), 73–92.

Worsley, Peter M., "Authority and the Young," *New Society*, 6, no. 147 (July, 1965), 10–13.

The Aged

Dietrich, T. Stanton, "Senior Citizens: A Potential Minority Group?" *Research Reports in Social Science*, 12, no. 2 (August 1969), 32–46.

Field, M., *Aged, the Family, and the Community*. New York: Columbia University Press, 1972.

Francher, J. Scott, "American Values and the Disenfranchisement of the Aged," *Eastern Anthropologist*, 22, no. 1 (January-April 1969), 29–36.

Gowgell, Donald O., "The Demography of Aging" in *The Daily Needs and Instincts of Older People*, Adeline M. Hoffman, Springfield, Ill.: Charles C. Thomas, 1970.

Hoffman, Adeline M., *The Daily Needs and Instincts of Older People*. Springfield, Ill.: Charles C. Thomas, 1970.

Poorkaj, Houshang, "Social-Psychological Factors and 'Successful Aging,' " *Sociology and Social Research*, 56, no. 3 (April, 1972), 289–300.

Reid, Otto M., "Aging Americans," *Welfare in Review*, 4, no. 5 (May, 1966), 1–12.

Rose, A. M., "Mental Health of Normal Older Persons," in *Older People and Their Social World*, A. M. Rose and W. A. Peterson, eds., Philadelphia: F. A. Davis, 1965, pp. 193–200.

Rose, A. M., and W. A. Peterson, eds., *Older People and Their Social World*. Philadelphia: F. A. Davis, 1965.

Rosenfelt, Rosche H., "The Elderly Mystique," *Journal of Social Issues*, 21, no. 4 (October 1965), 37–43.

ROSOW, IRVING, "And Then We Were Old," *Trans-Action*, 2, no. 2 (January-February 1965), 20–26.

——, *Social Integration of the Aged*, New York: Free Press, 1967.

SHANAS, ETHEL, "A Note on Restriction of Life Space: Attitudes of Age Cohorts," *Journal of Health and Social Behavior*, 9, no. 1 (March, 1968), 86–90.

——, "What's New in Old Age?" *American Behavioral Scientist*, 14, no. 1 (September-October 1970), 5-12.

——, "Family-Kin Networks and Aging in Cross-Cultural Perspective," *Journal of Marriage and the Family*, 35, no. 3 (August 1973), 505–11.

SHANAS, ETHEL, and PHILIP M. HAUSER, "Zero Population Growth and the Family Life of Old People," *The Journal of Social Issues*, 30, no. 4 (1974), 79–92.

TIBBITS, CLARK, and WILMA DONAHUE, eds., *Social and Psychological Aspects of Aging Around the World* New York: Columbia University Press, 1962.

9

Cultural Minorities in the United States

Ethnicity or cultural differentiation has been inherent in American culture from the society's colonial foundation: With its WASP colonial elite, high European immigration for economic purposes, and close correlation between cultural background and the socioeconomic hierarchy, ethnic prejudice and discrimination represent an American tradition. Cultural prejudice has also been inherent in racism from negative contact with native Americans through Black slavery to contemporary ethnocentrism concerning Chicanos. In fact, WASP values of materialism and moralism may be viewed as a major factor behind the society's colonial foundation and structure of minority group differentiation.

As stated earlier, ethnic groups or cultural minorities are produced, in similar fashion to racial minorities, through migration. Given that American society has been subject to high levels of immigration with at least twenty foreign countries significantly represented,[1] ethnicity is a major factor in its cultural makeup, resulting in high levels of economic competition, ethnocentrism, and prejudice, with the WASP majority maintaining an emphasis on its assumed cultural superiority. Among whites ethnicity functions in a similar fashion to racism as each subgroup migrates into the society under particular historical circumstances for economic purposes and is subject to the control and exploitation of the WASP elite. Despite the "melting-pot" notion, assumed cultural differences operate among whites in a socioeconomic fashion.

Whites in the society may be divided into four major groups: Anglo-Saxon Protestants, European Protestants, Roman Catholics, and non-Protestant ethnics. The first include English and Scots immigrants —the society's founding colonial settlers—the second consists of groups such as Germans, Swedes, Dutch Protestants, Norwegians, and Finns, the third include the Irish and Italians, while examples of the last are Jewish, Russian, and other European groups. The first two represent the core of American culture with its Protestant ethic values of individualism, moralism, materialism, economic development, whiteness and purity—the basis of prejudice, discrimination, and oppression. The further a minority deviates from these values, the more negativism it tends to experience. The second group represents European immigrants with religions and cultures similar to the WASP elite, experiencing similar high levels of assimilation, and contributing agricultural skills and Lutheran religion. On the other hand, the Italians and Irish with their poverty-stricken origins, high levels of immigration, non-Protestant religion, and linguistic difficulties have experienced greater problems regarding acceptance and assimilation. The last group—non-Protestant ethnics—given their relatively smaller size, variation in immigration, and cultural values regarding economic behavior and materialism, have tended to be highly successful in terms of social status and economic achievement.

In general, America's ethnic hierarchy consists of a Protestant majority, highly successful non-Protestant ethnic groups, and Roman Catholics who have tended to be less successful. This structure represents a combination of three major elements: (1) the historical circumstances surrounding each group's migration into the society (whether

---

[1]This includes Russians, Greeks, Swedes, British, Danish, Irish, Norwegians, French, Austrians, Lithuanians, Germans, Dutch, Cubans, Canadians, Hungarians, Italians, Czechoslovakians, Yugoslavians, and Poles.

positive or negative, the group's demographic characteristics and economic resources); (2) the extent of cultural similarity with the WASP elite, particularly regarding economic behavior; and (3) each group's major economic role in the society, particularly the extent to which it provides cheap, unskilled labor for a capitalist economy. As with race, cultural minorities are a product of migration and represent economic resources—particularly labor—for the dominant society. While rationalized less in psychological terms, assumed cultural inferiority remains a powerful argument for their continued subordination.

As has been indicated, the historical circumstances surrounding the creation of these minorities may be extremely negative: high rates of immigration, poverty-stricken resources, disproportionate ratios of the aged, large family size, linguistic problems, color variation, traditional familistic values, geographic concentration after arrival, health problems, non-Protestant religious practices, and highly visible cultural characteristics. These have all served to place groups such as the Irish and Italians at a severe disadvantage in the society, particularly in the past.[2] While social mobility among ethnic groups has been relatively high, as we shall indicate, these groups were created for economic reasons and represented economic resources for the host society. Fear of economic competition from these has also produced severe reactions (lynching of Italians, prejudice against the Irish) and political attempts to control the immigration process because immigrants were viewed as polluting the purity of the "American race."[3] As with racial minorities, ethnic groups are a product of migration under negative conditions, represent economic-labor resources, and experience the conservative backlash of the WASP elite.

Demographic data on the society's ethnic hierarchy indicate a high proportion of English and German groups, with the Irish and Italians of medium size, and significantly smaller percentages of French, Polish, and Russian inhabitants.[4] Regarding religion, Protestants and Catholics predominate, with much smaller percentages of Jews and Eastern Christians.[5] Ethnic groups engaged in professional and white-collar occupations are predominantly Russian, Greek, Swedish, British, Danish, Irish, Norwegian, French, Austrian, Lithuanian, and German while those with significantly lower percentages in this

[2]See, for example, W. Strawbridge, "Competition as a Cause of Discrimination and Prejudice," *University of Washington Journal of Sociology*, 2, (1970), pp. 28–37.

[3]J. Higham, *Strangers in the Land: Patterns of American Nativism, 1860–1925* (New Brunswick: Rutgers University Press, 1955).

[4]Based on U.S. Bureau of the Census, *Statistical Abstract of the United States: 1974, 95th ed.*, (Washington, D.C.: 1974), Table 41.

[5]*Statistical Abstract of the United States*, Table 65.

category tend to be Cuban, Hungarian, Italian, Czechoslovakian, Yugoslavian, or Polish.[6] In general, white Americans tend to be English and German in origin, and predominantly Christian, while the occupationally successful are mostly Anglo-Saxon European Protestants, and non-Protestant ethnics. The ethnic majority is clearly visible: European Protestant along with non-Protestant ethnics, placing others in a minority status. While socioeconomic mobility is much higher than among racial minorities,[7] a clear ethnic structure exists in the society.

Majority attitudes reveal extensive *ethnocentrism*—belief in the inherent superiority of their own culture. As a result, non-WASPs are defined as dumb, lazy, dirty, immoral, grasping, mercenary, and disloyal—the assumed opposite of ingroup traits.[8] Furthermore, in terms of desired levels of association with ethnic groups, the majority favor British Americans most, Europeans next, with Italians, Spaniards, and Jews least.[9] The socioeconomic hierarchy is reflected in attitudinal and social distance patterns.

Minority reactions may proceed through a number of stages: Conformity and assimilation during the earlier years of economic deprivation and dependency, moving to secessionism (withdrawal) with greater awareness of ethnic discrimination, to contemporary emphases on nationalism and ethnic power (Jewish Defense League, Italian-American Civil Rights League, National Center for Urban Ethnic Affairs.)[10] Depending on a minority's economic resources, the discrimination it experiences relative to other groups, the manner in which it defines its identity and position in the society, and the general society's

[6]Based on U.S. Bureau of the Census, *1970 Census of Population, Subject Reports. National Origin and Language,* PC(2)-1A (Washington, D.C.: 1971), Table 13.

[7]See B. Duncan and O. T. Duncan, "Minorities and the Process of Stratification," *American Sociological Review,* 33, (1968), pp. 356–64; S. Lieberson, "Stratification and Ethnic Groups," *Sociological Inquiry,* 40 (1970), 172–81.

[8]See, for example, D. Katz and K. Braly, "Racial Stereotypes of One Hundred College Students," *Journal of Abnormal and Social Psychology,* (1933), pp. 280–90; R. A. Mulligan, "Socioeconomic Background and Minority Attitudes," *Sociology and Social Research,* 45 (1961), pp. 289–94; S. Ettinger, "The Origins of Modern Anti-Semitism," *Dispersion and Unity,* 9 (1969), pp. 17–37; C. H. Anderson, *White Protestant Americans* (Englewood Cliffs, N.J.: Prentice-Hall, 1970).

[9]See, E. S. Bogardus, *Immigration and Race Attitudes* (Boston: Heath, 1928). See also L. H. Carlson and G. A. Colburn, eds., *In Their Place: White America Defines Her Minorities, 1850–1950* (New York: Wiley, 1972); L. Dinnerstein and F. C. Jaher, eds., *The Aliens: A History of Ethnic Minorities in America* (New York: Appleton-Century-Crofts, 1970); G. Potter, *To the Golden Door: The Story of the Irish in Ireland and America* (Boston: Little, Brown, 1960); H. E. Ransford, "Skin Color, Life Chances, and Anti-White Attitudes," *Social Problems* 18 (1970), 164–78.

[10]For examples of such "types" see P. I. Rose, *They and We* (New York: Random House, 1964); L. Wirth, "The Problem of Minority Groups," in R. Linton, ed., *The Science of Man in the World Crisis* (New York: Columbia University Press, 1945).

level of economic development, its major orientations may focus on assimilation, pluralism, self-hatred, secessionism, or militancy[11] as it reacts to the majority in the context of a changing society. Accordingly, groups which experience most discrimination, possess few resources, and begin to perceive their relative deprivation with economic change tend to be most vocal in their reaction, while higher status groups may be more assimilationist or pluralist in viewpoint, with less overt protest.[12] Minority reaction reflects the ethnic hierarchy as well as the larger society's general level of economic development, paralleling in some respects the changing dynamics of race relations.

The structure of institutionalized discrimination is clear: political dominance, economic exploitation through ethnic-specific occupational roles, residential, religious, and educational segregation, along with negative stereotypes reinforced in the family and media. The economic exploitation of ethnic minorities is reinforced by political control and segregation, rationalized by negative cultural stereotypes.

Ethnic social movements include precinct politics and political organizations, unions based on ethnic-specific occupations, traditional ethnic community institutions, and contemporary nationalist groups working for ethnic power.[13] These movements reflect each minority's position in the ethnic socioeconomic hierarchy, as well as the larger society's level of economic development.

The basis of majority-minority ethnic relations, as with racial minorities, is essentially economic, that is, the economic roles and exploitation of non-WASP groups is rationalized in terms of assumed cultural inferiority with reference to assumed limitations in intelligence, and associated work skills. While significant ethnic social mobility has occurred, it remains evident that backlash reactions to economic competition, continued anti-Semitism on a number of levels in the society, as well as media ethnic stereotypes, indicate the extent to which political and economic power is ethnically based and rationalized in social terms. Ethnic relations involve competition for resources such as political power, housing, educational facilities, and union leadership, within the context of a clear socioeconomic hierarchy.[14] Vested economic interests

[11]See, for example, I. Rinder, "Minority Orientations: An Approach to Intergroup Relations Theory through Social Psychology," *Phylon*, 26 (1965), pp. 5–17.

[12]P. M. Lewin, "Psychological Aspects of Minority Group Members: The Concepts of Kurt Lewin," *Jewish Social Studies*, (1974), 72–79.

[13]J. Lopreato, *Italian Americans* (New York: Random House, 1971); V. R. Greene, *The Slavic Community on Strike* (Notre Dame: University of Notre Dame Press, 1968); T. Andrews, *The Polish National Catholic Church in America* (London: Clowes, 1953); L. Killian, *White Southerners* (New York: Random House 1970).

[14]A. M. Greeley, "White against White, The Enduring Ethnic Conflict," in L. K. Howe, ed., *The White Majority, Between Poverty and Affluence* (New York: Vintage, 1970), pp. 111–18.

thus maintain the viability of assumed cultural differences as a major way of defending inequality among white Americans.

Interminority relations are also competitive within the Protestant-non-Protestant-Catholic hierarchy as each group competes for these resources on a community basis. Such competition, furthermore, is complicated by the overlap of ethnicity and racism, sexism, traditional family roles, social class, and types of deviance, reinforcing the hierarchy, particularly as those groups which rank low in this structure are more influenced by other dimensions of minority group status.[15] The shape and boundaries of the hierarchy thus remain relatively stable, maintaining the general correlation between culture and economic exploitation. In this manner the more the disadvantages of minority group status accumulate, the lower an individual and/or group stands in the hierarchy.

CONCLUSIONS

Ethnic minorities in America have been produced through migration under generally negative circumstances and represent varying economic-labor resources for the larger society. The ethnic majority tends to be English and German in origin, and predominantly Christian, while the occupationally successful tend to be Anglo-Saxon and European Protestants as well as non-Protestant ethnics. A clear hierarchy is thus evident. Majority attitudes reveal a high degree of ethnocentrism and social distance which parallels this structure while minorities have reactions ranging from self-hatred and assimilation to secessionism, to contemporary militancy. Minority movements have included political, economic, and social groups which reflect their position in the society as well as their level of economic development. Finally, the basis of majority-minority ethnic relations is competition for economic resources while interminority relations are complicated by other major dimensions of minority group status.

Ethnic differentiation among American whites reflects the *migration experiences* of various cultural groups and their *economic relation* to the *WASP majority*, defined in assumed *cultural terms* with specific reference to *occupational skills*. Heterogeneous migration results in intrawhite differentiation, differing levels of economic status and exploitation, and cultural prejudice. Despite the "melting-pot" notion, the society is culturally, as well as racially, defined. The major characteristics of such differentiation are summarized in Figure 9.1.

[15] P. Gleason, "Immigration and American Catholic Intellectual Life," *Review of Politics*, (1964), pp. 147–73; M. K. Opler and J. L. Singer, "Ethnic Differences in Behavior and Psychopathology: Italian and Irish," *International Journal of Social Psychiatry*, (1956), pp. 11–22.

DIMENSIONS	CHARACTERISTICS
1. Historical:	migration under negative historical circumstances for economic purposes
2. Demographic:	majority is European Protestant and non-Protestant ethnics
3. Attitudinal:	
(a) Majority	high ethnocentrism concerning non-WASPs
(b) Minority	conformity, assimilationism, seccessionism, nationalism, ethnic power
4. Institutional:	political dominance, economic exploitation, negative cultural stereotypes
5. Social Movements:	political organizations, unions, community institutions, nationalist groups
6. Relational:	
(a) Majority-Minority	vested WASP economic interests, backlash reactions
(b) Interminority	
racial	economic, social competition
sexual	traditional sexual roles
age based	traditional family roles
cultural	*
economic	relationship to social class
behavioral	ethnic forms of deviance

FIGURE 9.1. Characteristics of Cultural Minorities in the U.S.

STUDY QUESTIONS

1. Select an ethnic minority with which you are familiar and:
   (a) Delineate the major historical circumstances behind its creation.
   (b) Outline its major demographic characteristics.
   (c) Describe majority and minority attitudes toward each other.
   (d) Outline the dimensions of institutionalized domination.
   (e) Describe the characteristics of majority-minority relations.
2. How does this minority differ from racial, sexual, and age-based types?

READINGS

CULTURAL MINORITIES: GENERAL

ANDERSON, C. H., *White Protestant Americans.* Englewood Cliffs, N.J.: Prentice-Hall, Inc. 1970.

BARTH, F., ed., *Ethnic Groups and Boundaries.* London: Allen, 1969.

CORDASCO, FRANCISCO, and ROCCO G. GALATIOTO, "Ethnic Displacement in the Interstitial Community: The East Harlem Experience," *Phylon,* 31, no. 3 (Fall, 1970), 302–12.

DINNERSTEIN, L., and D. M. REIMERS, *Ethnic Americans: A History of Immigration and Assimilation.* New York: Harper & Row, 1975.

DUNCAN, BEVERLY, and OTIS DUDLEY DUNCAN, "Minorities and the Process of Stratification," *American Sociological Review,* 33, no. 3 (June, 1968), 356–64.

FEATHERMAN, DAVID L., "The Socioeconomic Achievement of White Religio-Ethnic Subgroups: Social and Psychological Explanations," *American Sociological Review,* 36, no. 2 (April, 1971), 207–22.

FELLOWS, D. K., *A Mosaic of America's Ethnic Minorities.* New York: Wiley, 1972.

FRANCIS, E. K., *Interethnic Relations, An Essay in Sociological Theory.* New York: Elsevier, 1976.

GELFAND, D. E., and R. D. LEE, eds., *Ethnic Conflicts and Power: A Cross-National Perspective.* New York: Wiley, 1973.

GOERING, JOHN M., "The Emergence of Ethnic Interests," *Social Forces,* 49, no. 3 (March, 1971), 379–84.

GREELEY, ANDREW M., "American Sociology and the Study of Ethnic Immigrant Groups," *International Migration Digest,* 1, no. 2 (Fall, 1964), 107–13.

HALE, E. H. *Letters on Irish Emigration.* Boston: Phillips, Sampson, 1852.

HIGHAM, J., *Strangers in the Land: Patterns of American Nativism, 1860–1925.* New Brunswick: Rutgers University Press, 1955.

HOLDIN, MATTHEW, "Ethnic Accommodation in a Historical Case," *Comparative Studies in Society and History,* 8, no. 2 (January 1966), 168–80.

HUNT, C. I., and L. WALKER, *Ethnic Dynamics, Patterns of Intergroup Relations in Various Societies.* Homewood: Dorsey, 1974.

KANTROWITZ, N., *Ethnic and Racial Segregation Patterns in New York City Metropolis: Residential Patterns among White Ethnic Groups, Blacks, and Puerto Ricans.* New York: Praeger, 1973.

KENNEDY, R. E., JR., "Irish Americans, A Successful Case of Pluralism," in *The Minority Report,* eds., A. G. Dworkin, and R. J. Dworkin. New York: Praeger, 1976.

KRAUSZ, ERNEST, "Factors of Social Mobility in British Minority Groups," *British Journal of Sociology,* 23, no. 3 (September 1972), 275–86.

LAGUMINA, S. J., and F. J. CAVAIOLI, *The Ethnic Dimension in American Society.* New York: Holbrook, 1974.

LEVENTMAN, SEYMOUR, "Class and Ethnic Tensions: Minority Group Leadership in Transition," *Sociology and Social Research,* 50, no. 3 (April, 1966), 371–76.

LEWIN, PAPANEK, MIRIAM, "Psychological Aspects of Minority Group Membership: The Concepts of Kurt Lewin," *Jewish Social Studies,* (January 1974), 72–79.

147

LIEBERSON, S., "Stratification and Ethnic Groups," *Sociological Inquiry,* 40 (1970), 172–81.
MAKIELSKI, S. J., JR., *Beleagured Minorities, Cultural Politics in America.* San Francisco: Freeman, 1973.
MULLIGAN, RAYMOND A., "Socio-economic Background and Minority Attitudes," *Sociology and Social Research,* 45, no. 3 (April, 1961), 289–94.
NELSEN, FRANK C., "The German-American Immigrants—Struggle," *International Review of History and Political Science,* 10, no. 2 (May, 1973), 37–49.
NOEL, D. L., "A Theory of the Origin of Ethnic Stratification," *Social Problems,* 16, (1968), 157–71.
PRATT, H. J., "Politics, Status and the Organization of Ethnic Minority Group Interests. The Case of the New York Protestants," *Polity,* 3, no. 2 (Winter 1970), 222–46.
RANSFORD, H. E., "Skin Color, Life Chances, and Anti-White Attitudes," *Social Problems* 18 (1970), 164–78.
REDEKOP, CALVIN, and JOHN A. HOSTETLER, "Minority-Majority Relations and Economic Interdependence," *Phylon,* 27, no. 4 (Winter 1966), 367–78.
ROUCEK, J. S., "Difficulties in the Education of Minority Groups in the United States," *Sociological Review,* 9, nos. 13–14 (1965), 34–49.
SCHERMERHORN, R. A., *Comparative Ethnic Relations: A Framework for Theory and Research.* New York: Random House, 1970.
———, "Minorities and National Integration," *Journal of Social Research,* 13, no. 2 (March, 1970), 25–35.
SHIBUTANI, TAMOTSU, and KIAN M. KWAN, *Ethnic Stratification: A Comparative Approach.* New York: The Macmillan Co., 1965.
SKLARE, MARSHALL, "Assimilation and the Sociologists," *Commentary,* 39, no. 5 (May, 1965), 63–66.
STRAWBRIDGE, WILLIAM, "Competition as a Cause of Discrimination and Prejudice," *University of Washington Journal of Sociology,* 2 (November 1970), 28–37.
VECOLI, RUDOLPH J., "European Americans: From Immigrants to Ethnics," *International Migration Review,* 6, no. 4 (Winter 1972), 403–34.
YINGER, J. MILTON, "Social Forces Involved in Group Identification or Withdrawal," *Daedalus,* 90, no. 2 (Spring, 1961), 247–62.

Catholic Americans

GLEASON, P., "Immigration and American Catholic Intellectual Life," *Review of Politics.* 2, no. 26 (April, 1964), 147–73.
GREELEY, A. M., "White against White, The Enduring Conflict," in *The White Majority, Between Poverty and Affluence,* ed. L. K. Howe. New York: Vintage, 1970, pp. 111–18.

Czechoslovakian Americans

CAPEK, THOMAS, *The Czechs (Bohemians) in America.* New York: The Arno Press, 1969, (reprint, originally published in 1920).
KUTAK, ROBERT I., *The Story of a Bohemian-American Village; A Study of Social Persistence and Change.* New York: The Arno Press, 1969, (reprint, originally published in 1933).

Greek Americans

BURGESS, THOMAS, *Greeks in America.* New York: The Arno Press, (reprint, originally published in 1913).
ZENIDES, J. P., *The Greeks in America.* San Francisco: R & E Associates, 1972.

Irish Americans

OPLER, MARVIN K., and JEROME L. SINGER, "Ethnic Differences in Behavior and Psychopathology: Italian and Irish," International Journal of Social Psychiatry, 2, no. 1 (Summer 1956), 11–22.

Italian Americans

BAYOR, RONALD H., "Italians, Jews, and Ethnic Conflict," *International Migration Review,* 6 (Winter 1972), 377–93.
CHILD, J. L., *Italian or American? The Second Generation Conflict.* London: Oxford University Press, 1943.
DIGGINS, JOHN P., "The Italo-American Anti-Facist Opposition," *Journal of American History,* 54, no. 3 (December 1967), 579–98.
FENTON, EDWIN, *Immigrants and Unions, A Case Study: Italian and American Labor.* New York: The Arno Press, 1975.
GALLO, J., *Ethnic Alienation: The Italian-Americans.* New York: Fairleigh Dickinson, 1974.
LOPRESTO, J., *Italian Americans.* New York: Random House, 1970.
PALISI, BARTOLOMEO J., "Ethnic Generation and Family Structure," *Journal of Marriage and the Family,* 28, no. 1 (February 1966), 49–50.
SCHIAVO, G. E., *Italian-American History.* New York: Arno, 1975.
VAIRO, PHILIP D., "The Italian Immigrant in the United States," *Indian Sociological Bulletin,* 2, no. 4 (July, 1965), 196–205.

Jewish Americans

BITTON, LIVIA E., "The Jewess as a Fictional Sex Symbol," *Bucknell Review,* 21, no. 1 (Spring, 1973), 63–86.
BUTWIN, F., *Jews in America.* New York: Lerner Publications, 1969.
EHRLICH, H. J., "Stereotyping and Negro-Jewish Stereotypes," *Social Forces,* 41, (1963), 171–76.
ETTINGER, SHMUEL, "The Origins of Modern Anti-Semitism," *Dispersion and Unity,* 9, (1969), 17–37.
FRIEDMAN, NORMAN L., "German Lineage and Reform Affiliation: American Jewish Prestige Criteria in Transition," *Phylon,* 261, no. 2 (Summer 1965), 140–47.
GROSS, BARRY, "What Shylock Forgot, or Making It and Losing It in America," *The Journal of Ethnic Studies,* 2, no. 3 (Fall, 1974), 50–57.
KOGAN, LAWRENCE A., "The Jewish Conception of Negroes in the North: An Historical Approach," *Phylon,* 28, no. 4 (Winter 1967), 376–85.
ROSENTHAL, ARLENE, "The Jewish Community in the Broader Society. An Attitude Survey," *Proceedings of the Southwestern Sociological Association,* 19, (1968), 5–9.

VOGEL, MANFRED, "Some Reflections on the Jewish-Christian Dialogue in the Light of the Six-Day War," *Annals of the American Academy of Political and Social Science*, 387 (January 1970), 96–108.

Polish Americans

ANDREWS, THEODORE, *The Polish National Catholic Church in America.* London: W. Clowes, 1953.

BERCOVICI, KONRAD, *On New Shores.* New York: The Century Co., 1925.

BLANSHARD, BRAND, *The Church and the Polish Immigrant,* New York: Oxford University Press, 1920.

CHROBOT, LEONARD, "The Elusive Polish-American," *Polish-American Studies,* (Spring, 1973), 54–59.

FOX, PAUL, *The Poles in America.* New York: The Arno Press, 1970.

KOLM, RICHARD, "The Identity Crisis of Polish-Americans," *The Quarterly Review,* (April, June 1969), 1–4.

KOTLARZ, ROBERT J., "Writings About the Changing of Polish Names in America," *Polish-American Studies,* (January-June 1963), 1–4.

LOPATA, HELENA ZNANIECKI, *Polish Americans: Status Competition in an Ethnic Community.* Englewood Cliffs, N.J.: Prentice-Hall, 1976.

MAGIERA, STANLEY A., "Some Reasons for First Name Changes," *Polish-American Studies,* (January-June 1963), 8–9.

OBIDINSKI, EUGENE, "Polish-Americans in Buffalo: The Transformation of an Ethnic Subcommunity," *Polish Review,* (Winter, 1969), 28–39.

SANDERS, IRWIN T., and EWA T. MORAWSKA, *Polish-American Community Life: A Survey of Research.* Community Sociology Training Program, Boston University, 1975.

WAGNER, STANLEY P. "The Polish-American Vote in 1960," *Polish-American Studies,* (January-June 1964), 1–9.

WOOD, ARTHUR, E., *Hamtranck: A Sociological Study of A Polish-American Community.* New Haven: College and University Press, 1955.

ZAGRANICZNY, STANLEY, "Some Reasons for Polish Surname Changes," *Polish-American Studies,* (January-June 1963), 12–14.

Ukranian Americans

BORHEK, J. D., "Ethnic Group Cohesion," *American Journal of Sociology,* (July, 1970), 33–48.

HALICH, WASYL, *Ukranians in the United States.* New York: The Arno Press, 1970.

Yugoslavian Americans

ADAMIC, LOUIS, *Laughing in the Jungle: The Autobiography of an Immigrant in America.* New York: The Arno Press, 1974.

BABICZ, WALTER VLADIMIR, *Assimilation of Yugoslavs in Franklin County, Ohio,* San Francisco: R & E Associates, 1972.

COLAKOVIC, BRANKO MITA, *Yugoslav Migrations to America.* San Francisco: R & E Associates, 1973.

GOVORCHIN, GERALD GILBERT, *Americans From Yugoslavia.* Gainesville: University of Florida Press, 1961.

GREEN, ROGER H. JR., *South Slav Settlement in Western Washington: Perception and Choice.* San Francisco: R & E Associates, 1974.

PRPIC, GEORGE J., *The Croatian Immigrants in America.* New York: Philosophical Library, 1971.

10

Economic Minorities in the United States

America, despite its economic wealth, high gross national product, superior technology, and spectacular rate of economic development, at least in the past, has a serious poverty problem. It has been estimated, for instance, that between twelve and twenty percent of the population was "below the poverty line" in 1970. This minority significantly overlaps with other dimensions of discrimination such as sex, race, age, and mental illness.[1] Such deprivation, furthermore, represents a self-reinforcing cycle in which factors such as economic deprivation, emotional problems, and illness during childhood are closely related to reduced intelligence levels and educational achievement.[2] Poverty has devastating effects on a number of levels in society.

[1]See C. S. Chilman, "Families in Poverty in the Early 1970's: Rates, Associated Factors, Some Implications," *Journal of Marriage and the Family,* 37 (1975), pp. 49–60.
[2]See B. D. Coll, "Deprivation in Childhood: Its Relation to the Cycle of Poverty," *Welfare in Review,* 3, (1965), pp. 1–10.

We have also indicated the extent to which poverty is endemic in the society's social system, namely, capitalism through its monopoly of the economic system creates poverty through its control of economic resources and the labor market—the basis of capitalism in which changing economic needs result in instability, depression, and unemployment. Gans, for example, has outlined a wide variety of the economic, social (emotional), and political functions of poverty in American society, including subsidizing activities which benefit the affluent, creating jobs for those who serve the poor, evoking feelings of altruism among the rich, and shaping the American political process through their low level of participation in the system.[3] Poverty thus plays a number of important roles in the society in which the vast majority of the population represent little more than a labor resource at the mercy of the capitalist system. This resource, furthermore, is heavily defined by other major dimensions of minority group status, that is, race, sex, age, ethnicity, and deviance. An individual's labor "marketability" is clearly a function of his background characteristics and resources with respect to these factors. Also, since many of these other minorities have been developed for economic reasons, the structure of economic domination is heavily institutionalized in the society as a whole. Finally, the poor are generally labeled as lazy, immoral, and extravagant, or as behaviorally inferior. Given other types of labeling indicating intellectual and emotional deficiency, it can be seen that poverty is not only well institutionalized, it is heavily rationalized as well. As a result, economic minorities are large, heterogeneous groups spread throughout the society and are subject to intense levels of discrimination and prejudice, representing a basic and significant social problem.

The conditions under which poverty has been created are extremely negative: racial conflict (white-Indian wars), slavery, the migration and subsequent exploitation of poverty-stricken ethnic groups, and negative effects of economic specialization, depression, and recession. Furthermore, WASP culture views the poor as immoral, lazy, and dependent—the opposite of protestant ethic virtues such as morality, hard work, and individualism. This moralistic labeling has had very negative repercussions over the centuries and has brought about the punitive control of vagrants and the unemployed, incorporation of the almshouse and workhouse with the jail, negative attitudes toward poor immigrants, food riots, and rising crime rates. Other results have been increased use of incarceration as a "solution" to the poverty problem,

[3]See H. J. Gans, "The Positive Functions of Poverty," *American Journal of Sociology* 78 (1972), 275–89.

the negative effects of Social Darwinism, low relief payments during the Great Depression, a very limited social security program, and the punitive nature of the contemporary welfare system.[4] Majority reaction to the "poverty problem"—a minority which it has essentially created — continues to be moralistic and punitive, rationalizing economic exploitation and using the poor as negative "normative examples" to reinforce ingroup conformity. Economic and normative exploitation go together. The norms of capitalism create, as well as exploit, poverty.

Demographic data on the poor indicate the size and extent of the problem: Approximately 13.6 percent of the population (almost 27 million) are classified in the poor category, while racial rates reveal that 39.7 percent of Indians are poor, 34.6 percent of Blacks, 30.0 percent of Koreans, 14.5 percent of Hawaiians, 13.7 percent of Filipinos, 12.5 percent of Chinese, 10.4 percent of whites, and 6.5 percent of Japanese are all poor.[5] Furthermore, "foreign stock" statistics reveal that Mexicans, those from the Dominican Republic, and South Americans fall into this category also.[6] These data reveal that economic minorities are large, heterogeneous, and clearly defined by race and national origin with characteristics that reflect the society's racial and ethnic hierarchies as already outlined. "Double discrimination" exists in the manner that race, ethnicity, and poverty are intercorrelated.

Majority attitudes toward the poor are well known: They are defined as lazy, immoral, gratification oriented, extravagant, lacking in initiative, and dependent on the state, that is, they are *behaviorally inferior.*[7] This "blame the victim"[8] orientation represents the assumed opposite of WASP characteristics and belief in the Horatio Alger view of society in which it is unrealistically assumed that all that is required for achievement is adequate motivation. The poor, it is assumed, lack this because they are able to obtain resources from the state and thus avoid hard work. In this manner, WASP values, and belief in the openness of society result in a punitive and moralistic view of the poor as being responsible for their own fate, and behaviorally inferior. Such a viewpoint is further reinforced by religious moralism as well as by

[4]For a useful discussion of this see J. R. Feagin, *Subordinating the Poor* (Englewood Cliffs, N.J.: Prentice-Hall Inc., 1975), chapter 2.

[5]Based on U.S. Bureau of the Census, *1970 Census of Population, Subject Reports, Low-Income Population,* PC(2)-9A (Washington, D.C.: 1971), Table 3.

[6]*1970 Census of Population,* Table 5.

[7]See Feagin, *Subordinating the Poor,* p. 30.

[8]See, for example, W. Ryan, *Blaming the Victim* (New York: Pantheon, 1971).

assumptions regarding the negative characteristics of related racial and ethnic minorities.

Economic minorities, in turn, may respond in a number of ways. They may accept these labels, have high dependency, live on a daily basis, have feelings of helplessness, or exhibit apathetic behavior.[9] They may suffer from self-blame and a lack of self-respect,[10] or attempt to escape the poverty cycle through education, participation in deviant or criminal activities, or attempt to organize individuals on welfare and obtain more legal and economic rights. Any organization, however, tends to be diffused by the boundaries of other minorities, particularly the racial or ethnic ones. Thus, while there has been some recent organization of the poor, they remain fairly passive and at the mercy of the economic system.

The dimensions of institutionalized economic discrimination are clearly evident in American society. Poverty is linked to educational tracking, delinquency,[11] low IQ and school achievement.[12] These factors in turn limit occupational achievement severely, contributing to the ongoing "cycle of poverty."[13] Furthermore, political control of welfare programs, legal discrimination,[14] and religious reinforcement of moralistic antipoverty prejudice institutionalize the problem further. The changing demands of a capitalistic economy, as well as its instability, further contribute to the ongoing creation of poor families, and those on welfare. Also, as we have pointed out, the societal dimensions of institutionalized racism, sexism, age, and ethnic discrimination ensure that the poor are kept within these boundaries at a permanent disadvantage, reinforced by their own feelings of helplessness. Poverty is heavily institutionalized throughout the society permanently and is the most fundamental type of minority since economic factors are basic to the creation of all major minorities and to this one in particular.

Minority social movements have included welfare and consumer groups, union activity, particularly among exploited unskilled workers,

[9]An example of this is contained in A. Campbell, P. E. Converse *et al.*, *The American Voter* (New York: Wiley, 1960).

[10]An excellent example of this is discussed in R. Sennett and J. Cobb, *The Hidden Injuries of Class* (New York: Knopf, 1973).

[11]See W. E. Schafer, C. Olexa, *et al.*, "Programmed for Social Class: Tracking in High School," *Transaction*, 7 (1970), pp. 39–46.

[12]See B. D. Coll, "Deprivation in Childhood," pp. 1–10.

[13]D. P. Moynihan, ed., *On Understanding Poverty* (New York: Basic Books, 1968).

[14]See J. Weiss, "The Law and the Poor," *Journal of Social Issues*, 26 (1970) pp. 59–68.

radical political groups concerned with the poor, free legal aid organizations, and other minority political movements concerned with the economic welfare of their members. As can be seen, however, the general reaction of this minority is differentiated by membership in particular minorities. Their plight as a class is thus given little visibility or attention.

The basis of majority-minority relations with respect to the poor are the vested normative interests of the former. The behavior of the latter, insofar as they are able to wrest a living from the state through welfare, challenges the validity of majority economic behavioral norms, resulting in anger, latent jealousy, and outrage.[15] In consequence, the poor have to be reformed or rehabilitated and made to conform to majority norms, particularly in their economic behavior. Relations are thus authoritarian, control oriented, and moralistic. To the extent that racial, sexual, ethnic, or age characteristics are involved also, economic and psychological factors may further reinforce the relevance of these normative considerations. Relations are highly ethnocentric, authoritarian, and control oriented with the poor in an extremely disadvantaged economic and normative position.

Interminority relations are obviously competitive in the daily struggle to survive while the high correlation between poverty and racial, sexual, age-based, and ethnic discrimination, as well as deviant behavior and its suppression, compounds this competition. Intergroup relations may be negative and conflict ridden despite the relatively similar material position of the minorities concerned. Once again the negative dimensions of minority group status synthesize to form an overwhelming structure of domination and exploitation.[16]

CONCLUSIONS

Economic minorities in America were created through the negative conditions of racial conflict, slavery, ethnic migration, economic specialization, depression, and recession, and are large, heterogenous, and clearly defined by race and national origin. They have been defined as lazy, immoral, gratification oriented, extravagant, lacking in initiative, and too dependent on the state, or behaviorally inferior. In turn, they have responded by accepting these labels, remaining within the "poverty cycle," attempting to escape through education or deviant

[15]An excellent example of this kind of outrage is provided by Sennett and Cobb in their book, *The Hidden Injuries of Class*, Chapter 2.

[16]See, for example, B. B. Seligman, *Permanent Poverty: An American Syndrome.* New York: Quadrangle Books (1968).

behavior, or organizing groups to obtain more legal or economic rights. However, economic discrimination is heavily institutionalized throughout the society, reinforced by other major types of minority dominance. While the poor have participated in various social movements, their visibility and effectiveness has tended to be extremely limited. Majority-minority relations thus tend to be ethnocentric, authoritarian, and control oriented, while intergroup interaction is competitive, conflict ridden, and defined by other dimensions of minority group status.

Economic relations reflect the basis and rationale of a society's social structure, particularly in its economic system and related beliefs. In America the individual is confronted by a number of anomalies: Capitalism has created poverty yet blames it on the individual, the society accepts unemployment but believes in the Horatio Alger myth, while racial, sexual, and ethnic discrimination belie the notion of an open, equalitarian society. Nevertheless, majority beliefs are entrenched and stable, particularly since those with economic power are rewarded on the basis of them. Reaction to those whose economic behavior is deviant, therefore, is strong, negative, moralistic, and highly political since basic interests are involved. The poor thus serve an important normative (as well as economic) function in the society, legitimizing the status quo and its reward system, that is, its type of economic discrimination. Economic discrimination is a basic form of control legitimized in normative and moralistic terms, and reinforced by other types of minority group status. Its major characteristics are summarized in Figure 10.1 (See page 158).

STUDY QUESTIONS

1. Define "poverty." What are its major characteristics?
2. How does poverty relate to other major dimensions of minority group differentiation (for example, race, sex, age, ethnicity, deviance)?
3. Compare economic minorities in American society to the minorities analyzed in Chapters 8 and 9. What major conclusions do you draw?
4. How does poverty reflect core American values?
5. What is the basis of economic majority-minority relations?

DIMENSIONS	CHARACTERISTICS
1. Historical:	created under negative racial, migration, and economic conditions
2. Demographic:	large, heterogeneous, and defined by race and national origin
3. Attitudinal:	
(a) Majority	lazy, immoral, gratification oriented, extravagant, lack initiative, dependent
(b) Minority	self-blame, helplessness, apathy, deviance, attempts to organize
4. Institutional:	political control, legal discrimination, religious moralism
5. Social Movements:	unions, welfare and consumer groups, radical political movements
6. Relational:	
(a) Majority-Minority	majority vested normative interests
(b) Interminority	
racial	high correlation with poverty
sexual	economic deprivation
age based	economic deprivation
cultural	ethnic discrimination
economic	*
behavioral	high correlation with poverty

FIGURE 10.1. Characteristics of Economic Minorities in the U.S.

READINGS

ECONOMIC MINORITIES

ANDERSON, C. H., *The Political Economy of Social Class.* Englewood Cliffs, N.J.: Prentice-Hall, 1974.

BENSIN, J. KENNETH, "Militant Ideologies and Organizational Contexts: The War on Poverty and the Ideology of 'Black Power'," *Sociological Quarterly,* 12, no. 2 (Summer 1971), 328–39.

BREMNER, R. H., *From the Depths.* New York: New York University Press, 1966.

CAMPBELL, A., P. E. CONVERSE, et al., The American Voter, New York: Wiley, 1960.

CHILMAN, CATHERINE S., "Families in Poverty in the Early 1970's: Rates, Associated Factors, Some Implications," Journal of Marriage and the Family, 37, no. 1 (February 1975), 49–60.

COLL, BLANCHE D., "Deprivation in Childhood: Its Relation to the Cycle of Poverty," Welfare in Review, 3, no. 3 (March, 1965), 1-10.

FEAGIN, J. R., Subordinating the Poor, Welfare and American Beliefs. Englewood Cliffs, N.J.: Prentice-Hall, 1975.

FELDMAN, LEONARD, "Portrait of Poverty: A Review of 'La Vida'," Welfare in Review, 5, no. 6 (June-July 1967), 14–16.

GALBRAITH, JOHN KENNETH, "The Causes of Poverty: A Clinical View," Population Research, 6, no. 2 (July, 1962), 62–66.

GANS, H. J., "The Positive Functions of Poverty," American Journal of Sociology, 78 (1972), 275–89.

HAUSER, PHILIP, "Mounting Chaos At Home," Bulletin of the Atomic Scientists, 24, no. 2 (January 1968), 56–58.

HURLEY, R. L., Poverty and Mental Retardation: A Causal Relationship. New York: Random House, 1970.

KOHN, M., Class and Conformity: A Study in Values. Homewood: Dorsey, 1969.

KOSA, J., and I. K. ZOLA, eds., Poverty and Health: A Sociological Analysis. Cambridge: Harvard University Press, 1975.

LENS, S., Poverty: America's Enduring Paradox. New York: Crowell, 1969.

LENSKI, G., Power and Privilege, A Theory of Social Stratification. New York: McGraw-Hill, 1966.

LEWIS, O., The Children of Sanchèz. Harmondsworth: Penguin Books, 1961.

MEISSNER, H. H., ed., Poverty in the Affluent Society. New York: Harper & Row, 1973.

MOGULL, ROBERT G., "American Poverty in the 1960's," Phylon, 33, no. 2 (Summer 1972), 161–68.

MOYNIHAN, D. P., ed., On Understanding Poverty. New York: Basic Books, 1968.

ROACH, JACK L., and ORVILLE R. GURSSLIN, "An Evaluation of the Concept 'Culture of Poverty'," Social Forces, 45, no. 3 (January 1967), 383–91.

ROBY, P., ed., Poverty Establishment, Englewood Cliffs, N.J.: Prentice-Hall, 1974.

SCHAFER, WALTER E., CAROL OLEXA, and KENNETH POLK, "Programmed for Social Class: Tracking in High School," Trans-Action, 7, no. 12 (October 1970), 39–46, 63.

SELIGMAN, BEN B., Permanent Poverty: An American Syndrome. New York: Quadrangle Books, 1968.

SENNETT, R., and J. COBB, The Hidden Injuries of Class. New York; Knopf, 1973.

WEISS, JONATHAN, "The Law and the Poor," Journal of Social Issues, 26, no. 3 (Summer 1970), 59–68.

WILLARD, WILLIAM, and HARLAND PADFIELD, "Poverty and Social Disorder: Introduction," Human Organization, 29, no. 1 (Spring, 1970), 1–4.

WILLIAMSON, JOHN B., " Beliefs about the Motivation of the Poor and Attitudes toward Poverty Policy," Social Problems, 21, no. 5 (June, 1974), 634–48.

11

Behavioral Minorities in the United States

Behavioral deviance in America has been highlighted continuously as a threat to social stability: In the media, politics, and religious institutions, deviance, whether social or criminal, continues to be given high visibility as a threat to majority values. As with poverty, behavioral minorities serve a normative function in the society by reinforcing ingroup conformity—the social example and negative consequences argument—as well as providing rationales for the control and exploitation of particular subgroups. In this manner, deviance reveals more about majority norms than characteristics of behavioral minorities themselves.

Deviance is primarily a *political* issue: Problems of law-and-order, perceived threats to social stability, corruption, crime rates, drug traffic, and sexual deviance are defined as central to the social order. Politicians have a vested interest in highlighting and controlling behavioral minorities to increase their personal efficacy. The extent to which political considerations define the operation of social control agencies (law enforcement agencies) further politicizes the processes of law and order. As a consequence these agencies are more concerned with their political profiles than with the rehabilitation of their clients. Also, as "Watergate" has indicated, political issues are confounded by moralism and when the former are paramount, the latter is given little consideration. However, given the society's strong overt emphasis on virtuous behavior, when impropriety is discovered—a direct challenge to this myth—the reaction is devastating and punitive. As a result, behavioral minorities may be subject to extreme levels of punishment. In general the majority orientation toward deviance is both political and moralistic—a powerful combination.

The correlation between deviance and other types of minority status is readily apparent: The convicted and/or incarcerated tend to be nonwhite and poor, those with *least resources.* In fact it might well be said that deviance is a major adaptation of the poor to structured inequality. Generally, deviants tend to be members of other minorities also, reinforcing the labeling process of their inferior behavior, making it accountable on a number of grounds.

As we have indicated in previous discussions, behavioral minorities, particularly in this society, may be viewed as an outgrowth of increasing *economic differentiation.* As this has occurred, social cohesion has declined while perceived social problems such as poverty, unemployment, addiction, sexual deviance, crime, and mental illness have increased. Given the society's utopian myths of equality and security for all, these problems have presented a serious challenge to its legitimacy. Crime also threatens material, capitalist development but is defined in moral terms. Such material and moral deviance have resulted in punitive reactions such as long-term incarceration with little concern for rehabilitation beyond attempting to force the individual to conform to majority norms. In this manner deviance in American society represents a political-moral issue, challenging its material and normative viability, resulting in punitive-moralistic solutions. Behavioral minorities are a result of majority values and are punished by them, serving an important normative (and political) function in the society as a whole.

As has been indicated, the historical circumstances surrounding the creation of behavioral minorities have been extremely negative: As the society began to change in the Jacksonian era, social problems and instability appeared to increase. A major concern with social stability led to incarceration as a solution to these problems in an attempt to ensure increased community cohesion.[1] Enlightenment ideas, particularly the control of reason, eventually coupled with science and medicine, reinforced the institutional approach to deviance through the medical model.[2] Deviants have become both "patients" and "victims" of a medical, control-oriented, institutional approach to social problems which are perceived to threaten community cohesion and social stability.[3] Thus, deviance becomes a scientific, medical, and institutional problem in the attempt to maintain societal integration. Whether an individual is defined as a criminal, alcoholic, drug addict, sexual pervert, or as being mentally ill, the same combination of solutions tends to be applied, since they are all defined to some extent at least, as threatening social order. Economic development also tends to increase a legalistic approach to deviance.[4]

Statistics on institutional inmates reveal a population of over two million of which 20 percent are mental patients, 9 percent are in correctional settings, and 3 percent are delinquents.[5] Sexual differences reveal that men are primarily in correctional institutions while women are more often mental patients.[6] Race is also a major factor: whites are more often mental patients while blacks and those of Spanish origin tend to be criminals or delinquents in correctional settings. Blacks also tend to commit "serious offenses" more often than other race groups.[7] Behavioral minorities thus tend to be large and clearly defined by race and sex. As a group they represent a significant proportion of the general population.

Majority attitudes toward deviants are extremely negative: They have been defined as physiologically and genetically defective,[8] possess-

---

[1]See, for example, D. J. Rothman, *The Discovery of the Asylum, Social Order and Disorder in the New Republic* (Boston: Little Brown, 1971).

[2]M. Foucault, *Madness and Civilization* (New York: Vintage Books, 1973).

[3]R. Perrucci, *Circle of Madness, On Being Insane and Institutionalized in America* (Englewood Cliffs, N.J.: Prentice-Hall, 1974).

[4]See D. Black, *The Behavior of Law* (New York: Academic Press, 1976), pp. 38–40.

[5]Based on U.S. Bureau of the Census, *1970 Census of Population, Subject Reports, Persons in Institutions and Other Group Quarters,* PC(2)–4E, (Washington, D.C.: 1971), Tables 1, 3, 4, 10.

[6]U.S. Bureau of the Census, *1970 Census of Population.*

[7]U.S. Bureau of the Census, *1970 Census of Population. Statistical Abstract of the United States: 1974,* 95th ed., (Washington, D.C.: 1974), Table 254.

[8]See, for example, F. J. Kallmann, *The Genetics of Schizophrenia: A Study of Heredity and Reproduction in the Families of 1,087 Schizophrenics,* (New York: Augustine, 1938).

ing inferior personality,[9] lacking in intelligence, or behaviorally inferior due to class or cultural background.[10] Behavioral deviance is accounted for in all major terms: physical, intellectual, psychological, and cultural, with little or no regard for their disadvantaged minority position. Once again the opposite definitional process is operating: Deviants are assumed to be abnormal in body, mind, and behavior, confirming majority normality and superiority.[11]

Behavioral minorities may react to this labeling process with shame and attempt to become part of the majority again through rehabilitation. However, given the long-term stigmatic effects of punishment and incarceration as well as the development of subgroups and cliques in these institutions, individuals with enough reinforcement may become committed to a deviant identity and life style—the effects of "secondary deviance."[12] Drug addicts are used as family scapegoats,[13] mental illness may be attributed to minority group frustration and stereotypes,[14] prostitutes tend to rationalize their illegal activity,[15] homosexuals change their self-definitions,[16] and delinquents develop complex subcultures.[17] Long-term subcultures tend to develop around various forms of deviance as behavioral minorities are subject to stigmatization, segregation, institutionalization, as well as economic and legal discrimination. Rather than being rehabilitated and returned to conformity, they are "locked in" to their deviant roles, segregated, and subjected to long-term discrimination. As with other types of minori-

[9]See I. Chein, "Psychological Functions of Drug Use," in H. Steinberg, ed., *Scientific Basis of Drug Dependence: A Symposium* (London: Churchill, 1969), pp. 13–30.

[10]M. Kohn, *Class and Conformity: A Study in Values* (Homewood: Dorsey, 1969).

[11]It should be emphasized that controversy over the accuracy of this labeling perspective has developed: Gove, for instance, argues that most people who are mental patients have a "serious disturbance" (W. R. Gove, "Societal Reaction as an Explanation of Mental Illness: An Evaluation," *American Sociological Review* 35 (1970), 879). However, in this critique he fails to deal adequately with the extent to which psychiatrists participate in the labeling process in their diagnosis of such "disturbances," thereby participating in the "opposite definitional process" also and to a significant degree.

[12]See T. J. Scheff, *Being Mentally Ill* (Chicago: Aldine, 1966), p. 79.

[13]R. Langer and L. Shugart, "Complementary Pathology in Families of Male Heroin Addicts," *Social Casework*, (1969), pp. 356–61.

[14]See J. Rothman, "Minority Group Status, Mental Health and Intergroup Relations: An Appraisal of Kurt Lewin's Thesis," *Journal of Intergroup Relations*, (1962), pp. 299–310.

[15]T. Hirschi, "The Professional Prostitute," *Berkeley Journal of Sociology*, 7 (1962), pp. 33–50.

[16]See B. M. Dank, "Coming Out in the Gay World," *Psychiatry*, 34, (1971), pp. 180–97.

[17]P. Lerman, "Gangs, Networks, and Subculture Delinquency," *American Journal of Sociology*, 73 (1967), pp. 63–72.

ties, the typical creation of *permanent subcultures* occurs as these groups are subjected to segregation, control, and discrimination.

The dimensions of institutionalized discrimination against behavioral minorities are highly oppressive: political exploitation, economic discrimination, long-term legal disadvantages, forcible discharge from the military, religious moralism, entertainment exploitation in the media, restricted educational opportunity, and negative stereotypes perpetuated through childhood socialization. The major result of this is widespread and stable labeling of deviants[18] as well as demands for stronger punishment and deterrents among the general population.[19] Also, in view of the predominance of the incarceration solution to this "problem," it is reasonable to view behavioral minorities as subject to the highest levels of institutionalized discrimination.

Social movements include Gay Liberation groups, the American Civil Liberties Union, groups working for legal reform with respect to children and adolescents, drug law reform, the struggle for prisoners' rights, legal protection for the mental patient, and the fight for the decriminalization of drugs and alcohol. From this two major trends are evident: (1) the struggle for minority legal rights; and, (2) the decriminalization of deviance. While there has been limited success with the former, the latter continues to be met with high levels of political and public resistance.

As already indicated, the basis of majority-minority relations with respect to behavioral minorities are the *normative* interests of the majority: deviance is wrong, threatens community norms and welfare, and must be punished. Consequent relations are authoritarian, moralistic, ethnocentric, and control oriented with major effort made to convince the deviant that he is "sick" and requires rehabilitation from his erroneous ways by a variety of scientific and medical techniques including chemotherapy, electric shock treatment, conditioning, and even surgery. The major form of this relationship is doctor to patient with society as the former.

Interminority relations are based on competition for resources in the society compounded by the high correlation between race, sex, age, ethnicity, poverty, and behavioral deviance. As a consequence group interaction is both complicated and competitive as deviants are subject to a complex of types of discrimination.

---

[18]W. K. Bentz, J. W. Edgerton, *et al.*, "Perceptions of Mental Illness among Public School Teachers," *Sociology of Education*, 42 (1969), pp. 400–406.

[19]A useful example is contained in G. Newman, *Comparative Deviance, Perception and Law in Six Cultures* (New York: Elsevier, 1976).

CONCLUSIONS

From our discussion it has been evident that behavioral minorities in America were created under the negative conditions of rising social problems and associated "rational" incarceration. They are large and clearly differentiated by race and sex, are defined as physically, intellectually, psychologically, and culturally defective, and develop deviant subcultures. In addition, they are subject to oppressive discrimination, interact on the basis of majority normative interests, and compete for resources and other dimensions of minority group status. As the society became economically differentiated, lost its cohesion, and produced widespread social problems, the need to maintain community cohesion and solidarity resulted in the political and moral creation of behavioral minorities, which were reinforced by the medical scientific model, and subjected to punitive moralistic solutions. In this manner deviance reflects majority values and processes, challenges their validity and legitimacy, and experiences establishment anger as a result. Economic differentiation has resulted in the evolution of a myriad of *normative* minorities with disastrous results. Their major characteristics are summarized in Figure 11.1.

DIMENSIONS	CHARACTERISTICS
1. Historical:	concern with social stability leads to incarceration and medical approach
2. Demographic:	large, clearly defined by race and sex
3. Attitudinal:	
(a) Majority	physically, intellectually, psychologically, culturally inferior
(b) Minority	rehabilitation oriented, secondary deviance, subcultures
4. Institutional:	political exploitation, economic and legal discrimination, media exploitation
5. Social Movements:	legal groups, liberation organizations
6. Relational:	
(a) Majority-Minority:	majority vested normative interests, authoritarian, control-oriented
(b) Interminority	
racial	high correlation with deviance
sexual	correlation with mental illness
age based	age-specific labeling
cultural	ethnic deviance
economic	high correlation with deviance
behavioral	*

FIGURE 11.1. Characteristics of Behavioral Minorities in the U.S.

MINORITY GROUP RELATIONS IN AMERICA: A GENERAL PORTRAIT

In the last few chapters we have attempted to apply the general conceptual framework presented in Chapter 7 to American society. We described that society as consisting of a colonial, WASP majority motivated by material and economic exploitation, having experienced high levels of migration, subordination, importation, economic differentiation and specialization, and has used science and religion to rationalize minority group dominance. Status within this structure is dependent upon an individual's majority-minority membership profile. The advantages are cumulative as a person's general status within it becomes higher, while consequent relationships are very competitive. Finally, economic functions (racial-ethnic status) define the operation of the normative (poverty and deviance) and psychological (sexual and age-based minorities), while the structure is modified by economic change but remains essentially stable and conservative.

American society ranks high on all major factors in our framework: population growth, economic needs, division of labor, private property, economic differentiation, colonial migration, subordination, and importation. Economic specialization results in a complex minority hierarchy consisting of all major types, and is reinforced by science, medicine, psychology, and religion, while serving economic, normative, and psychological functions, and is modified by demographic economic change. This hierarchy is a result of underlying economic factors that operate through racial and ethnic groups, defining the operation of normative and psychological functions. Furthermore, it is *elitist*—those at higher levels have more power, particularly since the structure is economically based, making their advantages cumulative—and more *integrated* the lower a person is placed in the system. The correlation between poverty, sexism, age discrimination, and deviance is extremely high, resulting in *diffusion* and *conflicting loyalties*.

Minority group relations within this setting are *economically based, hierarchical, competitive,* and *diffuse.* They are controlled by majority economic, normative, and psychological *interests*, are *rationalized* in scientific-religious terms, and are founded on the *assumed* physical, intellectual, emotional, and behavioral *inferiority* of minority group members. The society, then, given its demographic and economic development, has produced a highly complex hierarchy of domination designed to meet majority economic interests, normative and psychological needs, is based upon assumed human inferiority (*all* aspects of the human person), and rationalized in scientific-religious terms. Human beings are reduced to (assumed) inferior types in order to meet elite material needs, resulting in dehumanization, and the equation of people with animal characteristics that causes devastating individual and group effects as minorities reject themselves and/or develop segregated subcultures for relief and protection. Relations, both interpersonal and group, are highly complex, competitive, and negative as a result, as people compete for all types of resources (economic, normative, and psychological) within the boundaries of this structure.

Personal as well as group problems should be understood within this *structural context,* since they reflect varying levels and kinds of resources within it. Minority group relations reflect combinations of particular levels and types of such resources in social interaction. The high racial (economic), economic (normative), sexual, age-based, behavioral (normative) power, interact with low racial, economic, sexual, age-based and behavioral resources. Personal and group relations occur within a *resource matrix* such as this, based on broad and institutionalized *power inequalities,* reflecting demographic and economic factors. American society represents one of the most highly developed types of minority group systems despite official myths regarding equality, human rights, and democracy. Its major characteristics are outlined in Figure 11.2.

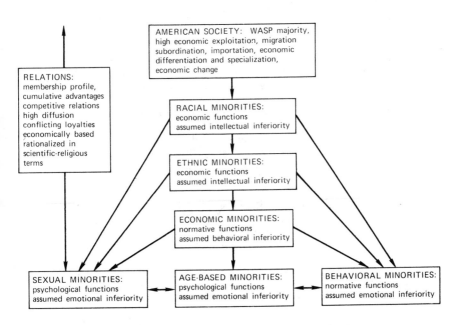

FIGURE 11.2.   Minority Group Relations in America

STUDY QUESTIONS

1. What is deviant behavior? Who decides that it is deviant?
2. What are the background characteristics of many deviants? Why is this so?
3. What societal function does deviance serve in American society? Document your response.
4. How does the minority group hierarchy operate in American society?
5. Outline the ways in which science, medicine, psychology, sociology, and religion reinforce this hierarchy.

READINGS

BEHAVIORAL MINORITIES: GENERAL

AKERS, RONALD L., "Problems in the Sociology of Deviance: Social Definitions and Behavior," *Social Forces*, 46, no. 4 (June, 1968), 455–64.

——, *Deviant Behavior: A Social Learning Approach*. Belmont: Wadsworth, 1972.

BECKER, H. S., *The Other Side: Perspectives on Deviance*. New York; Free Press, 1964.

COUNT VAN MANEN, GLORIA, "Towards an Interpersonal Theory of Deviance," *Proceedings of the Southwestern Sociological Association*, 19 (1968), 132–36.

DAVIS, NANETTE J., "Labeling Theory in Deviance Research: A Critique and Reconsideration," *Sociological Quarterly*, 13, no. 4 (Fall, 1972), 447–74.

——, *Social Constructions of Deviance*. Dubuque: W. C. Brown, 1975.

DOUGLAS, J. D., ed., *Deviance and Respectability: The Social Construction of Moral Meanings*. New York: Basic Books, 1970.

ERIKSON, K. T., *Wayward Puritans: A Study in the Sociology of Deviance*. New York: Wiley, 1966.

GREENBERG, DAVID F., and FAY STENDER, "The Prison as a Lawless Agency," *Buffalo Law Review*, 21, no. 3 (Spring, 1972), 799–838.

GUSKIN, SAMUEL, "Dimensions of Judged Similarity Among Deviant Types," *American Journal of Mental Deficiency*, 68, no. 2 (September 1963), 218–24.

LIAZOS, ALEXANDER, "The Poverty of the Sociology of Deviance; Nuts, Sluts, and Perverts," *Social Problems*, 20, no. 1 (Summer 1972), 103–20.

LOFLAND, J., *Deviance and Identity*. Englewood Cliffs, N.J.: Prentice-Hall, 1969.

NEWMAN, G., *Comparative Deviance, Perception and Law in Six Cultures*. New York: Elsevier, 1976.

ROCK, PAUL, "Phenomenalism and Essentialism in the Sociology of Deviancy," *Sociology*, 7, no. 1 (January 1973), 17–29.

RUBINGTON, E., ed., *Deviance: The Interactionist Perspective*. New York: Macmillan, 1973.

SCOTT, R. A., "A Proposed Framework for Analyzing Deviance as a Property of Social Order," in *Theoretical Perspectives in Deviance*, eds. R. A. Scott and J. D. Douglas. New York: Basic Books, 1972, pp. 9–36.

SCOTT, R. A., and J. D. Douglas, eds., *Theoretical Perspectives on Deviance*. New York: Basic Books, 1972.

SEIBEL, H. D., "Social Deviance in Comparative Perspective," in *Theoretical Perspectives in Deviance*, eds. R. A. Scott and J. D. Douglas. New York: Basic Books, 1972, pp. 251–81.

TURK, AUSTIN T., "Prospects for Theories of Criminal Behavior," *Journal of Criminal Law, Criminology and Police Science*, 55, no. 4 (December 1964), 454–61

WARD, RICHARD H., "The Labeling Theory: A Critical Analysis," *Criminology*, 9, nos. 2–3 (August-November 1971), 268–90.

Alcoholism

BACON, SELDEN D., "The Process of Addiction to Alcohol," *Quarterly Journal of Studies in Alcohol*, 34, no. 1 (March, 1973), Part A, 1–27.

KAMMEIER, MARY LEO, "Adolescents from Families With and Without Alcoholic Problems," *Quarterly Journal of Studies on Alcohol*, 32, no. 2 (June 1971), 364–72.

LOWE, GEORGE D., and H. EUGENE HODGES, "Deaths Associated with Alcohol in Georgia, 1970." *Quarterly Journal of Studies on Alcohol*, 25, no. 1 (March, 1974), Part A, 215–20.

MULFORD, HAROLD A., and DONALD E. MILLER, "Measuring Public Acceptance of the Alcoholic as a Sick Person," *Quarterly Journal of Studies on Alcohol*, 25, no. 2 (June 1964), 314–24.

PATRICK, C. H., *Alcohol, Culture, and Society*. New York: AMS Press, 1970.

Crime

ALLISON, JUNIUS L., "Poverty and the Administration of Justice in the Criminal Courts," *Journal of Criminal Law, Criminology and Police Science*, 55, no. 2 (June 1964), 241–45.

BEATTIE, RONALD H., and JOHN P. KENNEY, "Aggressive Crimes," *Annals of America Academy of Political and Social Science*. 364 (March 1966), 73–85.

CRESSEY, D. R., ed., *Crime and Criminal Justice*, New York: New York Times Book Service, 1971.

DE WOLF, L. H., *Crime and Justice in America: A Paradox in Conscience*. New York: Harper & Row, 1975.

DOUGLAS, J. D., ed., *Crime and Justice in American Society*. Indianapolis, Bobbs-Merrill, 1971.

EYSENCK, H. J., *Crime and Personality*. Boston: Houghton Mifflin, 1964.

FOX, RICHARD G., "The XYY Offender: A Modern Myth?" *Journal of Criminal Law, Criminology and Police Science*, 62, no. 1 (March 1971), 59–73.

Glaser, Daniel, "Criminology and Public Policy," *American Sociologist*, 6, Suppl., (June 1971), 30–37.

Green, Edward, "Race, Social Status, and Criminal Arrest," *American Sociological Review*, 35, no. 3 (June 1970), 476–90.

Hartjen, C., *Crime and Criminalization*. New York: Praeger, 1974.

Jeffrey, C. R., "Criminal Behavior and Learning Theory," *Journal of Criminal Law, Criminology and Police Science*, 56, no. 3 (September 1965), 294–300.

Lombroso-Ferrero, G., *Criminal Man*. Montclair: Patterson-Smith, 1911.

Pepinsky, H. E., *Crime and Conflict*. New York: Academic Press, 1976.

Quinney, R., *Crime and Justice in Society*. Boston: Little Brown, 1969.

———, ed., *Criminal Justice in America: A Critical Understanding*, Boston: Little Brown, 1974.

Schur, E. M., *Crimes without Victims—Deviant Behavior and Public Policy: Abortion, Homosexuality, Drug Addiction*. Englewood Cliffs, N.J.: Prentice-Hall, 1965.

Simon, Rita J., "American Women and Crime," *The Annals of the American Academy of Political and Social Science*, 423 (January 1976), 31–46.

Tappan, P., *Crime, Justice, and Correction*. New York: McGraw-Hill, 1960.

Delinquency

Cortes, J. B., and F. M. Gatti, *Delinquency and Crime, a Biopsychosocial Approach: Empirical, Theoretical, and Practical Aspects of Criminal Behavior*. New York: Academic Press, 1972.

Cressey, D., and D. A. Ward, eds., *Delinquency, Crime and Social Process*. New York: Harper and Row, 1969.

Erikson, Maynard L., "Group Violations and Official Delinquency: The Group Hazard Hypothesis," *Criminology*, 11, no. 2 (August 1973), 127–60.

Guttentog, Marcia, "The Relationship of Unemployment to Crime and Delinquency," *Journal of Social Issues*, 24, no. 1 (January 1968), 105–14.

Jenkins, Robert L., and Andrew Boyer, "Types of Delinquent Behavior and Background Factors," *International Journal of Social Psychiatry*, 14, no. 1 (Winter 1967–68), 65–76.

Kassebaum, G., *Delinquency and Social Policy*. Englewood Cliffs, N.J.: Prentice-Hall, 1974.

Kratcoski, Peter C., and John E. Kratcoski, "Changing Patterns in the Delinquent Activities of Boys and Girls: A Self-Reported Delinquency Analysis," *Adolescence*, 10, no. 37 (Spring 1975), 83–91.

Lerman, Paul, "Gangs, Networks, and Subculture Delinquency," *American Journal of Sociology*, 73, no. 1 (July 1967), 63–72.

Matza, D., *Delinquency and Drift*. New York: Wiley, 1964.

Platt, Anthony M., "Saving and Controlling Delinquent Youth: A Critique," *Issues in Criminology*, 5, no. 1 (Winter 1970), 1–24.

Poveda, Tony G. "The Image of the Criminal: A Critique of Crime and Delinquency Theories," *Issues in Criminology*, 5, no. 1 (Winter 1970), 59–84.

Short, James F. Jr., Ramon Rivera, and Harvey Marshall, "Adult-Adolescent Relations and Gang Delinquency," *Pacific Sociological Review*, 7, no. 2 (Fall 1964), 59–65.

SHORT, J. F. JR., ed., *Delinquency, Crime and Society*. Chicago: University of Chicago Press, 1976.

STERNE, RICHARD S., *Delinquent Conduct and Broken Homes*. New Haven, Conn.: College and University Press, 1964.

TURK, AUSTIN R., "Toward Construction of a Theory of Delinquency," *Journal of Criminal Law, Criminology and Police Science*, 55, no. 2 (June 1964), 215–29.

VOSS, HARWIN L., "Socioeconomic Status and Reported Delinquent Behavior," *Social Problems*, 13, no. 3 (Winter 1966), 314–24.

WILLIAMS, JAY R., and MARTIN GOLD, "From Delinquent Behavior to Official Delinquency," *Social Problems*, 20, no. 2 (Fall 1972), 209–29.

WILLIE, CHARLES V., "The Relative Contribution of Family Status and Economic Status of Juvenile Delinquency," *Social Problems*, 14, no. 3 (Winter 1967), 326–34.

WILLIE, CHARLES V., and ANITA GERSHENOVITZ, "Juvenile Delinquency in Racially Mixed Areas," *American Sociological Review*, 29, no. 5 (October 1964), 740–44.

Drug Addiction

AUSUBEL, D. P., *Drug Addiction: Physiological, Psychological, and Sociological Aspects*. New York: Random House, 1958.

BALL, JOHN C., "Two Patterns of Narcotic Drug Addiction in the United States," *Journal of Criminal Law, Criminology and Police Science*, 56, no. 2 (June 1965), 203–11.

BEJEROT, N., *Addiction and Society*. Springfield: C. C. Thomas, 1970.

CHEIN, I., "Psychological Functions of Drug Use," in *Scientific Basis of Drug Dependence: A Symposium*, ed. H. Steinberg, London: Churchill, 1969.

GANGER, ROSLYN, and GEORGE SHUGART, "Complementary Pathology in Families of Male Heroin Addicts," *Social Casework*, 49, no. 6 (June 1969), 356–61.

GRUPP, STANLEY, "Experiences with Marihuana in a Sample of Drug Users," *Sociological Focus*, 1, no. 2 (Winter 1967), 39–52.

HOLMER, J., *Drugs and Minority Oppression*. New York: Seabury, 1976.

KUPPERSTEIN, LENORE R., "Assessing the Nature and Dimensions of the Drug Problem," *The Annals of the American Academy of Political and Social Science*, 417 (January 1975), 76–85.

MCAREE, C. P., R. A. STEFFENHAGEN, and L. S. ZHENER, "Personality Factors in College Drug Users," *International Journal of Social Psychiatry*, 15, no. 2 (Spring 1969), 102–6.

SUCHMAN, EDWARD A., "The 'Hang-Loose' Ethic and the Spirit of Drug Use," *Journal of Health and Social Behavior*, 9, no. 2 (June 1968), 146–55.

SMITH, ROGER, "Status Politics and the Image of the Addict," *Issues in Criminology*, 2, no. 2 (Fall 1966), 157–76.

WILLIAMS, JOYCE E., and WILLIAM M. BATES, "Toward a Typology of Female Narcotic Addicts," *Proceedings of the Southwestern Sociological Association*, 18 (March 1967), 152–56.

Mental Illness

BENTZ, W. KENNETH, J. WILBERT EDGERTON, and FRANCIS T. MILLER, "Perceptions of Mental Illness Among Public School Teachers," *Sociology of Education*, 42, no. 4 (Fall 1969), 400–406.

BORD, RICHARD JAMES, "Rejection of the Mentally Ill: Continuities and Further Developments," *Social Problems*, 18, no. 4 (Spring 1971), 496–509.

CLAUSIN, JOHN A., and CAROL L. HUFFINE, "Sociocultural and Social-Psychological Factors Affecting Social Responses to Mental Disorder," *Journal of Health and Social Behavior*, 16, no. 4 (December 1975), 405–20.

FOUCAULT, M., *Madness and Civilization.* New York: Vintage, 1973.

FREEMAN, HOWARD E., and OZZIE G. SIMMONS, *The Mental Patient Comes Home.* New York: Wiley, 1963.

GOVE, WALTER R., "Societal Reaction as an Explanation of Mental Illness: An Evaluation," *American Sociological Review* 35, no. 5 (October 1970), 873–83.

GROB, GERALD N., "The State Mental Hospital in Mid-Nineteenth Century America: A Social Analysis," *American Psychologist*, 21, no. 6 (June 1966), 510–23.

JUHANI, HIRVAS, "Identity and Mental Illness: A Study on the Interaction Between the Mentally Ill and their Environment," *Transactions of the Westermarck Society*, 12, (1966), 11–116.

KALLMAN, F. J., *The Genetics of Schizophrenia.* New York: Augustin, 1938.

KHATON, ODESSA M., and RAPHAEL P. CARRIERA, "An Attitude Study of Minority Group Adolescents Toward Mental Health," *Journal of Youth and Adolescence*, 1, no. 2 (June 1972), 131–41.

LINN, LAWRENCE, "The Mental Hospital from the Patient Perspective," *Psychiatry* 31, no. 3 (August 1968), 213–23.

LINSKY, ARNOLD S., "Community Homogeneity and Exclusion of the Mentally Ill," *Journal of Health and Social Behavior*, 11, no. 4 (December 1970), 304–10.

MANIS, MELVIN, PETER S. HOUTS, and JOAN B. BLAKE, "Beliefs About Mental Illness as a Function of Psychiatric Status and Psychiatric Hospitalization," *Journal of Abnormal Psychology*, 67, no. 3 (1963), 226–33.

MYERS, JEROME K., and L. BEAN, *A Decade Later: A Follow-Up of Social Class and Mental Illness*, New York: Wiley, 1968.

PERRUCCI, R., *Circle of Madness, On Being Insane and Institutionalized in America.* Englewood Cliffs, N.J.: Prentice-Hall, 1974.

PHILLIPS, DEREK, "Rejection of the Mentally Ill: The Influence of Behavior and Sex," *American Sociological Review*, 29, no. 5 (October 1964), 679–86.

ROTHMAN, D. J., *The Discovery of the Asylum.* Boston: Little Brown, 1971.

ROTHMAN, JACK, "Minority Group Status, Mental Health and Intergroup Relations: An Appraisal of Kurt Lewin's Thesis," *Journal of Intergroup Relations*, 3, no. 4 (Autumn 1962), 299–310.

SCHEFF, T. J., *Being Mentally Ill.* Chicago: Aldine, 1966.

———, "Stereotypes of Insanity," *New Society*, 9, 232 (March 9, 1967), 348–50.

———, ed., *Mental Illness and Social Processes.* New York: Harper & Row, 1967.

WEINSTEIN, RAYMOND M., "Patients' Perceptions of Mental Illness: Paradigms for Analysis," *Journal of Health and Social Behavior,* 13, no. 1 (March 1972), 38–47.

WITTKOWER, E. D., and GUY DUBREUIL, "Psychocultural Stress in Relation to Mental Illness," *Social Science and Medicine,* 7, no. 9 (September 1973), 691–704.

Sexual Deviance

BECHER, HAROLD K., "A Phenomenological Inquiry into the Etiology of Female Homosexuality," *Journal of Human Relations,* 17, no. 4 (1969), 570–80.

BRYAN, JAMES H., "Occupational Ideologies and Individual Attitudes of Call Girls," *Social Problems,* 13, no. 4 (Spring 1966), 441–50.

CHURCHILL, W., *Homosexual Behavior among Males: A Cross Cultural and Cross Species Investigation.* Englewood Cliffs, N.J.: Prentice-Hall, 1971.

DANK, BARRY M., "Coming Out in the Gay World," *Psychiatry,* 34, no. 2 (May 1971), 180–97.

ELLIS, ALBERT, "Homosexuality: The Right to be Wrong," *Journal of Sex Research,* 4, no. 2 (May 1968), 96–107.

GRAY, DIANA, "Turning-Out: A Study of Teenage Prostitution," *Urban Life and Culture,* 1, no. 4 (January 1973), 401–25.

HIRSCHI, TRAVIS, "The Professional Prostitute," *Berkeley Journal of Sociology* 7, no. 1 (Spring 1962), 33–50.

JAMES, LIONEL, "On the Game," *New Society,* 24, no. 555 (May 24, 1973), 426–29.

MCCAGHY, CHARLES H., and JAMES K. SKIPPER, JR., "Lesbian Behavior as an Adaptation to the Occupation of Stripping," *Social Problems,* 17, no. 2 (Fall 1969), 262–70.

MANOSEVITZ, MARTIN, "The Development of Male Homosexuality," *Journal of Sex Research,* 8, no. 1 (1972), 31–40.

PACHT, ASHER R., and JAMES E. COWDEN "An Exploratory Study of Five Hundred Sex Offenders," *Criminal Justice and Behavior,* 1, (March 1972), 13–20.

PARKER, PHILIP D., "The Homosexual: Attitudes, Needs and Role Strain," *Proceedings of the Southwestern Sociological Association,* 19 (1968), 202–206.

PATTISON, E. MANSEL, "Confusing Concepts about the Concept of Homosexuality," *Psychiatry,* 37, no. 4 (November 1974), 340–49.

SAGARIN, EDWARD, "Homosexuality as a Social Movement: First Reports from the Barricades," *The Journal of Sex Research,* 9, no. 4 (November 1973), 289–94.

SIMON, WILLIAM, and JOHN H. GAGNON, "Homosexuality: the Formulation of a Sociological Perspective," *Journal of Health and Social Behavior,* 8, no. 3 (September 1967), 177–84.

SONENSCHUN, DAVID, "The Ethnography of Male Homosexual Relationships," *Journal of Sex Research,* 4, no. 2 (May 1968), 69–83.

TRIPP, C. A., *Homosexual Matrix.* New York: McGraw-Hill, 1975.

WEINBERG, MARTIN S., "The Male Homosexual: Age-Related Variations in Social and Psychological Characteristics," *Social Problems,* 17, no. 4 (Spring 1970), 527–37.

West, D. J., "Parental Figures in the Genesis of Male Homosexuality," *International Journal of Social Psychiatry,* 5, no. 2 (Autumn 1959), 97.

Winick, Charles, "Prostitutes' Clients' Perception of Themselves," *International Journal of Social Psychiatry,* 8, no. 4 (Autumn 1962), 289–97.

Winick, Charles, and Paul M. Kinsie, *The Lively Commerce: Prostitution in the United States.* Chicago: Quadrangle Books, 1971.

12

The World Context

So far we have attempted to apply our general conceptual framework to one society in particular. In this discussion we shall broaden our focus to include minority group relations in major types of societies worldwide. We shall accomplish this by outlining comparative discussions of societies and minorities, relating them to our framework, and applying both to major types of society throughout the world. We then draw some general conclusions concerning minorities on the intersocietal level in preparation for a general theory of minority group relations to be presented in Section Five.

COMPARATIVE LITERATURE

Comparative analyses of societal characteristics and minorities focus broadly on two major sets of factors: (1) the type of migration and elite minority contact situation which produced the present social structure;

and, (2) the society's economic development as related to minority group relations. We examine each in turn.

Type of Migration and Contact

Writers who focus primarily on these factors highlight elite characteristics, initial intergroup contact, and the kind of migration which made that situation so negative. Thus, Furnivall, for example, is well known for distinguishing between direct and indirect forms of colonial rule, with the former resulting in higher levels of conflict and lower postindependence development.[1] Lieberson, in attempting a "societal theory" of race relations, also distinguishes between migrant and indigenous (local) elites with the first type producing high conflict and low assimilation, while indigenous elites tend toward the opposite.[2] Mason also outlines the factors most closely related to domination as consisting of disproportionate demographic ratios, colonial migration, heterogeneous indigenous minorities, and a colonial elite imbued with Protestant Ethic values of economic development, bureaucratic centralization, and strict social control.[3] Finally, Rex has analyzed the "social institutions of colonialism" also, pointing to the relevance of social differentiation based upon physical and/or cultural differences and discrimination rationalized in biological terms.[4] From these works a major proposition emerges: *High levels of racism and conflict-prone minority relations are primarily a creation of colonial migration.* Colonial elites are viewed as most responsible for the evolution of discrimination.

A second group of writers concentrates on the implications of the initial migrant indigenous contact situation for ensuing intergroup relations. Banton, for instance, delineates "six orders of race relations" in which initial domination is perceived to result in racial pluralism, while paternalistic contact leads to eventual integration.[5] Barth and Noel also view "exploitative contact" as closely correlated with racial conflict in the context of the "race cycle framework"[6] while in a separate analysis

[1]J. S. Furnivall, *Colonial Policy and Practice* (London: Cambridge University Press, 1948).

[2]S. Lieberson, "A Societal Theory of Race and Ethnic Relations," *American Sociological Review*, 26 (1961), pp. 902–10.

[3]P. L. Mason, *Race Relations* (London: Oxford University Press, 1970), chapter 8.

[4]J. Rex, *Race Relations in Sociological Theory* (London: Weidenfeld and Nicolson, 1970).

[5]M. Banton, *Race Relations* (New York: Basic Books, 1967), chapter 4.

[6]E. Barth and D. L. Noel, "Conceptual Frameworks for the Analysis of Race Relations: An Evaluation," *Social Forces*, 50 (1972), pp. 333–55.

Noel delineates basic ingredients in ethnic stratification as competition, ethnocentrism, and differential power.[7] Tumin also sees perceived intergroup threat as a "major source of variability in racial thinking,"[8] while Schermerhorn emphasizes that initial degree and type of intergroup value conflict produces power relations, legitimacy beliefs, and social action, with high value conflict producing most negative action.[9] Taken together these discussions suggest that *negative initial contact, particularly of the exploitive colonial type, results in high levels of conflict and domination.*

Inherent in the above discussions is a particular type of migration process—colonial migration for economic purposes and the forced importation of outside groups for (slave) labor purposes. A number of writers have focused on this: Petersen, for example, in attempting to develop a "general typology of migration" relates "forced" and "impelled" migration to "displacement," "flight," as well as slavery and the "coolie trade."[10] van den Berghe also delineates particular kinds of migration leading to racism: military conquest, frontier expansion, and voluntary or involuntary migration of particular groups.[11] Finally, Marden and Meyer outline four types of dominant-minority relations that reflect varying kinds of migration also: slavery, annexation, colonialism, and voluntary immigration. The first three have particularly negative consequences.[12] In short, it is clear that *colonial and forced migration tends to result in high levels of institutionalized exploitation and discrimination.* "Minority group situations" are produced primarily through colonial migration.

It is evident that negative minority group situations are created primarily by migrant colonial elites whose initial contact with the indigenous population is extremely negative, while further minorities are created through forced migration for labor purposes. *Extent of colonial-forced migration* is thus an underlying comparative dimension which may be used to examine a range of societies with respect to degree of racial and ethnic discrimination. It appears that the more colonial a society (that is, the more it has been subject to a migrant,

[7]D. L. Noel, "A Theory of the Origin of Ethnic Stratification," *Social Problems,* 16 (1968), pp. 157–72.

[8]M. Tumin, ed., *Comparative Perspectives on Race Relations* (Boston: Little Brown, 1969).

[9]R. A. Schermerhorn, "Toward a General Theory of Minority Groups," *Phylon,* 25 (1964), pp. 238–46.

[10]W. Petersen, "A General Typology of Migration," *American Sociological Review,* 23 (1958), pp. 256–66.

[11]P. L. van den Berghe, *Race and Racism* (New York: Wiley, 1967), chapter 1.

[12]C. F. Marden and G. Meyer, *Minorities in American Society* (New York: Van Nostrand Reinhold, 1968), 3rd ed., pp. 11–19.

colonial elite), the more racism and ethnic discrimination tend to be present.[13]

Economic Development

A second comparative dimension involves a society's type and rate of economic development. Two major elements are relevant to this: level of economic development, and degree of economic specialization and division of labor.

With respect to the first of these, Rose has indicated that in societies with "well-defined class systems," personal discrimination (physical violence, imprisonment, press suppression) tends to be "extremely harsh."[14] In an empirical study of forty-eight countries, Bagley concludes that racialism tends to be associated with "relatively advanced economic development" as exemplified in the United States, South Africa, Australia, Brazil, Rhodesia, and Indonesia. Highly "pluralist" societies, on the other hand, lack such development but have experienced recent colonial domination (Nigeria, Surinam, Madagascar, Burma, Cyprus). Non-pluralist-non-racialist societies exist also (France, West Germany, Austria, East Germany). He also suggests that gross power imbalances cause racialism to emerge out of pluralism (America, South Africa, Brazil).[15] From these analyses it would appear that *economic development is positively associated with minority group discrimination, particularly as such development contributes to power monopolies in the colonial context.* In this manner economic development results in greater differentiation and thereby to the creation of minorities.

Economic specialization may contribute to increased minority group differentiation. Meadows, for example, in a study of ethnicity, concludes that extent of "pluriethnicity" in a particular society is positively associated with its division of labor and territorial scope—factors related to industrialization, colonial migration, and nationalism. Economic specialization produces greater minority differentiation.[16] van den Berghe is well known for his delineation of "paternalistic" and

[13]For an application of this dimension see G. C. Kinloch, *The Dynamics of Race Relations, A Sociological Analysis* (New York: McGraw-Hill, 1974), chapter 2.

[14]A. M. Rose, "The Comparative Study of Intergroup Conflict," *Sociological Quarterly*, 1 (1960), pp. 57–66.

[15]C. Bagley, "Racialism and Pluralism: A Dimensional Analysis of Forty-eight Countries," *Race*, 13 (1972), pp. 347–54.

[16]P. Meadows, "Insiders and Outsiders: Towards a Theory of Overseas Cultural Groups," *Social Forces*, 46 (1967), pp. 61–71.

"competitive" types of race relations.[17] The former type is characteristic of agricultural societies, within which there is little mobility since race defines the society's division of labor. Race relations thus exhibit a tightly integrated pattern since there is a high level of economic interdependence between the racial castes in the society at large. In contrast, the "competitive" type is most evident in societies based on an industrial-urban economy with competition between the subordinate racial caste and dominant working class. In this situation economic specialization has led to structural and economic fragmentation, producing structural strain, disequilibrium, and high levels of racial conflict. Thus, economic specialization produced through industrialization results in structural fragmentation, competitive economic relations, and greater majority-minority conflict. In short, *economic specialization produces greater minority differentiation, competition, and conflict.* It appears that economic development contributes to power monopolies in the colonial context, leading to greater minority group discrimination while further economic specialization produces greater minority differentiation, competition, and conflict. *Level of general economic development* may thus be used to compare societies with respect to their minority group structures and relations. Linked with extent of colonial-forced migration, this dimension is crucial to the comparative understanding of minority group relations.

A COMPARATIVE FRAMEWORK

So far in our discussion we have highlighted two major factors related to the comparative understanding of minority group relations: the extent of colonial-forced migration as related to degree of racial and ethnic discrimination; and, the level of general economic development leading to greater minority differentiation, competition, and conflict. In the general conceptual framework outlined in Chapter 7, we emphasized two major sets of factors: (1) colonial migration, subordination, and importation; and, (2) economic differentiation and specialization. It was also assumed that the first of these contributed to the creation of racial and ethnic minorities while economic differentiation and specialization were more closely related to the evolution of economic, behavioral, sexual, and age-based minorities.

From this it is evident that our framework and comparative analysis of minority group relations overlap significantly, pointing to two major kinds of factors involved in understanding those relations on the

[17]van den Berghe, *Race and Racism,* chapter 1.

societal level: the extent of colonial migration, subordination, and importation; and the level of general economic development involving differentiation and specialization. Using these dimensions of *migration* and *economic development*—central elements in our preliminary framework—it is possible to compare minority group relations in all major societies in terms of where they stand in each dimension. Given our discussion in this chapter, it is possible to view minority group relations on a worldwide scale as a characteristic of type of migration and economic development, concluding that *where both colonial migration and development are high, a complex minority group hierarchy will evolve, containing all major types of minorities,* as indicated in our framework. On the other hand, *where migration with low economic development occurs, minority group differentiation will be primarily racial and/or ethnic,* with little economic, behavioral, sexual, or age-based discrimination. *Economic development with little or no migration, however, will tend to result in the opposite case,* that is, low racial ethnic differentiation, and medium to high economic, behavioral, sexual, and age-based differentiation. *The absence of both factors may result in a relative lack of minorities* as in the case of isolated, traditional-type societies, based primarily on kinship.

From this it is possible to delineate four major types of societies with respect to minority group differentiation:

1. *The colonial-developed type:* Societies high on both factors, possessing a complex minority hierarchy.
2. *The colonial-non-developed type:* The societies high on migration and differentiated primarily in racial and/or ethnic terms.
3. *The non-colonial-developed type:* Those societies high on economic differentiation and/or specialization, with economic, behavioral minorities, and sexual as well as age-based discrimination.
4. *The non-colonial-non-developed type:* Isolated societies which have experienced little of either factor and are relatively undifferentiated in consequence.

In general, minority group relations worldwide may be viewed as a result of a society's foundation (type of migration) and level of economic development. Such a typology is both general and crude, requiring refinement with extensive empirical data, but appears useful in the understanding of minority group relations. We proceed to apply it to particular societies.

A COMPARATIVE ANALYSIS

Figure 12.1 presents an application of the two dimensions—colonial migration and economic development—to major types of society worldwide. We emphasize that such an analysis is crude, preliminary, and illustrative only, with considerable variation in characteristics among each major *societal type*. Furthermore, a particular society may fit into more than one classification (for example, Great Britain is colonial insofar as it contains a significant subordinate nonwhite population) while geographical regions vary tremendously in societal characteristics. Accordingly, the typology should not be viewed as exclusive; rather, it is based on the predominant traits of major societies with respect to the creation of minorities within them and appears generally useful in understanding minority groups on the broad societal level.

The Colonial-Developed Type

This consists primarily of societies such as the United States, Canada, Australia, New Zealand, Rhodesia, and South Africa. They are economically developed, colonial-founded societies structured, more or less, by race and ethnicity, as well as economic, behavioral, sexual, and age-based criteria. While they obviously vary in the degree to which

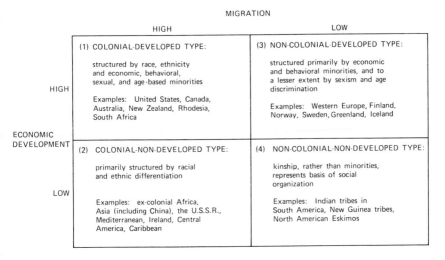

FIGURE 12.1. Minority Group Relations in World Context

they are differentiated by all these types of minorities—America is perhaps the most developed case—they are all structured by race and ethnicity, and depending upon their degree of industrialization, the other dimensions of minority group status also. Race and ethnicity also vary in relevance—race is more powerful in the United States and Southern Africa, less so in Canada and Australia. Ethnicity appears to operate more strongly in South Africa, the United States, and Canada. However, in all cases a complex minority hierarchy is operative consisting of racial, ethnic, economic, sexual, age-based, and behavioral types of minority. Given the colonial foundation of each society, thereby creating racial and ethnic minorities, economic development, depending on its level and degree of specialization, has produced the other types within these racial and cultural boundaries. Colonial-developed societies thus possess all major types of minority, arranged in a complex hierarchy. While each society obviously varies in colonial history and economic development, the general combination of these two elements tends to produce a variety of minorities within racial and/or ethnic boundaries.

The Colonial-Non-Developed Type

This type includes ex-colonial Africa, Asia (including China), Russia, the Mediterranean, Ireland, Central America, and the Caribbean. These societies have experienced extensive migration, both colonial and ethnic, but lower rates of economic differentiation and specialization. Consequently, racial, and particularly ethnic differentiation, are evident, resulting in high levels of domination but in a caste-like fashion with lower incidences of specialized economic, behavioral, sexual, and age-based minorities. While poverty, deviance, sexism, and age discrimination obviously exist in these societies, they tend to be overshadowed by racial and/or ethnic factors and are products of industrialization and capitalist development to a lesser extent. Accordingly, the minority hierarchy is less complex and more defined by caste-like elements, particularly by ethnicity. Racism is more a characteristic of earlier colonial eras, aggravating ethnic boundaries during postindependence development. This second type of society tends to be a product of external (and often colonial) migration, creating ethnic minorities and using culture as the basis of social organization under conditions of slow economic development. Ethnic dominance becomes a major problem. While there are obvious variations in both racial and ethnic heterogeneity, the colonial-non-developed type of society tends to be structured primarily by race and ethnicity, with few of the types of minority produced by economic differentiation and/or specialization.

The Non-Colonial-Developed Type

This type of society has been subject to relatively little migration but high levels of economic development. Major examples include Western Europe, Finland, Norway, Sweden, Greenland, and Iceland. Basic types of minority include the economic and behavioral and, among the more specialized, sexual, and age-based groups also. They tend to be less differentiated by racial and/or ethnic factors and more by economically produced groups such as class, deviance, sexism, and age with the evolution of a more specialized division of labor through industrialization. While ethnic differences certainly exist in countries such as Great Britain and Germany, they do not represent the foundation of minority group differentiation; rather, economically produced groupings are more significant to each society's system of social organization.

While there are obvious variations in the level of economic development, in particular specialization, it appears that minorities created through economic development rather than (colonial) migration predominate. With a lack of this migration and greater racial and/or ethnic homogeneity, minorities are consequently based on economic differentiation, particularly class and behavior and, later, sex and age as specialization results in the creation of specialized minorities produced by these economic developments. These societies, then, are *primarily* differentiated by economic and behavioral minorities, and, in the more advanced and specialized, by sexual and age-based types also. However, they are not static; with developments such as voluntary migration (for example, West Indians and Asian Ugandans migrating to Great Britain), racial and/or ethnic minorities may emerge. The basis of minority group relations remains economic development.

The Non-Colonial-Non-Developed Type

There are few societies which have not been subject to some kind of migration and economic development through contact with other societies. However, groups exist which have experienced little of either. Indian tribes in South America, indigenous New Guinea tribes, and to a lesser extent, isolated Eskimos in North America represent prime examples. In such situations kinship represents the basis of social organization with intertribal competition and, on occasion, conflict. While elements of ethnic discrimination may be present in the latter, little contemporary, formal, and specialized minority discrimination exists. Consequently, minority group differentiation of all kinds—racial, ethnic, sexual, age based, economic, and behavioral—is virtually nonexistent since forced migration and economic development are not operating in the immediate society. Social structure is kinship based, communal, homogeneous, unspecialized, and highly cohesive with none of the "reasons" we have specified as basic to the emergence of minority groups, namely, high population growth, increased economic needs, high division of labor, as well as private property, economic differentiation, migration, and economic specialization. By virtue of their relative isolation and lack of economic development, they have not been subject to minority group differentiation. However, it is obvious that this state cannot last indefinitely. The encroachment of external societies is increasing with the potential of turning entire tribes into minorities through migration as well as forced economic assimilation. This contact, particularly with industrialized societies, results in domination and economic differentiation—the basis of minority group differentiation. Isolated societies are absorbed into the mainstream of economic development and are transformed into minorities in the process. Contemporary domination and exploitation thus appear inevitable with tragic consequences for all concerned.

CONCLUSIONS

In this chapter we have outlined comparative analyses of societies and minority groups, highlighting two major factors involved in the creation of the minorities: extent of colonial-forced migration as related to racial and/or ethnic discrimination, and the level of general economic development leading to greater minority differentiation, competition, and conflict. Bringing these two dimensions of *migration* and *economic development* together, we outlined several major types of society and minority group differentiation: *the colonial-developed type*—societies with a high degree of both, possessing a complex hierarchy; *the colonial-non-developed type*—those with much migration and differentiated primarily in racial and/or ethnic terms, *the non-colonial-developed societies*—those with high economic differentiation and/or specialization, with economic, behavioral minorities and sexual as well as age-based discrimination, and *the non-colonial-non-developed societies*—isolated communities which have experienced little of either factor and are relatively undifferentiated in consequence. While such a typology is admittedly crude and contains wide variations within each major type, it points to the following relationships:

1. Migration and economic development together produce a complex hierarchy of racial, ethnic, economic, sexual, age-based, and behavioral minorities.
2. Forced migration with low economic development results primarily in racial and/or ethnic differentiation as the basis of social stratification.
3. High economic development with little or no forced migration creates economic, sexual, age-based, and behavioral minorities with little or no racial or ethnic differentiation.
4. A lack of forced migration and economic development results in little minority group differentiation generally, with kinship as the basis of social organization.

In general, then, forced migration produces racial and ethnic minorities while economic differentiation and specialization create economic, sexual, age-based, and behavioral types more often. *In this manner migration and economic development appear primarily responsible for the creation of all major types of minority on a worldwide basis.* Furthermore, it is possible to outline *developmental sequences* within this typology as follows:

Colonial-Developed Societies   are unlikely to experience further migration; however, ongoing economic development may result in the partial (economic) assimilation of subordinate groups such as women, the aged, deviants, and non-WASPs, and to a far lesser extent, non-whites, moving the society toward a less complex hierarchy that is based primarily upon class and economic power, and ultimately perhaps, some form of socialism.[18] Such trends will be complicated, uneven, and slow, continuing to reflect elements of the original minority hierarchy. They will also vary greatly from society to society. Nevertheless, continuing economic development will influence the structure of the minority group hierarchy significantly.

Colonial-Non-Developed Societies   will also experience further economic development in which racial/ethnic divisions may become exacerbated by class differentiation and behavioral minorities as well as the evolution of more "psychological" types such as sexual and age-based discrimination with industrialization. In this manner these societies may move in the direction of the colonial-developed type with the

[18]C. H. Anderson, *The Political Economy of Social Class* (Englewood Cliffs, N.J.: Prentice-Hall, 1974), chapter 13.

expansion of their minority group hierarchies through economic differentiation and specialization. Once again these developments will be halting and slow, complicated by the racial/ethnic/economic heritage of past colonial decades. Nevertheless, it appears reasonable to expect the emergence of some version of the racial/ethnic-economic-sexual, age-based, behavioral hierarchy with ongoing and long-term economic development.

Non-Colonial-Developed Societies will also experience further economic development, particularly in the specializing influence of industrialization on the less developed societies producing more specialized minority sexual and age-based discrimination. Voluntary migration (for economic purposes) may occur producing racial and ethnic minorities at contemporary stages of these societies' economic development. They may also move in the direction of the colonial-developed type but in a modified fashion since they remain fairly racially and ethnically homogeneous and are structured primarily by economic factors. Nevertheless, creation of more traditional-type minorities at this contemporary stage is not impossible, complicating minority group relations considerably. In this case, *migration patterns* move the society in the direction of the colonial-developed, although with modification.

The Non-Colonial-Non-Developed Societies will eventually experience the influence of outside groups, turning them into minorities and subjecting them to economic differentiation. Given their isolated situation, two developments are theoretically possible: change through colonial contact; or, internal economic development in response to demographic pressures. The former appears more likely, transforming the group into a racial or ethnic minority within the context of the colonial society. Further economic development may then result in elaboration of the initial hierarchy in the direction indicated for colonial-non-developed societies. Isolated societies may also take the other possible route, economic development and then migration. This appears less likely and occurs usually within a colonial context in any case. Thus, relatively undifferentiated societies lose their structural homogeneity through colonial contact and migration, moving them in the direction of more complex and hierarchical forms of social organization.

From the preceding, it is evident that types of minority group structures are not static but experience the effects of economic assimilation, industrialization, voluntary migration, and colonial contact, producing changing forms and increased levels of social differentiation. These potential developmental sequences are outlined in Figure 12.2.

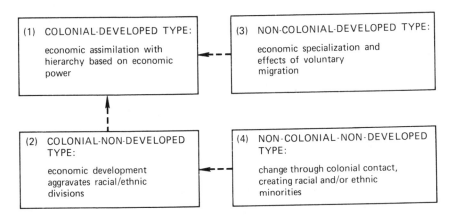

FIGURE 12.2. Developmental Sequences in Types of Minority Group Relations in World Context

From this comparative analysis we conclude that minority group relations are a creation of colonial-forced migration and economic development, operate in the context of four major types of hierarchy, and experience the effects of economic assimilation, industrialization, voluntary migration, and colonial contact, resulting in changing forms and increased levels of social differentiation. Such relations are a development of macroscopic and wide-ranging phenomena but may be reduced to types of intergroup contact and level of economic development—major factors in stratification and social organization. While the typology we have introduced is both crude and tentative, it has highlighted the relevance of these phenomena.

READINGS

BAGLEY, CHRISTOPHER, "Racialism and Pluralism: A Dimensional Analysis of Forty-Eight Countries," *Race,* 13, no. 3 (January 1972), 347–354.
BANTON, M., *Race Relations.* New York: Basic Books, 1967.
BARRON, MILTON L., "Recent Developments in Minority and Race Relations," *The Annals of the American Academy of Political and Social Science,* 420 (July 1975), 125–76.

Barth, Ernest, and Donald L. Noel, "Conceptual Frameworks for the Analysis of Race Relations: An Evaluation," *Social Forces*, 50, no. 3 (March 1972), 333–55.

Berry, B., *Race Relations: The Interaction of Ethnic and Racial Groups*, Boston: Houghton Mifflin, 1951.

Blalock, H. M., Jr., "A Power Analysis of Racial Discrimination," *Social Forces*, 39, no. 1 (October 1960), 53–59.

Bonacich, Edna, "A Theory of Middleman Minorities," *American Sociological Review*, 38, no. 5 (October 1974), 583–94.

Dodge, Peter, "Comparative Racial Systems in the Greater Caribbean," *Social and Economic Studies*, 16 (September 1967), 249–61.

Duvall, Raymond, and Mary Welfling, "Social Mobilization, Political Institutionalization, and Conflict in Black Africa: A Simple Dynamic Model," *Journal of Conflict Resolution*, 17 (December 1973), 673–702.

Eisinstadt, S. N., "Current Research in Comparative Sociological Analysis," *Sociological Inquiry*, 39, no. 1 (Winter 1969), 96–99.

Holden, Arnold G., "A Typology of Individual Migration Patterns," *Summation*, 1 (June 1968), 15–28.

Hunt, Chester L., and Lewis Walker, *Ethnic Dynamics: Patterns of Intergroup Relations in Various Societies*. Homewood: Dorsey, 1974.

Lieberson, S., "Societal Theory of Race and Ethnic Relations," *American Sociological Review*, 26 (1961), 902–10.

Mason, P. L., *Patterns of Dominance*. New York: Oxford University Press, 1970.

Meadows, Paul, "Insiders and Outsiders: Towards a Theory of Overseas Cultural Groups," *Social Forces*, 46, no. 1 (1967), 61–71.

Morrison, Donald G., et al., *Black Africa: A Comparative Handbook*, 1972.

Noel, D. L., "A Theory of the Origin of Ethnic Stratification," *Social Problems*, 16 (Fall 1968), 157–72.

Peterson, W., "A General Typology of Migration," *American Sociological Review*, 23 (1958), 255–66.

Rex, John, *Race Relations in Sociological Theory*, London: Weidenfeld and Nicholson, 1970.

Rose, A. M., "The Comparative Study of Intergroup Conflict," *Sociological Quarterly*, 1 (1960), 57–66.

Schermerhorn, R. A., *Comparative Ethnic Relations. A Framework for Theory and Research*, New York: Random House, 1970.

Tabb, William K., "Race Relations Models and Social Change," *Social Problems*, 18, no. 4 (Spring 1971), 431–44.

Tumin, Melvin, ed., *Comparative Perspectives on Race Relations*. Boston: Little Brown, 1969.

van den Berghe, P. L., *Race and Ethnicity: Essays in Comparative Sociology*. New York: Basic Books, 1970.

White, Terrence H., "Minority Groups: Beyond Description," *Wisconsin Sociologist*, 6, no. 1 (Spring-Summer 1968), 25–33.

SUMMARY
OF
SECTION FOUR

In this section of our analysis we have attempted to apply the preliminary conceptual framework presented in Section Three to minority group relations in the United States and worldwide. We made the following major points:

1. American society consists of a colonial, WASP majority, motivated by material and economic exploitation, which has experienced high levels of migration, subordination, importation, economic differentiation and specialization, and has used science and religion to rationalize minority group domination and exploitation.
2. The result is a complex minority group hierarchy consisting of racial, ethnic, economic, sexual, age-based, and behavioral groups, integrated under majority group dominance.
3. Status within this structure is dependent upon an individual's majority-minority membership profile, advantages are cumulative the higher a person's general status is within it, while consequent relationships are very competitive.
4. Finally, economic functions (racial and ethnic status) define the operation of the normative (poverty and deviance) and psychological (sexual and age-based minorities), while the structure is modified by economic change but remains essentially stable and conservative.

    In general, then, American society ranks high on all major factors in our framework: population growth, economic needs, division of labor, private property, economic differentiation, colonial migration, subordination, importation, as well as economic specialization. This has produced a complex minority hierarchy consisting of all major types, reinforced by science, medicine, psychology, and religion, serving economic, normative, and psychological functions, and modified by demographic-economic change. Minority

189

group relations in this society exemplify the most highly developed and differentiated type of society, providing a reference point for examining these relations worldwide.

5. Minority group relations worldwide are a function of two major factors: the extent of colonial-forced migration as related to racial and/or ethnic discrimination, and the level of general economic development leading to greater minority differentiation, competition, and conflict.

6. America represents societies which are high on both dimensions—*the colonial-developed*—possessing a complex racial, ethnic, economic, sexual, age-based, behavioral hierarchy. Further economic development may lead to increased (economic) assimilation within this type of structure but also within racial and/or ethnic boundaries.

7. Societies high on migration but low in economic development—*the colonial-non-developed*—are differentiated primarily in racial and/or ethnic terms with little of the economically produced type of minorities. However, economic development may aggravate these racial/ethnic divisions through class differentiation and the evolution of other minorities, moving this type of society in the direction of the colonial-developed form, if only in a halting and slow manner, complicated by its original divisions.

8. *Non-colonial-developed* societies are low on migration and high on economic differentiation and/or specialization, with economic, behavioral, sexual, age-based minorities relatively undifferentiated by racial or ethnic factors. However, with economic development, voluntary immigration may occur, producing limited racial and ethnic minorities within them, moving the society in a limited economic-colonial direction but in a restricted fashion only as compared to colonial-developed societies.

9. Finally, societies low on both dimensions—*the non-colonial-non-developed*—contain little formal and specialized minority discrimination, are based upon kinship instead, and are communal, homogeneous, and relatively unspecialized. However, external societies are subjecting them to the influences of migration and economic assimilation. Such contact, particularly with industrialized societies, results in domination and economic development—the basis of minority group differentiation.

From this comparative analysis it is evident that four major types of minority group hierarchy may exist: (1) the racial, ethnic, economic, sexual, age-based, and behavioral type—the most complex hierarchy evident in colonial-developed societies; (2) racial, ethnic structures with fewer economically produced minorities (colonial-non-developed societies); (3) economic, sexual, age-based, and behavioral hierarchies developed in non-colonial-developed societies; and, (4) traditional, and relatively isolated societies based primarily on kinship with few if any minority groups. Furthermore, each type in turn is subject to the changing influences of economic assimilation, industrialization, voluntary migration, and colonial contact, all of which result in changing forms and increased levels of social differentiation.

From these analyses we draw the following major conclusions: American society represents the most highly developed type of minority group hierarchy, reflecting high levels of colonial migration and economic development. Other major types of minority group hierarchy are the outcome of varying levels of colonial migration and economic development.

In conclusion, this application of our preliminary conceptual framework has highlighted the significant extent to which minority group relations are a consequence of migration and economic development.

Section Five

TOWARD HUMAN LIBERATION

13

Causes and Effects:
Toward a General Theory

In our discussion so far, we have delineated a number of factors —societal, group, and individual—behind minority group relations, their interrelationship, stages in these relations, and major types of minority group situations worldwide. We also formulated a preliminary conceptual framework linking demographic changes, economic development, and migration to the evolution of minority group hierarchies. In this chapter we shall draw all these discussions together in the form of a general theory which attempts to account for various patterns of minority group relations before turning to the practical implications of our analysis.

MAJOR FACTORS

We defined minorities as groups socially created by power elites on the basis of perceived physical, cultural, economic, and behavioral characteristics for economic reasons as a development of economic migration and specialization, rationalized in scientific, medical, and religious terms, producing minority roles, institutions, subcultures and identities, and forming a minority hierarchy in society. From this it is evident that three major types of factors are involved:

1. *Societal:* Migration, economic development.
2. *Group:* Roles, institutions, and subcultures subject to majority control, segregation, and exploitation.
3. *Individual:* Personal identities and patterns of socialization. Minority group relations thus operate at all levels of society as indicated in our introductory discussion.

MAJOR LINKS

A number of major links among these factors are evident: Minority group relations are a consequence of migration and economic development (differentiation and specialization), resulting in minority group roles, institutions, and subcultures, perpetuated through individual socialization and identities, serving economic, normative, and psychological functions, and rationalized in terms of assumed physiological and psychological inferiority. In general minority groups represent forms of social differentiation produced by demographic and economic change, they serve majority interests (normative and psychological), and are based upon perceived physiological and psychological characteristics—the assumed opposite of majority qualities. Major types of minorities are produced by particular processes: Migration results primarily in the creation of racial and ethnic minorities, economic differentiation produces subordinate economic and behavioral groups, and economic specialization appears to create sexual and age-based minorities. Consequently, the minority group hierarchy so formed reflects these particular processes, operates in terms of an individual's majority-minority profile, offers advantages which are cumulative the higher a person is positioned in the hierarchy and represents major societal functions (economic, normative, and psychological). In this manner it is assumed that societal factors are responsible for the complex operation of minority group relations at group and individual levels throughout society.

MAJOR STAGES

According to our preliminary conceptual framework, a number of specific stages in the evolution of minority group relations are possible:

1. Demographic change (population growth) without economic differentiation, for example, the growing traditional society.
2. Demographic change with economic differentiation (population growth, increased economic needs, division of labor, and private property, with the creation of economic and behavioral minorities and roles, institutions, and subcultures operating through socialization and identity), as in European societies experiencing industrialization.
3. Demographic change with economic differentiation, and colonial migration, subordination, and importation (the factors resulting in colonial migration and so forth), creating racial and low ethnic minorities differentiated by economic and behavioral criteria, as the South American colonial societies.
4. Demographic change with economic differentiation, migration, subordination, and importation, as well as economic specialization, resulting in the creation of a complex racial, ethnic, economic, sexual, age-based, behavioral hierarchy, reinforced by science, medicine, psychology, and religion serving major societal, economic, normative, and psychological functions, as in American society.

It is assumed that there are a number of links between each stage: Demographic growth leads to economic differentiation through increased division of labor and private property as the latter respond to this growth. Economic differentiation, in turn, produces economic and normative minorities through a materialistic economic system and elitism, leading to various migration processes (voluntary and involuntary) for economic and labor resources, creating racial and ethnic minorities also. Economic differentiation and migration together may contribute to further economic development, particularly in industrialization, making for greater economic specialization, especially in the industrial-urban context. This leads to role segregation, specialization, and the creation of sexual and age-based minorities.

Demographic development operating through economic differentiation, migration, and economic specialization may result in the creation of a complex minority group hierarchy containing all major physically defined, cultural, economic, and behavioral minorities, reinforced in a number of ways, and serving a variety of societal functions.

Finally, demographic change within this hierarchy results in greater economic assimilation while minority group reaction to their subordinate status may result in its modification in time, thereby contributing feedback into the system and reducing some of the criteria for discrimination. In this manner minority group relations are dynamic and subject to ongoing change through the demographic-minority group structure dialectic. Such changes, however, tend to be inhibited by the complexity of the general hierarchy.

Accordingly, minority group relations are viewed as a consequence of particular stages of a society's demographic and economic development.

MAJOR TYPES

Implicit in these "stages" are a number of types of minority group situation:

The non-colonial-non-developed type of Stage 1 in our previous discussion, with little or no minority group differentiation; the non-colonial-developed type of society or Stage 2 where demographic change and economic differentiation have occurred with little or no migration. Economically-produced minorities, in which particular economic and behavioral types tend to predominate, while later specialization may result in sexual and age-based discrimination; the colonial-non-developed type or Stage 3, consisting of limited economic development with high migration, producing racial and ethnic minorities primarily; and (4) the colonial-developed type—Stage 4—consisting of all major demographic, migration, and economic developments, forming a complex minority group hierarchy consisting of all major types.

Finally, all four types may proceed to later stages in the cycle without significant migration taking place. Variation in sequences may obviously occur but still within the context of our sequential model.

TOWARD A MODEL

In our analysis we have delineated major societal, group, and individual factors involved in minority group relations, interrelations among them, and major stages in their development. It is possible to integrate these elements in the form of a general model as indicated in Figure 13.1. Here it can be seen that demographic, economic, and migration factors define the group and individual operation of minority group

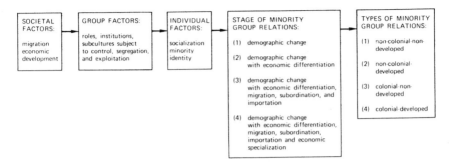

FIGURE 13.1.   A General Model of Factors Defining Minority Group Relations

relations, the evolution of different kinds of minorities and their respective functions, and the structure of minority group hierarchies. These factors also define stages in their development, major types of minority group situation, and consequent social change. It is concluded that *minority group relations are a consequence of demographic, economic, and migration factors,* based on *the major proposition that the more a society (or community) is subject to demographic change, economic development, and migration, the more complex its minority group hierarchy will be.* Furthermore, demographic change tends to lead to economic differentiation, migration, and specialization, producing various types of minority group hierarchy at each stage, leading to the most complex and comprehensive. We turn to define these factors, links, and propositions in more formal theoretical terms.

TOWARD A GENERAL THEORY OF MINORITY GROUP RELATIONS

Bringing together the major factors we have discussed, their links, stages of operation, and types of combination, as well as the general model outlined, it is possible to develop a general theory in the form of a set of sequential propositions as follows:

Stage 1. Demographic Development

The greater a society's level of population growth, the higher the increase in its economic needs. The higher its economic needs, the greater the increase in its division of labor. The greater its division of labor, the higher its level of private property.

Stage 2. Economic Differentiation

The higher a society's level of private property, the greater its economic differentiation. The greater its economic differentiation, the more differentiated it will be by economic (poverty) and behavioral minorities (deviance), formalized through roles, institutions, and subcultures, and operating through individual socialization and identity.

Stage 3. Colonial Migration, Subordination, and Importation

The more a society is differentiated by economic and behavioral criteria, the more likely it is to participate in colonial migration, subordination, and/or importation processes. The more it participates in colonial migration, subordination, and/or importation processes, the more likely that it will create racial and/or ethnic minorities, formalized through roles, institutions, and subcultures, operating through individual socialization and identity.

Stage 4. Economic Specialization

The more a society creates racial and/or ethnic minorities, the more likely it is to experience economic specialization through industrialization. The more economic specialization it experiences, the more likely it will create sexual and age-based minorities within the context of the nuclear family system, formalized through roles, institutions, and subcultures, operating through individual socialization and identity.

Stage 5. Complex Minority Hierarchy

The more a society creates sexual and age-based minorities, the more likely it will produce a complex racial, ethnic, economic, sexual, age-based, behavioral minority group hierarchy, reinforced by science, medicine, psychology, and religion, serving economic, normative, and psychological functions. The more complex a society's minority group hierarchy, the more hierarchical and competitive minority group relations within it will be.

Stage 6. Social Change

The more hierarchical and competitive a society's minority group relations, the greater the eventual level of economic assimilation in the society at large. The greater the eventual economic assimilation, the greater the eventual reduction in general discrimination. The greater the eventual reduction in general discrimination, the higher the society's level of ongoing demographic development, provided by this "feedback."

This approach is a *demographic-economic, sequential* theory, underlining the relevance of a society's demographic-economic development to the kinds of social differentiation and intergroup relations within it. Furthermore, it is a general model which does not apply completely to any specific situation; rather, it is a broad approach to the general understanding of minority group relations worldwide—a model which may be applied to specific minority group situations in particular. This approach also focuses on the structure of minority group relations, particularly in the manner in which these structures are a result of underlying demographic and economic factors. This theory is dynamic, focusing on the emergence and changing stages of minority group relations. We have attempted to develop a general, ideal-type, structural, and dynamic theory of minority group relations, applicable to any minority situation in particular.

Its major implications include the following:

Minority groups are primarily *a consequence of a society's demographic-economic development.* As it experiences such growth, increasing social differentiation occurs, including the creation of minority groups. As a society grows, then, it becomes increasingly differentiated in terms of minority group criteria.

This implies that *social development* is closely linked to the creation of minorities. Such development, therefore, requires critical and ongoing assessment in contrast to the notion that such growth is positive and functional by definition.

It is evident that minority group relations operate on *all levels of society*—societal (demographic-economic factors), group (roles, institutions, and subcultures), and individual (socialization and identity). In this manner they reflect major characteristics of the social system as a whole rather than elite and/or subgroup traits only.

Minority group relations are a question of *social structure*, particularly in the roles and institutions majorities have created primarily for their own economic purposes. Interaction at all levels occurs within the context of this structure as it is imposed on subgroups and in turn is acted upon by them.

This structure is *legitimized in terms of assumed physical and/or psychological inferiority*—the presumed opposite of majority characteristics. Such inferiority exists only in the minds of exploitive majorities (consciously or otherwise) and those on whom it is imposed insofar as it might be accepted as valid. It is doubtful that significant variation with regard to physical and psychological potential actually exists; rather, assumed inferiority is the argument used by majorities to rationalize their position of dominance, wreaking untold damage on those under their control, whether nonwhites, children, women, the poor, or deviants. *Projected inferiority* thus represents the foundation of majority-minority relations.

The major motive behind this perception is *domination and exploitation for economic gain.* Projected inferiority is highly *utilitarian* —it serves to further and legitimize the variety of types of exploitation, reinforced by institutionalized control and segregation.

Furthermore, minorities serve a *variety of purposes or societal functions*—economic, psychological, and normative. In this way they are "useful" to majorities at the societal (economic) level, group level (normative), and individual (psychological), contributing to material gain, ethnocentrism, and ego gratification. As a result, they are heavily institutionalized at a number of levels throughout society.

These functions, as we have pointed out, are *further legitimized by science, medicine, psychology, sociology, and religion,* implying that they represent majority interests rather than the notion of objectivity. Accordingly, their assumptions and conclusions must be viewed as suspect and self-serving in contrast to ideas concerning their utopian potential.

Given the exploitive nature of this minority group structure, it is possible to view *problems in society,* whether institutional, group-related, or personal as *a creation of this system's characteristics.* Whether we are attempting to deal with race riots, male chauvinism, child abuse, poverty, or personal relationship difficulties, it is possible to perceive the negative influence of assumed inferiority at work under conditions of domination and exploitation. Minority group relations operate on all levels and within all types of group contexts in society at large.

Finally, it is evident that minority group differentiation is *dehumanizing*—groups and individuals are defined in animalistic terms (for example, kids, bitches, chicks, goats, and so on), thereby reducing their human worth, resulting in self-denigration and high levels of frustration.

In conclusion, minority group relations are a creation of demographic-economic development, are legitimized in terms of assumed physical and/or psychological inferiority, represent majority economic interests, serve a variety of societal functions, are behind major social problems, and reflect a dehumanizing process. Within such contexts human beings can hardly be viewed as free and unexploited, bringing us to the question of human liberation.

STUDY QUESTIONS

1. Apply the general theory developed in this chapter to an understanding of minority group relations:
   (a) In South Africa;
   (b) In Brazil;
   (c) In Great Britain;
   (d) In New Guinea.
2. What combination(s) of demographic and economic factors are present in each situation?

14

Social Change

In our analysis we have made a number of major points concerning minority group relations; in this chapter we shall summarize them and examine their practical implications.

To begin with, we defined minorities as any group that is defined by an elite as different (inferior) on the basis of certain perceived characteristics and is consequently treated in a negative fashion. Accordingly, minority group relations were viewed as the interaction (individual, group, or institutional) between groups so defined.

We then expanded these definitions to view minorities as groups socially created by power elites on the basis of perceived physical, cultural, economic, and behavioral characteristics for economic reasons. They were a necessary part of economic migration and specialization, rationalized in scientific, medical, and religious terms, produced minority roles, institutions, subcultures, and identities, and formed a minority hierarchy in society.

This approach was incorporated in a preliminary conceptual framework, based on the general proposition that minority groups are a result of demographic growth, migration, and economic development, and are based upon assumed physical, cultural, economic, and behavioral characteristics. This framework was then applied to minority group relations in the United States and other societies, with the conclusion that American society represents the most highly developed type of minority group hierarchy, reflecting very high levels of colonial migration and economic development while other major types of minority group hierarchy appear to be a function of varying levels of colonial migration and economic development.

Drawing the above discussion together we developed a general theory of minority group relations based on the major proposition that the more a society (or community) is subject to demographic change, economic development, and migration, the more complex its minority group hierarchy will be. This set of sequential propositions dealt with several stages of minority group relations: demographic development, economic differentiation, colonial migration, subordination, importation, economic differentiation and specialization, a complex minority hierarchy, and social change. These relations are viewed as an outgrowth of demographic-economic development, are legitimized in terms of assumed physical and/or psychological inferiority, represent majority economic interests, serve a variety of societal functions, and are behind major social problems that reflect a dehumanizing process.

From the above analyses we conclude that *minority group relations evolve out of demographic change and economic differentiation in which assumed physical and/or psychological inferiority (the assumed opposite of majority traits) is used to legitimize inequality and serves as the foundation of social organization.* This process consists of five major elements:

Material-economic interests and resultant inequality: The monopolization of material resources as the society shifts from communal to private property and industrialization.

Economic, psychological, and normative functions: The particular societal functions each major type of minority serves: racial and ethnic serving economic functions, sexual and age-based types representing psychological resources, with economic and behavioral minorities serving normative purposes. Each type serves particular purposes in the society.

Assumed physical and/or psychological inferiority: We noted the frequency with which these assumptions were applied to all types of minorities as majority groups project the opposite image of themselves onto minorities to legitimize their domination and exploitation. Such inferiority, of course, does not exist in reality; rather, it is perceived and imposed.

Minority group roles, institutions, and subcultures: The resultant structure of minority group control and domination through roles or social types (women, children, criminals), institutionalized discrimination (controlled institutional access, resources, and stereotypes), and minority group reaction to their segregated, subordinate positions by development of their own separate subcultures and lifestyles.

Resultant minority group hierarchy, individual majority-minority profile, and cumulative advantages: The racial-ethnic-economic-sexual-age-based-behavioral hierarchy which places an individual in society according to his/her majority-minority membership profile, and defines intergroup relations in terms of degree of majority group advantages—resources which become cumulative the higher an individual is located in the structure.

In general, then, minority groups appear to be a development of demographic change and resultant material inequality, producing a variety of minority types according to societal function, rationalized in terms of assumed physical and/or psychological inferiority, and resulting in minority group roles, institutions, subcultures, and a well-defined hierarchy. Accordingly, minority group relations are products of general and ongoing societal processes and occur within institutionalized social structures.

PRACTICAL IMPLICATIONS

We shall discuss the practical implications of each of the previous elements.

Material Inequality

Resource inequality represents the basis of minority group relations, whether economic, psychological, or normative, and operates on all levels of society—individual, group, and institutional. Consequently, it is vital to provide open access to political, economic, and social resources in relation to general human welfare. This does not imply the lack of a reward system; only provision for individual physical and social welfare as well as open access to these resources based on need and ability without regard for background characteristics. This would result in the following practical implications (P.I.):

P.I. 1. Provide open access to political, economic, and social resources to meet human welfare needs without regard to individual background characteristics.

P.I. 2. Ensure that groups in control of political, economic, and social resources are as heterogenous and representative of all minority groups as possible in the society.

Specialized Functions

We have indicated the manner in which each minority type represents particular historical roles in a society's evolutionary development. Racial and ethnic minorities have served specific economic-labor roles in society through migration, sexual and age-based groups, have come to play particular psychological roles through economic specialization, while the poor and deviant represent normative minorities created through economic differentiation. Minorities have come to play specific roles in society, reinforced through segregation, exploitation, discrimination, and assumed inferior qualities. These roles are anachronistic, exploitive, and dehumanizing, resulting in the following implications:

P.I. 1. Assign political, economic, and social roles without regard to individual background characteristics.

Assumed Inferiority

We have highlighted the crucial part played by science, medicine, psychology, sociology, and religion in providing the assumed inferiority rationale for minority group differentiation. We would argue strongly that such inferiority does not exist in reality. While there may be variations in creative activity, the greater majority of any population possesses the potential to accomplish virtually any task, provided basic human needs are met. The above fields have tended to reflect vested majority interests with invidious consequences. As a result there is a need to:

P.I. 1. Critically examine the ideological content of all forms of science (physical and social) and religion for all forms of minority inferiority rationales.

P.I. 2. Highlight these invidious distinctions upon discovery and reject their validity.

P.I. 3. Encourage the development of more equalitarian and potential-developing forms of science and religion.

P.I. 4. Reject the validity of scientific and religious artifacts such as achievement tests (IQ and educational), psychological tests (personality), developmental curves and medical specialties based on age, which reinforce the "reality" of minority group criteria.

Minority Roles, Institutions, and Subcultures

The structural effects of minority group differentiation include the creation of highly specialized roles, institutions, and subcultures, based on the processes and arguments outlined. Consequently, minority groups required deinstitutionalization as follows:

P.I. 1. Remove all minority social types (racial, the notion of child, woman, the aged, the poor, the criminal, the pervert, the mentally ill) from language and the media, substituting more general, human-oriented terms.

P.I. 2. Remove the minority basis of access to, resources in, and stereotypes concerning all major social institutions, particularly in the political, military, legal, economic, medical, welfare, educational, and religious institutions as well as the family and media.

P.I. 3. Integrate these institutions as broadly as possible, maximizing social heterogeneity with respect to race, sex, age, culture, economic resources, and behavior.

Minority Group Hierarchy

The ultimate consequence of these elements is the creation of a complex, cumulative, minority group hierarchy. This structure ensures that minority domination, exploitation, and segregation are maintained in a stable and self-reinforcing fashion. In order to remove these hierarchical relations, its inequitable structure, and the cumulative advantages within it, it appears important to:

P.I. 1. Distribute political, economic, and social resources and rewards without regard to an individual's background characteristics.

In general we are advocating open access to political, economic, and social resources, heterogeneous control of these resources, universalistic role assignment, development of equalitarian and potential-developing types of ideas, reduction of majority controlled barriers to achievement, removal of minority social types, institutions and subcultures, and universalistic reward systems. It would be simplistic and naive to assume that these changes would be easy to implement or automatically effective in significantly changing the structure of minority group dominance. Accordingly, it can be argued that these implications are highly utopian. They also do not highlight the importance of providing for the political, economic, and social needs of the population as a whole since, as Benedict has pointed out with reference to race relations, we need to appreciate the nature of conflict and social inequality behind racism rather than race per se, since racial conflict is but a reflection of the social inequality behind it.[1] Thus, a major reason for the apparent stability of discrimination in contemporary society, despite the economic and legal advances of some minorities, is the extent to which majority group members continue to feel insecure about their political, economic, and social rights and maintain the control of minority groups in order to protect their interests. Consequently, it is highly important to remove the criteria for discrimination against all major groups in society as a *whole,* creating an open, equalitarian system for all sections of the population.

However, these changes are useful in highlighting alternate kinds of value systems; (1) the negative, exploitive type which maximizes assumed human physical and psychological inferiority to legitimize the monopolization of material resources, equates human beings with animals and dehumanizes them in the process. This is the value system underlying minority group differentiation versus positive, equalitarian values emphasizing common human needs, rights, and access to communal resources, or, the basis of *human liberation.* In contrast to this, are values which legitimize the dehumanization, exploitation, and control of human beings through their assumed inferiority and equation with animals. This is *the nexus of contemporary domination* at individual, group, and institutional levels throughout society. Humanitarian values would emphasize equality, common human needs, and access to the resources to meet them. Such alternatives highlight the generally negative societal influence of demographic change and economic development in the creation of primitive, materialistic, dehumanizing values with devastating effects on majorities and minority groups alike.

[1] R. Benedict, *Science and Politics* (New York: Viking, 1940).

It is reasonable to conclude that the most pressing social problem in contemporary society is not simply inflation and unemployment, but the implementation of a value system which will end the exploitation, degradation, and destruction of human beings. For, even if economic difficulties were to decline, the problem of creating a humane society would remain. Failure to recognize and deal with it could result in devastating human damage and intergroup conflict. The continued existence and exploitation of minority groups testifies to the relatively low development of human society. Much needs to be done if the wide gap between technological and human development is to be closed. An appreciation of the problem's significance and magnitude is but a small step in this direction.

STUDY QUESTIONS

1. Select an example of each of the four major types of minorities discussed in our analysis (physically defined, cultural, economic, and behavioral) and apply the eleven practical implications we have outlined to them. Provide specific suggestions as to how these might be applied to each particular group.
2. What general conclusions do you draw regarding the basis of minority group relations and necessary changes?

READINGS

BEJEROT, N., *Addiction and Society*. Springfield: C. C. Thomas, 1970.
CHILMAN, C., "Families in Poverty in the Early 1970's: Rates, Associated Factors, Some Implications," *Journal of Marriage and the Family*, 37 (1975), 49–60.
CORTES, J. B., and F. M. GATTI, *Delinquency and Crime, A Biopsychosocial Approach: Empirical, Theoretical, and Practical Aspects of Criminal Behavior*. New York: Academic Press, 1972.
ETZKOWITZ H., and G. M. SCHAFLANDER, "A Manifesto for Sociologists: Institution-Formation—A New Sociology," *Social Problems*, 15, (1968), 399–407.

FEATHERMAN D. L., and R. M. HAUSER, "Sexual Inequalities and Socioeconomic Achievement in the U.S. 1962–1973," *American Sociological Review,* 1 (1976), 462–83.

GIL, D. G., "A Holistic Perspective on Child Abuse and its Prevention," *Journal of Sociology and Social Welfare,* 2, (1974), 110–25.

GLASER, D., "Criminology and Public Policy," *American Sociologist,* 6 (1971) 30–37.

GOERING, J. M., "The Emergence of Ethnic Interests," *Social Forces,* 49 (1971) 379–84.

HARE, N., "The Sociological Study of Racial Conflict," *Phylon,* 23 (1972), 27–31.

HOLT, H., "Sex Roles and Social Change," *Acta Sociologica,* 14 (1971), 2–12.

KASSEBAUM, G., *Delinquency and Social Policy.* Englewood Cliffs N.J.: Prentice-Hall, 1974.

KATZMAN, M. T., "Discrimination, Sub-Culture, and Economic Performance of Minority Groups," *American Journal of Economics and Sociology,* 26 (1968), 371–76.

LIAZOS, A., "The Poverty of the Sociology of Deviance: Nuts, Sluts and Perverts," *Social Problems,* 20 (1972), 103–20.

LOVRICH, N. P., JR., "Differing Priorities in an Urban Electorate: Service Preferences among Anglo, Black, and Mexican American Voters," *Social Science Quarterly,* 55 (1974), 704–17.

MAHONEY, A. R., "The Effect of Labeling upon Youths in the Juvenile Justice System: A Review of the Evidence," *Law and Society Review,* 8, (1974), 583–614.

MARX, G. T., "Social Movements and Mass Opinion: The Case of the Black Movement," Paper read at the Annual Meetings of the American Sociological Association, 1969.

MASON, K. O., J. L. CZAJKA, *et al.,* "Change in U.S. Women's Sex-Role Attitudes, 1964–1974," *American Sociological Review,* 41 (1976), 573–96.

MEISEENER, H. H., ed., *Poverty in the Affluent Society.* New York: Harper & Row, 1973.

METZGER, P. L., "American Sociology and Black Assimilation: Conflicting Perspectives," *American Journal of Sociology,* 76 (1971), 627–47.

MOORE, J. W., "Colonialism: The Case of the Mexican Americans," *Social Problems,* 17 (Spring, 1970), 463–72.

NEAL, J., "Mexican American Achievement Hindered by Culture Conflict," *Sociology and Social Research,* 56 (1972), 471–79.

PATRICK, C. H., *Alcohol, Culture, and Society.* New York: AMS Press, 1970.

PENALOSA, F., "Recent Changes among the Chicanos," *Sociology and Social Research,* 55, (1970), 47–52.

ROACH, J. L., and O. R. GURSSLIN, "An Evaluation of the Concept 'Culture of Poverty'," *Social Forces,* 45, (1967), 383–91.

RUDHAM, H., "Children under the Law," *Harvard Educational Review,* 43 (1973), 487–514.

SIEGEL, P. M., "On the Cost of Being a Negro," *Sociological Inquiry,* 35, (1965), 41–57.

Bibliography

AKERS, RONALD L., "Problems in the Sociology of Deviance: Social Definitions and Behavior," *Social Forces,* 46, no. 4 (June 1968), 455–64.
———, *Deviant Behavior: A Social Learning Approach.* Belmont: Wadsworth, 1972.
ALEXANDER, C. NORMAN, and ERNEST Q. CAMPBELL, "Peer Influences on Adolescent Drinking," *Quarterly Journal of Studies on Alcohol,* 28, no. 3 (September 1967), 444–54.
ALLISON, JUNIUS L., "Poverty and the Administration of Justice in the Criminal Courts," *Journal of Criminal Law, Criminology and Police Science,* 55, no. 2 (June 1964), 241–45.
ALLPORT, G. W., *The Nature of Prejudice.* Cambridge, Addison-Wesley, 1958.
ALVAREZ, RODOLFO, "The Psycho-Historical and Socioeconomic Development of the Chicano Community in the United States," *Social Science Quarterly,* 13, no. 4 (March 1973), 940–42.
ANDERSON, C. H., *White Protestant Americans.* Englewood Cliffs, N.J.: Prentice-Hall, 1970.
———, *The Political Economy of Social Class.* Englewood Cliffs, N.J.: Prentice-Hall, 1974.

ANDREWS, THEODORE, *The Polish National Catholic Church in America.* London: W. Clowes, 1953.

ANGRIST, SHIRLEY, "Role Conception as a Predictor of Adult Female Roles," *Sociology and Social Research,* 50, no. 4 (July 1960), 448–59.

ARIES, P., *Centuries of Childhood, A Social History of Family Life,* trans. by R. Baldick, New York: Knopf, 1962.

AUSUBEL, D. P., *Drug Addiction: Physiological, Psychological, and Sociological Aspects.* New York: Random House, 1958.

BABCHUK, NICHOLAS, and JOHN A. BALLWEG, "Black Family Structure and Primary Relations," *Phylon,* 33, no. 4 (Winter 1972), 334–47.

BABICZ, WALTER VLADIMIR, *Assimilation of Yugoslavs in Franklin County, Ohio.* San Francisco: R & E Associates, 1973.

BACON, SELDEN D., "The Process of Addiction to Alcohol," *Quarterly Journal of Studies in Alcohol,* 34, no. 1 (March 1973), 1–27.

BAGLEY, C., "Race Relations and Theories of Status Consistency," *Race,* 11, (1970), 267–89.

———, "Radicalism and Pluralism: A Dimensional Analysis of Forty-Eight Countries," *Race,* 13, no. 3 (January 1972), 347–54.

BAKER, DONALD B., "Identity, Power, and Psychocultural Needs: White Responses to Nonwhites," *The Journal of Ethnic Studies,* 1, no. 4 (Winter 1974), 16–44.

BALL, JOHN C., "Two Patterns of Narcotic Drug Addiction in the United States," *Journal of Criminal Law, Criminology and Police Science,* 56, no. 2 (June 1965), 203–11.

BALL, JOHN C., and M. P. LAU, "The Chinese Narcotic Addict in the United States," *Social Forces,* 45, no. 1 (September 1966), 68–72.

BANNER, L. W., *Women in Modern America: A Brief History.* New York: Harcourt Brace Jovanovich, 1974.

BANTON, M., *Race Relations.* New York: Basic Books, 1967.

BARRON, MILTON L., "Recent Developments in Minority and Race Relations," *The Annals of the American Academy of Political and Social Science,* 420, (July 1975) 125–76.

BARTH, ERNEST, and DONALD L. NOEL, "Conceptual Frameworks for the Analysis of Race Relations: An Evaluation," *Social Forces,* 50, no. 3 (March 1972), 333–55.

BARTH, F., ed., *Ethnic Groups and Boundaries.* London: Allen, 1969.

BAYOR, RONALD H., "Italians, Jews, and Ethnic Conflict," *International Migration Review,* 6 (Winter 1972), 377–93.

BEATTIE, RONALD H., and JOHN P. KENNEY, "Aggressive Crimes," *Annals of the American Academy of Political and Social Science,* 364 (March 1966), 73–85.

BECHER, HAROLD K., "A Phenomenological Inquiry into the Etiology of Female Homosexuality," *Journal of Human Relations,* 17, no. 4 (1969), 570–80.

BECKER, H. S., *The Other Side: Perspectives on Deviance.* New York: Free Press, 1964.

BEJEROT, N., *Addiction and Society.* Springfield: C. C. Thomas, 1970.

BELL, DANIEL, "On Meritocracy and Equality," *Public Interest,* 29 (Fall 1972), 29–68.

BENSIN, J. KENNETH, "Militant Ideologies and Organizational Contexts: The War on Poverty and the Ideology of 'Black Power'," *Sociological Quarterly,* 12, no. 2 (Summer 1971), 328–39.

BENTZ, W. KENNETH, J. WILBERT EDGERTON, and FRANCIS T. MILLER, "Perceptions of Mental Illness Among Public School Teachers," *Sociology of Education*, 42, no. 4 (Fall 1969), 400–406.

BERCOVICI, KONRAD, *On New Shores*. New York: The Century Co., 1925.

BERRY, B., *Race Relations: The Interaction of Ethnic and Racial Groups*. Boston: Houghton Mifflin, 1951.

BITTON, LIVIA E., "The Jewess as a Fictional Sex Symbol," *Bucknell Review*, 21, no. 1 (Spring 1973), 63–86.

BLACK, D., *The Behavior of Law*. New York: Academic Press, 1976.

BLALOCK, H. M., JR., "A Power Analysis of Racial Discrimination," *Social Forces*, 39, (1960), 53–59.

———, *Toward a Theory of Minority-Group Relations*. New York: Capricorn Books, 1970.

BLANCHARD, BRAND, *The Church and the Polish Immigrant*. New York: Oxford University Press, 1920.

BLASSINGAME, J. W., *The Slave Community*. New York: Oxford University Press, 1972.

BOGARDUS, E. S., *Immigration and Race Attitudes*. Boston: Heath, 1928.

BONACICH, EDNA, "A Theory of Middleman Minorities," *American Sociological Review*, 38, no. 5 (October 1973), 583–94.

BORD, RICHARD JAMES, "Rejection of the Mentally Ill: Continuities and Further Developments," *Social Problems*, 18, no. 4 (Spring 1971), 496–509.

BORHEK, J. D., "Ethnic Group Cohesion," *American Journal of Sociology*, (July 1970), 33–48.

BOTTOMORE, T. B., *Sociology as Social Criticism*. New York: Morrow, 1976.

BOYD, MONICA, "Oriental Immigration: The Experience of the Chinese, Japanese, and Filipino Population in the United States," *International Migration Review*, 5, no. 1 (Spring 1971), 48–61.

BREMNER, R. H., *From the Depths*. New York: New York University Press, 1966.

BRIMMER, ANDREW F., "The Black Revolution and the Economic Future of Negroes in the United States," *American Scholar*, 38, no. 4 (August 1969), 629–43.

BROOM, LEONARD, "Status Profiles of Racial and Ethnic Populations," *Social Science Quarterly*, 52, no. 2 (September 1971), 379–88.

BROWN, D., *Bury My Heart at Wounded Knee*. New York: Holt, Rinehart & Winston, 1970.

BRUCE, VIRGINIA, "The Expression of Femininity in the Male," *Journal of Social Research*, 3, no. 2 (May 1967), 129–40.

BRYAN, JAMES H., "Occupational Ideologies and Individual Attitudes of Call Girls," *Social Problems*, 13, no. 4 (Spring 1966), 441–50.

BURGESS, THOMAS, *Greeks in America*. New York: The Arno Press, 1970.

BUTWIN, F., *Jews in America*. New York: Lerner Publications, 1969.

CAIN, LEONARD D. JR., "Japanese-American Protestants: Acculturation and Assimilation," *Review of Religious Research* 3 (1962), 113–21.

CAMPBELL, A., P. E. CONVERSE, *et al.*, *The American Voter*. New York: Wiley, 1966.

CAPEK, THOMAS, *The Czechs (Bohemians) in America*. New York: The Arno Press, 1969.

CHAFETZ, J. S., *Masculine/Feminine or Human?* Itasca: Peacock, 1974.

CHEIN, I., "Psychological Functions of Drug Use," in *Scientific Basis of Drug Dependence: A Symposium*, ed. H. Steinberg, London: Churchill, 1969.

CHILD, J. L., *Italian or American? The Second Generation Conflict.* London: Oxford University Press, 1943.

CHILMAN, CATHERINE S., "Economic and Social Deprivations: Its Effects on Children and Families in the United States—A Selected Bibliography," *Journal of Marriage and the Family,* 26, no. 4 (November 1964), 495–98.

———, "Families in Poverty in the Early 1970's: Rates, Associated Factors, Some Implications," *Journal of Marriage and the Family,* 37, no. 1 (February 1975), 49–60.

CHROBOT, LEONARD, "The Elusive Polish-American," *Polish American Studies* (Spring 1973), 54–59.

CHURCHILL, W., *Homosexual Behavior among Males: A Cross Cultural and Cross Species Investigation.* Englewood Cliffs, N.J.: Prentice-Hall, 1971.

CLAUSIN, JOHN A., and CAROL L. HUFFINE, "Sociocultural and Social-Psychological Factors Affecting Social Responses to Mental Disorder," *Journal of Health and Social Behavior,* 16, no. 4 (December 1975), 405–20.

COLAKOVIC, BRANKO MITA, *Yugoslav Migrations to America.* San Francisco: R & E Associates, 1973.

COLBY, VERONICA, "Minority Group Residential Patterns in Milwaukee," *Wisconsin Sociologist,* 2, no. 2 (Fall 1963), 17–20.

COLEMAN, J. S., *The Adolescent Society.* New York: Free Press, 1971.

———, "Equality of Opportunity and Equality of Results," *Harvard Educational Review,* 43, no. 1 (February 1973), 129–37.

COLL, BLANCHE D., "Deprivation in Childhood: Its Relation to the Cycle of Poverty," *Welfare in Review,* 3, no. 3 (March 1965), 1–10.

COLLINS, R., "A Conflict Theory of Sexual Stratification," *Social Problems,* 19, (1971), 3–21.

CONANT, RALPH W., SHELDON LEVY, and RALPH LEWIS, "Mass Polarization: Negro and White Attitudes in the Pace of Integration," *American Behavioral Scientist,* 13, no. 2 (November–December 1969), 247–64.

CORDASCO, FRANCISCO, and ROCCO G. GALATIOTO, "Ethnic Displacement in the Interstitial Community: The East Harlem Experience," *Phylon,* 31, no. 3 (Fall 1970), 302–12.

CORTES, J. B., and F. M. GATTI, *Delinquency and Crime, a Biopsychosocial Approach; Empirical, Theoretical, and Practical Aspects of Criminal Behavior.* New York: Academic Press, 1972.

COTHRAN, TILMAN C., "The Negro Protest against Segregation in the South," *Annals of the American Academy of Political and Social Science,* 357 (January 1965), 65–72.

COTTLE, T. J., "Parent and Child: The Hazards of Equality," in *Children's Liberation,* D. Gottlieb, ed., Englewood Cliffs, N.J.: Prentice-Hall, 1973, pp. 87–102.

COUNT VAN MANEN, GLORIA, "Towards an Interpersonal Theory of Deviance," *Proceedings of the Southwestern Sociological Association,* 19 (1968), 132–36.

CRESSEY, D., and D. A. WARD, eds., *Delinquency, Crime and Social Process.* New York: Harper and Row, 1969.

CRESSEY, D. R., ed., *Crime and Criminal Justice.* New York: New York Times Book Service, 1971.

DANK, BARRY M., "Coming Out in the Gay World," *Psychiatry,* 34, no. 2 (May 1971), 180–97.

DAVIS, NANETTE J., "Labeling Theory in Deviance Research: A Critique and Reconsideration," *Sociological Quarterly*, 13, no. 4 (Fall 1972), 447–74.
——, *Social Constructions of Deviance*. Dubuque: W. C. Brown, 1975.
DERBYSHIRE, ROBERT L., and EUGENE B. BRODY, "Marginality, Identity and Behavior in the American Negro: A Functional Analysis," *International Journal of Social Psychiatry*, 10, no. 1 (Winter 1964), 7–13.
DE WOLF, L. H., *Crime and Justice in America: A Paradox in Conscience*. New York: Harper & Row, 1975.
DIETRICH, T. STANTON, "Senior Citizens: A Potential Minority Group?" *Research Reports in Social Science*, 12, no. 2 (August 1969), 32–46.
DIGGINS, JOHN P., "The Italo-American Anti-Fascist Opposition," *Journal of American History*, 54, no. 3 (December 1967), 579–98.
DINNERSTEIN, L., and D. M. REIMERS, *Ethnic Americans: A History of Immigration and Assimilation*. New York: Harper & Row, 1975.
DODGE, PETER, "Comparative Racial Systems in the Greater Caribbean," *Social and Economic Studies*, 16 (September 1967), 249–61.
DOLLARD, J., *Caste and Class in a Southern Town*. Garden City: Doubleday, 1957.
DOUGLAS, J. D., ed., *Deviance and Respectability: The Social Construction of Moral Meanings*. New York: Basic Books, 1970.
——, *Crime and Justice in American Society*. Indianapolis, Bobbs-Merrill, 1971.
DOZIER, EDWARD P., "Problem Drinking among American Indians: The Role of Sociocultural Deprivation," *Quarterly Journal of Studies on Alcohol*, 27, no. 1 (March 1966), 72–87.
DUNCAN, BEVERLY, and OTIS DUDLEY DUNCAN, "Minorities and the Process of Stratification," *American Sociological Review*, 33, no. 3 (June 1968), 356–64.
DUVALL, RAYMOND, and MARY WELFLING, "Social Mobilization, Political Institutionalization, and Conflict in Black Africa: A Simple Dynamic Model," *Journal of Conflict Resolution*, 17 (December 1973), 673–702.
DWORKIN, ANTHONY GARY, "Stereotypes and Self-Images Held by Native-Born and Foreign-Born Mexican-Americans," *Sociology and Social Research*, 49, no. 2 (January 1965), 214–24.
DWORKIN, A. G., and R. J. DWORKIN, eds., *The Minority Report, An Introduction to Racial, Ethnic, and Gender Relations*. New York: Praeger, 1976.
EHRLICH, H. J., "Stereotyping and Negro-Jewish Stereotypes," *Social Forces*, 41, (1963), 171–76.
EISINSTADT, S. N., "Current Research in Comparative Sociological Analysis," *Sociological Inquiry*, 39, no. 1 (Winter 1969), 96–99.
EITZEN, D. STANLEY, "A Conflict Model for the Analysis of Majority-Minority Relations," *Kansas Journal of Sociology*, 8, no. 2 (Spring 1967), 76–92.
ELKIND, D., *Children and Adolescents: Interpretive Essays on Jean Piaget*. New York: Oxford University Press, 1974.
ELLIS, ALBERT, "Homosexuality: The Right to be Wrong," *Journal of Sex Research*, 4, no. 2 (May 1968), 96–107.
ERIKSON, K. T., *Wayward Puritans: A Study in the Sociology of Deviance*. New York: Wiley, 1966.
ERIKSON, MAYNARD L., "Group Violations and Official Delinquency: The Group Hazard Hypothesis," *Criminology*, 11, no. 2 (August 1973), 127–60.

ETTINGER, SHMUEL, "The Origins of Modern Anti-Semitism," *Dispersion and Unity*, 9, (1969), 17–37.

ETZKOWITZ, HENRY, and GERALD M. SCHAFLANDER, "A Manifesto for Sociologists: Institution-Formation—A New Sociology," *Social Problems*, 15, no. 4 (Spring 1968), 399–407.

EYSENCK, H. J., *Crime and Personality*. Boston: Houghton Mifflin, 1964.

FANG, STANLEY L., "Assimilation and Changing Social Roles of Chinese Americans," *Journal of Social Issues*, 29, no. 2 (1973), 115–27.

FEAGIN, J. R., *Subordinating the Poor, Welfare and American Beliefs*. Englewood Cliffs, N.J.: Prentice-Hall, 1975.

FEATHERMAN, DAVID L., "The Socioeconomic Achievement of White Religio-Ethnic Subgroups: Social and Psychological Explanations," *American Sociological Review*, 36, no. 2 (April 1971), 207–22.

FEATHERMAN, DAVID L., and ROBERT M. HAUSER, "Sexual Inequalities and Socioeconomic Achievement in the U.S., 1962–1973," *American Sociological Review*, 41, no. 3 (June 1976), 462–83.

FELDMAN, LEONARD, "Portrait of Poverty: A Review of 'La Vida'," *Welfare in Review*, 5, no. 6 (June-July, 1967), 14–16.

FELLOWS, D. K., *A Mosaic of America's Ethnic Minorities*. New York: Wiley, 1972.

FENTON, EDWIN, *Immigrants and Unions, A Case Study: Italian and American Labor*. New York: The Arno Press, 1975.

FIELD, M., *Aged, the Family, and the Community*. New York: Columbia University Press, 1972.

FIRESTONE, S., *The Dialectic of Sex, The Case for Feminist Revolution*. New York: Bantam, 1971.

FLORA, CORNELIA BUTLER, "The Passive Female: Her Comparative Image by Class and Culture in Women's Magazine Fiction," *Journal of Marriage and the Family*, 33, no. 3 (August 1971), 435–44.

FORBES, JACK D., "Race and Color in Mexican-American Problems," *Journal of Human Relations*, 16, no. 1 (1968), 55–68.

FOUCAULT, M., *Madness and Civilization*. New York: Vintage, 1973.

FOX, PAUL, *The Poles in America*. New York: The Arno Press, 1970.

FOX, RICHARD, "The XYY Offender: A Modern Myth?" *Journal of Criminal Law, Criminology and Police Science*, 62, no. 1 (March 1971), 59–73.

FOX, WILLIAM, S., and JOHN R. FAINE, "Trends in White-Nonwhite Income Equality," *Sociology and Social Research*, 57, no. 3 (April 1973), 288–99.

FRANCHER, J. SCOTT, "American Values and the Disenfranchisement of the Aged," *Eastern Anthropologist*, 22, no. 1 (January–April 1969), 29–36.

FRANCIS, E. K., *Interethnic Relations, An Essay in Sociological Theory*. New York: Elsevier, 1976.

FRAZIER, E. F., "Sociological Theory and Race Relations," *American Sociological Review*, 12 (1947), 265–71.

———, *Race and Culture Contacts in the Modern World*. Boston: Beacon Press, 1965.

FREDRICKSON, G. M., *The Black Image in the White Mind*. New York: Harper & Row, 1971.

FREEMAN, HOWARD E., and OZZIE G. SIMMONS, *The Mental Patient Comes Home*. New York: Wiley, 1963.

FREEMAN, J., "Growing Up Girlish," *Transaction*, 8 (1970), 36–43.

———, "The Origins of the Women's Liberation Movement," *American Journal of Sociology*, 78, no. 4 (January 1973), 782–811.

———, "Political Organization in the Feminist Movement," *Acta Sociologica*, 18, nos. 2–3, (1975), 222–44.

FRIEDAN, B., *The Feminine Mystique*. New York: Dell, 1964.

FRIEDENBERG, EDGAR Z., "The Generation Gap," *Annals of the American Academy of Political and Social Science*, 382 (March 1969), 32–42.

FRIEDMAN, NORMAN L., "German Lineage and Reform Affiliation: American Jewish Prestige Criteria in Transition," *Phylon*, 261, no. 2 (Summer 1965), 140–47.

FUJIMOTO, TETSUYA, "Social Class and Crime: The Case of the Japanese Americans," *Issues in Criminology*, 10, no. 1 (Spring 1975), 73–93.

FURNIVALL, J. S., *Colonial Policy and Practice*. London: Cambridge University Press, 1948.

GALBRAITH, JOHN KENNETH, "The Causes of Poverty: A Clinical View," *Population Research*, 6, no. 2 (July 1962), 62–66.

GALLO, J., *Ethnic Alienation: The Italian-Americans*. New York: Fairleigh Dickinson, 1974.

GANGER, ROSLYN, and GEORGE SHUGART, "Complementary Pathology in Families of Male Heroin Addicts," *Social Casework*, 49, no. 6 (June 1969), 356–61.

GELFAND, D. E., and R. D. LEE, eds., *Ethnic Conflicts and Power: A Cross-National Perspective*. New York: Wiley, 1973.

GIL, DAVID G., "A Holistic Perspective on Child Abuse and Its Prevention," *Journal of Sociology and Social Welfare*, 2, no. 2 (Winter 1974), 110–25.

GITTLER, J. B., ed., *Understanding Minority Groups*. New York: Wiley, 1956.

GLASER, DANIEL, "Criminology and Public Policy," *American Sociologist*, 6 (June 1971), 30–37.

GLEASON, P., "Immigration and American Catholic Intellectual Life," *Review of Politics*, 2, no. 26 (April 1964), 147–73.

GOERING, JOHN M., "The Emergence of Ethnic Interests," *Social Forces*, 49, no. 3 (March 1971), 379–84.

GOLDBERG, PHILIP, "Are Women Prejudiced Against Women?" *Trans-Action*, 5, no. 5 (April 1968), 28–30.

GOODNIGHT, BARBARA, "Toward a Sociological Theory of Adolescence in American Society," *Proceedings of the Southwestern Sociological Association*, 19 (1968), 137–141.

GORDON, M. M., *Assimilation in American Life*. New York: Oxford University Press, 1964.

GORNICK, VIVIAN, and BARBARA K. MORAN, eds., *"Woman in Sexist Society: Studies in Power and Powerlessness*. New York: Basic Books, 1971.

GOSSETT, T. P., *Race: The History of an Idea in America*. Dallas: Southern Methodist University Press, 1963.

GOTTLIEB, D., ed., *Children's Liberation*. Englewood Cliffs, N.J.: Prentice-Hall, 1973.

GOTTLIEB, DAVID, and ANNE LEINHARD HEINSOHN, "Sociology and Youth," *Sociological Quarterly*, 14, no. 2 (Spring 1973), 249–70.

GOULD, C. C., and M. W. WARTOFSKY, eds. *Women and Philosophy: Toward a Theory of Liberation*. New York: Putnam, 1976.

GOVE, WALTER R., "Societal Reaction as an Explanation of Mental Illness: An Evaluation," *American Sociological Review*, 35, no. 5 (October 1970), 878–83.

GOVORCHIN, GERALD GILBERT, *Americans from Yugoslavia*. Gainesville: University of Florida Press, 1961.

GOWGELL, DONALD O., "The Demography of Aging" in *The Daily Needs and Instincts of Older People*, Adeline M. Hoffman, 1970.

GRAHAM, HILLARY, "Children Under the Law," *Harvard Educational Review*, 43, no. 4 (November 1973), 487–514.

GRAY, DIANA, "Turning-Out: A Study of Teenage Prostitution," *Urban Life and Culture*, 1, no. 4 (January 1973), 401–25.

GREBLER, LEA, JOAN W. MOORE, and RALPH C. GUZMANN, *The Mexican-American People: The Nation's Second Largest Minority*, 1970.

GREELEY, ANDREW M., "American Sociology and the Study of Ethnic Immigrant Groups," *International Migration Digest*, 1, no. 2 (Fall 1964), 107–13.

——, "White against White, The Enduring Conflict," in *The White Majority, Between Poverty and Affluence*, ed., L. K. Howe. New York: Vintage, 1970, pp. 111–18.

GREEN, EDWARD, "Race, Social Status, and Criminal Arrest," *American Sociological Review*, 35, no. 3 (June 1970), 476–90.

GREEN, ROGER H., Jr., *South Slav Settlement in Western Washington: Perception and Choice*. San Francisco: R & E Associates, 1974.

GREENBERG, DAVID F., and FAY STENDER, "The Prison as a Lawless Agency," *Buffalo Law Review*, 21, no. 3 (Spring 1972), 799–838 .

GREER, G., *Female Eunuch*. New York: McGraw-Hill, 1971.

GRIER, W. H., and P. M. COBBS, *Black Rage*. New York: Bantam Books, 1968.

GRIESSMAN, B. E., *Minorities, a Text with Readings in Intergroup Relations*, Hinsdale: Dryden, 1975.

GROB, GERALD N., "The State Mental Hospital in Mid-Nineteenth Century America: A Social Analysis," *American Psychologist*, 21, no. 6 (June 1966), 510–23.

GRUPP, STANLEY, "Experiences with Marihuana in a Sample of Drug Users," *Sociological Focus*, 1, no. 2 (Winter 1967), 39–52.

GUSKIN, SAMUEL, "Dimensions of Judged Similarity Among Deviant Types," *American Journal of Mental Deficiency*, 68, no. 2 (September 1963), 218–24.

GUTTENTOG, MARCIA, "The Relationship of Unemployment to Crime and Delinquency," *Journal of Social Issues*, 24, no. 1 (January 1968), 105–14.

HALE, E. H., *Letters on Irish Emigration*. Boston: Phillips, Sampson, 1852.

HARE, NATHAN, "The Sociological Study of Racial Conflict," *Phylon*, 33, no. 1 (Spring 1972), 27–31.

HARTJEN, C., *Crime and Criminalization*. New York: Praeger, 1974.

HARTZ, L., ed., *The Founding of New Societies*. New York: Harcourt, Brace & World, 1964.

HAUSER, PHILIP, "Mounting Chaos at Home," *Bulletin of the Atomic Scientists*, 24, no. 2 (January 1968), 56–58.

HAVIGHURST, R. J., and Ph. H. DRYER, eds., *Youth*. Chicago: University of Chicago Press, 1975.

HAYDEN, T., *Rebellion in Newark: Official Violence and Ghetto Response*. New York: Random House, 1967.

HAYS, WILLIAM C., and CHARLES H. MINDEL, "Extended Kinship Relations in

Black and White Families," *Journal of Marriage and the Family*, 35, no. 1 (February 1973), 51–57.

HEER, DAVID M., "Inter-marriage and Racial Amalgamation in the United States," *Eugenics Quarterly*, 14, no. 2 (June 1967), 112–20.

HEIDE, WILMA SCOTT, "What's Wrong with Male-Dominated Society," *Impact of Science on Society*, 21, no. 1 (January–May 1971), 55–62.

HELLER, CELIA STOPNICKA, "Class as an Explanation of Ethnic Differences in Mobility Aspirations: The Case of Mexican Americans," *International Migration Review*, 2, no. 1 (Fall 1967), 31–37.

HENDERSON, DONALD, "Minority Response and the Conflict Model," *Phylon*, 25, no. 1 (Spring 1964), 18–26.

HERMAN, M., *Japanese in America*. Dobbs Ferry: Oceana, 1974.

HERNTON, C. C., *Sex and Racism in America*. Garden City: Doubleday, 1965.

HIGHAM, J., *Strangers in the Land: Patterns of American Nativism, 1860–1925*. New Brunswick: Rutgers University Press, 1955.

HIMES, JOSEPH S., "Some Work-Related Cultural Deprivations of Lower-Class Negro Youths," *Journal of Marriage and the Family*, 26, no. 4 (November 1964), 447–49.

HIRSCHI, TRAVIS, "The Professional Prostitute," *Berkeley Journal of Sociology*, 7, no. 1 (Spring 1962), 33–50.

HOCHSCHILD, A. R., "A Review of Sex Role Research," *American Journal of Sociology*, 78 (1973), 1011–29.

HOFFMAN, ADELINE M., *The Daily Needs and Interests of Older People*. Springfield, Ill: Charles C. Thomas, 1970.

HOLDEN, ARNOLD G., "A Typology of Individual Migration Patterns," *Summation*, 1 (June 1968), 15–28.

HOLDIN, MATTHEW, "Ethnic Accommodation in a Historical Case," *Comparative Studies in Society and History*, 8, no. 2 (January 1966), 168–80.

HOLMER, J., *Drugs and Minority Oppression*. New York: Seabury, 1976.

HOLTER, HARRIET, "Sex Roles and Social Change," *Acta Sociologica*, 14, nos. 1–2 (1971), 2–12.

HOUGH, RICHARD L., "Parental Influence, Youth Contraculture, and Rural Adolescent Attitudes Toward Minority Groups," *Rural Sociology*, 34, no. 3 (September 1969), 383–86.

HOWARD, J. R., ed., *Awakening Minorities, American Indians, Mexican Americans, Puerto Ricans*. New Brunswick: Transaction, 1970.

HUNT, C. I., and L. WALKER, *Ethnic Dynamics, Patterns of Intergroup Relations in Various Societies*. Homewood: Dorsey, 1974.

HUNTER, CHARLES A., "Self-Esteem and Minority Status," *Proceedings of the Southwestern Sociological Association*, 18 (March 1967), 194–99.

HURLEY, R. L., *Poverty and Mental Retardation: A Causal Relationship*. New York: Random House, 1970.

HURLOCK, E. B., *Adolescent Development*, (4th ed.), New York: McGraw-Hill, 1973.

JACOBS, P., and S. LANDAU, eds., *To Serve the Devil*, Vols. I, II, New York: Vintage, 1971.

JAMES, LIONEL, "On the Game," *New Society*, 24, no. 555 (May 24, 1973), 425–29.

JEFFREY, C. R., "Criminal Behavior and Learning Theory," *Journal of Criminal Law, Criminology and Police Science*, 56, no. 3 (September 1965), 294–300.

JENKINS, ROBERT L., and ANDREW BOYER, "Types of Delinquent Behavior and Background Factors," *International Journal of Social Psychiatry,* 14, no. 1 (Winter 1967–68), 65–76.

JENSEN, A. R., "How Much Can We Boost I.Q. and Scholastic Achievement?" *Harvard Educational Review,* 39 (1969).

JOHNSEN, KATHRYN P., "The Factors Associated with the Male's Tendency to Negatively Stereotype the Female," *Sociological Focus,* 2, no. 3 (Spring 1969), 21–36.

JORDAN, W. P., *White over Black: American Attitudes Toward the Negro 1550–1812.* Chapel Hill: University of North Carolina Press, 1968.

JUHANI, HIRVAS, "Identity and Mental Illness: A Study on the Interaction Between the Mentally Ill and Their Environment," *Transactions of the Westermarck Society,* 12, (1966), 11–116.

KALLMAN, F. J., *The Genetics of Schizophrenia.* New York: Augustin, 1938.

KAMMEIER, MARY LEO, "Adolescents from Families With and Without Alcoholic Problems," *Quarterly Journal of Studies on Alcohol,* 32, no. 2 (June 1971) 364–72.

KANTROWITZ, N., *Ethnic and Racial Segregation Patterns in New York City Metropolis: Residential Patterns among White Ethnic Groups, Blacks and Puerto Ricans.* New York: Praeger, 1973.

KASSEBAUM, G., *Delinquency and Social Policy.* Englewood Cliffs, N.J.: Prentice-Hall, 1974.

KATZ, D., and K. BRALY, "Racial Stereotypes of One Hundred College Students," *Journal of Abnormal and Social Psychology* (1933), 280–90.

KATZMAN, M. T., "Discrimination, Sub-Culture, and Economic Performance of Minority Groups," *American Journal of Economics and Sociology,* 27, no. 4 (October 1968), 371–76.

KEITH-LUCAS, ALAN, "Child Welfare Services Today: An Overview and Some Questions," *Annals of the American Academy of Political and Social Science,* 355 (September 1964), 1–8.

KENNEDY, R. E., Jr., "Irish Americans, A Successful Case of Pluralism," in *The Minority Report,* eds., A. G. Dworkin and R. J. Dworkin. New York: Praeger, 1976.

KHATON, ODESSA M., and RAPHAEL P. CARRIERA, "An Attitude Study of Minority Group Adolescents Toward Mental Health," *Journal of Youth and Adolescence,* 1, no. 2 (June 1972), 131–41.

KILLIAN, L., *White Southerners.* New York: Random House, 1970.

KINLOCH, G. C., *The Dynamics of Race Relations, A Sociological Analysis.* New York: McGraw-Hill, 1974.

———, "Changing Black Reaction to White Domination," *Rhodesian History,* 5 (1974), 67–78.

———, "Changing Intergroup Attitudes of Whites as Defined by the Press: The Process of Colonial Adaptation," *Zambezia,* 4 (1975–76), 105–17.

KITANO, HARRY H. L., and STANLEY SUE, "The Model Minorities," *Journal of Social Issues,* 29, no. 2 (1973), 1–9.

KLEEMAN, JAMES A., "The Establishment of Core Gender Identity in Normal Girls," *Archives of Sexual Behavior,* 1, no. 2 (1971), 103–29.

KLEIN, DORIE, "The Etiology of Female Crime: A Review of the Literature," *Issues in Criminology,* 8, no. 2 (Fall 1973), 3–30.

KOGAN, LAWRENCE A., "The Jewish Conception of Negroes in the North: An Historical Approach," *Phylon,* 28 no. 4 (Winter 1967), 376–85.

KOHN, M., *Class and Conformity: A Study in Values*. Homewood: Dorsey, 1969.

KOLM, RICHARD, "The Identity Crisis of Polish-Americans," *The Quarterly Review*, (April, June 1969), 1–4.

KOSA, J., and I. K. ZOLA, eds., *Poverty and Health: A Sociological Analysis*. Cambridge: Harvard University Press, 1975.

KOTLARZ, ROBERT J., "Writings About the Changing of Polish Names in America," *Polish-American Studies*, (January–June., 1963), 1–4.

KOVEL, J., "Therapy in Late Capitalism," *Telos*, 30 (1976–77), pp. 73–92.

KRATCOSKI, PETER C., and JOHN E. KRATCOSKI, "Changing Patterns in the Delinquent Activities of Boys and Girls: A Self-Reported Delinquency Analysis," *Adolescence*, 10, no. 37 (Spring 1975), 83–91.

KRAUSZ, ERNEST, "Factors of Social Mobility in British Minority Groups," *British Journal of Sociology*, 23, no. 3 (September 1972), 275–86.

KRYSTALL, ERIC R., NEIL FRIEDMAN, GLEEN HOWZE, and EDGAR C. EPPS, "Attitudes Toward Integration and Black Consciousness: Southern Negro High School Seniors and Their Mothers," *Phylon*, 31, no. 2 (Summer 1970), 104–13.

KUPPERSTEIN, LENORE R., "Assessing the Nature and Dimensions of the Drug Problem," *The Annals of the American Academy of Political and Social Science*, 417 (January 1975), 76–85.

KUROKAWA, M., ed., *Minority Responses*. New York: Random House, 1970.

KUTAK, ROBERT I., *The Story of a Bohemian-American Village: A Study of Social Persistence and Change*. New York: The Arno Press, 1969.

LA GUMINA, S. J., and F. J. CAVAIOLI, *The Ethnic Dimension in American Society*. New York: Holbrook, 1974.

LASCH, CHRISTOPHER, *The New Radicalism in America, 1889–1963*. New York: Alfred A. Knopf, 1965.

LAUFER, ROBERT S., "Sources of Generational Consciousness and Conflict," *Annals of the American Academy of Political and Social Science*, 395 (May 1971), 80–94.

LENS, S., *Poverty: America's Enduring Paradox*. New York: Crowell, 1969.

LENSKI, G., *Power Privilege, A Theory of Social Stratification*. New York: McGraw-Hill, 1966.

LEONARD, G. B., "How School Stunts your Child," in *Children's Liberation*, D. Gottlieb, ed., Englewood Cliffs, N.J.: Prentice-Hall, 1973, pp. 145–66.

LERMAN, PAUL, "Gangs, Networks and Subculture Delinquency," *American Journal of Sociology*, 73, no. 1 (July 1967), 63–72.

LERNIR, GERDA, "Women's Rights and American Feminism," *American Scholar*, 40, no. 2, (April 1971), 235–48.

LEVENSEN, DANIEL J., and EUGENE B. GALLAGHER, *Parenthood in the Mental Health Hospital*, 1964.

LEVENTMAN, SEYMOUR, "Class and Ethnic Tensions: Minority Group Leadership in Transition," *Sociology and Social Research*, 50, no. 3 (April 1966), 371–76.

LEVY, SHELDON G., "Polarization in Racial Attitudes," *Public Opinion Quarterly*, 36, no. 2 (Summer 1972), 221–34.

LEWIN, PAPANEK, MIRIAM, "Psychological Aspects of Minority Group Membership: The Concepts of Kurt Lewin," *Jewish Social Studies*, (January 1974), 72–79.

LEWIS, O., *The Children of Sanchez*. Harmondsworth: Penguin Books, 1961.

LIAZOS, ALEXANDER, "The Poverty of the Sociology of Deviance: Nuts, Sluts, and Perverts," *Social Problems*, 20, no. 1 (Summer 1972), 103–20.

LIEBERSON, S., "A Societal Theory of Race and Ethnic Relations," *American Sociological Review*, 26 (1961), 902–10.

LINN, LAWRENCE, "The Mental Hospital from the Patient Perspective," *Psychiatry* 31, no. 3 (August 1968), 213–23.

LINSKY, ARNOLD S., "Community Homogeneity and Exclusion of the Mentally Ill," *Journal of Health and Social Behavior*, 11, no. 4 (December 1970), 304–10.

LIPSET, S. M., *Rebellion in the University*. Boston: Little Brown, 1971.

LOFLAND, J., *Deviance and Identity*. Englewood Cliffs, N.J.: Prentice-Hall, 1969.

LOMAX, L., *The Negro Revolt*. New York: Harper, 1962.

LOMBROSO-FERRERO, G., *Criminal Man*. Montclair: Patterson-Smith, 1911.

LOPATA, HELENA ZNANIECKI, *Polish Americans: Status Competition in an Ethnic Community*. Englewood Cliffs, N.J.: Prentice-Hall, 1976.

LOPREATO, J., *Italian Americans*. New York: Random House, 1970.

LORENCE, BOGNA W., "Parents and Children in Eighteenth-Century Europe," *History of Childhood Quarterly*, 2, no. 1 (Summer 1974), 1–30.

LOVRICH, NICHOLAS P., Jr., "Differing Priorities in an Urban Electorate: Service Preferences Among Anglo, Black, and Mexican American Voters," *Social Science Quarterly*, 55, no. 3 (December 1974), 704–17.

LOWE, GEORGE D., and H. EUGENE HODGES, "Deaths Associated with Alcohol in Georgia, 1970," *Quarterly Journal of Studies on Alcohol*, 32, no. 2 (June 1971), 364–72.

LYMAN, S., *Chinese Americans*. New York: Random House, 1974.

MCAREE, C. P., R. A. STEFFANHAGEN, and L. S. ZHENER, "Personality Factors in College Drug Users," *International Journal of Social Psychiatry*, 15, no. 2 (Spring 1969), 102–106.

MCCAGHY, CHARLES H., and JAMES K. SKIPPER, Jr., "Lesbian Behavior as an Adaptation to the Occupation of Stripping," *Social Problems*, 17, no. 2 (Fall 1969), 262–70.

MCCOY, NORMA, and EDWARD ZIGLER, "Social Reinforcer Effectiveness as a Function of the Relationship Between Child and Adult," *Journal of Personality and Social Psychology*, 1, no. 6 (1965), 602–12.

MCDOWELL, MARGARET B., "The New Rhetoric of Woman Power," *Midwest Quarterly*, 12, no. 2 (January 1971), 187–98.

MCLENOU, DALE S., "The Origins of Mexican American Subordination in Texas," *Social Science Quarterly*, 53, no. 4 (March 1973), 656–70.

MCPHERSON, J., et al., *Blacks in America: Bibliographical Essays*. New York: Doubleday, 1971.

MACCOBY, E., ed., *The Development of Sex Differences*. Palo Alto: University of Stanford Press, 1966.

MACIERA, STANLEY A., "Some Reasons for First Name Changes," *Polish-American Studies*, (January–June, 1963), 8–9.

MAHONEY, ANNE RANKIN, "The Effect of Labeling upon Youths in the Juvenile Justice System: A Review of the Evidence," *Law and Society Review*, 8, no. 4 (Summer 1974), 583–614.

MAKIELSKI, S. J., Jr., *Beleaguered Minorities, Cultural Politics in America*. San Francisco: Freeman, 1973.

MANIS, MELVIN, PETER S. HOUTS, and JOAN B. BLAKE, "Beliefs About Mental Illness as a Function of Psychiatric Status and Psychiatric Hospitalization," *Journal of Abnormal Psychology*, 67, no. 3 (1963), 226–33.

MANOSEVITZ, MARTIN, "The Development of Male Homosexuality," *Journal of Sex Research*, 8, no. 1 (1972), 31–40.

MARANELL, GARY M., "An Examination of the Self and Group Attitudes of Adolescent Clique Members," *Kansas Journal of Sociology*, 1, no. 3 (Summer 1965), 123–30.

MARDEN, C. F., and G. MEYER, *Minorities in American Society* (4th ed.), New York: van Nostrand, 1968.

MARRETT, CORA B., "The Brown Power Revolt: A True Social Movement," *Journal of Human Relations*, 19, no. 3 (1971), 356–66.

MARTIN, J. G., and C. W. FRANKLIN, *Minority Group Relations*. Columbia: Merrill, 1973.

MARTIN, M. K., and B. VOORHIES, *Female of the Species*. New York: Columbia University Press, 1975.

MARTINEZ, G. T., and J. EDWARDS, *Mexican Americans*. New York: Houghton Mifflin, 1973.

MASON, KAREN OPPENHUM, JOHN L. CZAJKA, and SARA ARBER, "Change in U. S. Women's Sex-Role Attitudes, 1964–1974," *American Sociological Review*, 41, no. 4 (August 1976), 573–96.

MASON, KAREN O., and LARRY L. BUMPASS, "U.S. Women's Sex Role Doctrology, 1970" *American Journal of Sociology*, 80, no. 5 (March 1975), 1212–19.

MASOUKA, JITSUICHI, "Conflicting Role Obligations and Role Types: With Special Reference to Race Relations," *Japanese Sociological Review*, 11, no. 1 (July 1960), 78–108.

MATZA, D., *Delinquency and Drift*. New York: Wiley, 1964.

MEAD, M., *Coming of Age in Samoa*. New York: Morrow, 1928.

————, *Sex and Temperament in Three Primitive Societies*. New York: Dell, 1969.

MEAD, M., and M. WOLFSTEIN, eds., *Childhood in Contemporary Cultures*. Chicago: University of Chicago Press, 1963.

MEADOWS, PAUL, "Insiders and Outsiders: Towards a Theory of Overseas Cultural Groups," *Social Forces*, 46, no. 1 (1967), 61–71.

MEISSNER, H. H., ed., *Poverty in the Affluent Society*. New York: Harper & Row, 1973.

METZGER, PAUL L., "American Sociology and Black Assimilation: Conflicting Perspectives," *American Journal of Sociology*, 76, no. 4 (January 1971), 627–47.

MEYER, P. B., "The Exploitation of the American Growing Class," in *Children's Liberation*, ed. D. Gottlieb. Englewood Cliffs, N.J.: Prentice-Hall 1973, pp. 35–52.

MILLER, D., *Adolescence: Psychology, Psychopathology, and Psychotherapy*. New York: Aronson, 1974.

MOGULL, ROBERT G., "American Poverty in the 1960's," *Phylon*, 33, no. 2 (Summer 1972), 161–68.

MOORE, JOAN W., "Colonialism: The Case of the Mexican Americans," *Social Problems*, 17, no. 4 (Spring 1970), 463–72.

MOORE, J., and A. CUELLAR, *Mexican Americans*. Englewood Cliffs, N.J.: Prentice-Hall, 1970.

MOSCOVICI, SERGE, and PATRICIA NEVE, "Studies on Polarization of Judgments: III. Majorities, Minorities and Social Judgments," *European Journal of Social Psychology*, 3, no. 4 (1973), 479–84.

MOYNIHAN, D. P., ed., *On Understanding Poverty*. New York: Basic Books, 1968.

MULFORD, HAROLD A., and DONALD E. MILLER, "Measuring Public Acceptance of the Alcoholic as a Sick Person," *Quarterly Journal of Studies on Alcohol*, 25, no. 2 (June 1964), 314–24.

MULLER, J. F., *Children of Frankenstein: A Primer on Modern Technology and Human Values*. Bloomington: Indiana University Press, 1970.

MULLIGAN, RAYMOND A., "Socio-economic Background and Minority Attitudes," *Sociology and Social Research*, 45, no. 3 (April 1961), 289–94.

MURDOCK, GEORGE, P., and CATERINA PROVOST, "Factors in the Division of Labor by Sex: A Cross-Cultural Analysis," *Ethnology*, 12, no. 2 (April 1973), 203–25.

MURDOCK, GRAHAM, and GUY PHELPS, "Youth Culture and the School Revisited," *British Journal of Sociology*, 23, no. 4 (December 1972), 478–82.

MYERS, JEROME K., and L. BEAN, *A Decade Later: A Follow-Up of Social Class and Mental Illness*, New York: Wiley, 1968.

NAFFZIGER, CLAUDEEN CLINE, and KEN NAFFZIGER, "Development of Sex Role Stereotypes," *The Family Coordinator*, 23, no. 3 (July 1974), 251–58.

NEAL, JUSTIN, "Mexican American Achievement Hindered by Culture Conflict," *Sociology and Social Research*, 56, no. 4 (July 1972), 471–79.

NELSEN, HART M., and LYNDA DICKSON, "Attitudes of Black Catholics and Protestants: Evidence for Religious Identity," *Sociological Analysis*, 33, no. 3 (Fall 1972), 152–65.

NELSEN, FRANK C., "The German-American Immigrants—Struggle," *International Review of History and Political Science*, 10, no. 2 (May 1973), 37–49.

NESBITT, RITA, "Conflict and the Black Panther Party: A Social Psychological Interpretation," *Sociological Focus*, 5, no. 4 (Summer 1972), 105–19.

NEWMAN, G., *Comparative Deviance, Perception and Law in Six Cultures*. New York: Elsevier, 1976.

NEWMAN, W. M., *American Pluralism, A Study of Minority Groups and Social Theory*. New York: Harper, 1973.

NOEL, D. L., "A Theory of the Origin of Ethnic Stratification," *Social Problems*, 16 (Fall 1968), 157–72.

OBIDINSKI, EUGENE, "Polish-Americans in Buffalo: The Transformation of an Ethnic Subcommunity," *Polish Review*, (Winter 1969), 28–39.

OLSEN, MARVIN E., "Social and Political Participation of Blacks," *American Sociological Review*, 35, no. 4 (August 1970), 682–97.

OPLER, MARVIN K., and JEROME L. SINGER, "Ethnic Differences in Behavior and Psychopathology: Italian and Irish," *International Journal of Social Psychiatry*, 2, no. 1 (Summer 1956), 11–22.

PACHT, ASHER R., and JAMES E. COWDEN, "An Exploratory Study of Five Hundred Sex Offenders," *Criminal Justice and Behavior*, 1, (March 1972), 13–20.

PAIGE, JEFFERY, "Changing Patterns of Anti-White Attitudes Among Blacks," *Journal of Social Issues*, 26, no. 4 (August 1970), 69–86.

PALISI, BARTOLOMEO J., "Ethnic Generation and Family Structure," *Journal of Marriage and the Family*, 28, no. 1 (February 1966), 49–50.

PAPPENFORT, DONNELL M., ADELAIDE DINWOODIE, and DEE MORGAN KILPATRICK, "Children in Institutions, 1966: A Research Note," *Social Service Review*. 42, no. 2 (June 1968), 252–60.

PARKER, PHILIP D., "The Homosexual: Attitudes, Needs, and Role Strain," *Proceedings of the Southwestern Sociological Association*, 19 (1968), 202–206.

PATTISON, E. MANSEL, "Confusing Concepts about the Concept of Homosexuality," *Psychiatry*, 37, no. 4 (November 1974), 340–49.

PEARLIN, LEONARD I., MARIAN RADKE YARROW, and HARRY A. SCARR, "Unintended Effects of Parental Aspirations: The Case of Children's Cheating," *American Journal of Sociology*, 73, no. 1 (July 1967), 73–83.

PEARSON, G. H., *Adolescence and the Conflict of Generations*. New York: Norton, 1958.

PENALOSA, FERNANDO, "Recent Changes Among the Chicanos," *Sociology and Social Research*, 55, no. 1 (October 1970), 47–52.

———, "The Changing Mexican-American in Southern California," *Sociology and Social Research*, 51, no. 4 (July 1967), 405–17.

PEPINSKY, H. E., *Crime and Conflict*. New York: Academic Press, 1976.

PERRUCCI, R., *Circle of Madness, On Being Insane and Institutionalized in America*. Englewood Cliffs, N.J.: Prentice-Hall, 1974.

PETERSON, W., "A General Typology of Migration," *American Sociological Review*, 23 (1958), 255–66.

PETRONI, FRANK A., "Adolescent Liberalism—The Myth of a Generation Gap," *Adolescence*, 7, no. 26 (Summer 1972), 221–32.

PETTIGREW, T. F., *Racially Separate or Together?* New York: McGraw-Hill, 1971.

PHILLIPS, DEREK, "Rejection of the Mentally Ill: The Influence of Behavior and Sex," *American Sociological Review*, 29, no. 5 (October 1964), 679–86.

PICCONE, PAUL, "Students' Protest, Class Structure, and Ideology," *Telos*, 2, no. 1 (Spring 1969), 106–22.

PINKNEY, A., "Prejudice Toward Mexican and Negro Americans: A Comparison," *Phylon*, (1963).

PLATT, ANTHONY M., "Saving and Controlling Delinquent Youth: A Critique," *Issues in Criminology*, 5, no. 1, (Winter 1970), 1–24.

POORKAJ, HOUSHANG, "Social-Psychological Factors and 'Successful Aging'," *Sociology and Social Research*, 56, no. 3 (April 1972), 289–300.

POVEDA, TONY G., "The Image of the Criminal: A Critique of Crime and Delinquency Theories," *Issues in Criminology*, 5, no. 1 (Winter 1970), 59–84.

PRATT, ANNIS, "Archetypal Approaches to the New Feminist Criticism," *Bucknell Review*, 21, no. 1 (Spring 1971), 3–14.

PRATT, H. J., "Politics, Status and the Organization of Ethnic Minority Group Interests. The Case of the New York Protestants," *Polity*, 3, no. 2 (Winter 1970), 222–46.

QUINNEY, R., *Crime and Justice in Society*. Boston: Little Brown, 1969.

———, ed., *Criminal Justice in America: A Critical Understanding*. Boston: Little Brown, 1974.

REDEKOP, CALVIN, and JOHN A. HOSTETLER, "Minority-Majority Relations and Economic Interdependence," *Phylon*, 27, no. 4 (Winter 1966), 367–78.

REID, OTTO M., "Aging Americans," *Welfare in R.*, 4, no. 5 (May 1966), 1–12.

RELYEA, HAROLD C., "'Black Power:' The Genesis and Future of a Revolution," *Journal of Human Relations*, 16, no. 4 (1968), 502–13.

REX, JOHN, "Race as a Social Category," *Journal of Biosocial Science*, Supplement 1, (July 1969), 145–52.

——, *Race Relations in Sociological Theory.* London: Weidenfeld and Nicholson, 1970.

RINDER, I. D., "Minority Orientations: An Approach to Intergroup Relations Theory Through Social Psychology," *Phylon*, 26 (1965), 5–17.

RIVERA, RAMON J., and JAMES F. SHORT, Jr., "Significant Adults, Caretakers and Structure of Opportunity: An Exploratory Study," *Journal of Research in Crime and Delinquency*, 4, no. 1 (January 1967), 76–97.

ROACH, JACK L., and ORVILLE R. GURSSLIN, "An Evaluation of the Concept 'Culture of Poverty'," *Social Forces*, 45, no. 3 (January 1967), 383–91.

ROBY, P., ed., *Poverty Establishment.* Englewood Cliffs, N.J.: Prentice-Hall, 1974.

ROCK, PAUL, "Phenomenalism and Essentialism in the Sociology of Deviancy," *Sociology*, 7, no. 1 (January 1973), 17–29.

ROGERS, D., *Adolescence: A Psychological Perspective.* New York: Appleton-Century-Crofts, 1972, (2nd ed.).

ROSE, A. M., "The Comparative Study of Intergroup Conflict," *Sociological Quarterly*, 1 (1960), 57–66.

ROSE, A. M., and W. A. PETERSON, eds., *Older People and Their Social World.* Philadelphia: F. A. Davis, 1965.

ROSE, P. I., *They and We.* New York: Random House, 1964.

ROSENFELT, ROSCHE H., "The Elderly Mystique," *Journal of Social Issues*, 21, no. 4 (October 1965), 37–43.

ROSENTHAL, ARLENE, "The Jewish Community in the Broader Society. An Attitude Survey," *Proceedings of Southwestern Sociological Association*, 19 (1968), 5–9.

ROSOW, IRVING, "And Then We Were Old," *Trans-Action*, 2, no. 2 (January-February 1965), 20–26.

——, *Social Integration of the Aged.* New York: Free Press, 1967.

ROSSI, A., ed., *Feminist Perspectives: From Adams to De Beauvoir.* New York: Columbia University Press, 1973.

ROTHMAN, JACK, "Minority Group Status, Mental Health and Intergroup Relations: An Appraisal of Kurt Lewin's Thesis," *J. Intergroup Relat.*, 3, no. 4 (Autumn 1962), 299–310.

ROTHMAN, SHIELA M., "Other People's Children: The Day Care Experience in America," *Public Interest*, 30 (Winter 1973), 11–27.

ROUCEK, JOSEPH S., "The Power and Ideological Aspects of the Majority-Minority Relationships," *Sociologia Internationalis*, 3, no. 11 (1965), 97–120.

——, "Special Characteristics of the Problem of Racial Minorities in the U.S.A.," *Revista Internacional de Sociologia*, 23, no. 89 (1965), 37–54.

——, "Difficulties in the Education of Minority Groups in the United States," *Sociological Review*, 9, nos. 13–14 (1965), 34–49.

RUBINGTON, E., ed., *Deviance: The Interactionist Perspective.* New York: Macmillan, 1973.

RUSH, GARY B., "The Radicalization of Middle-Class Youth," *International Social Science Journal*, 24, no. 2 (1972), 312–25.

RYAN, M. P., *Womanhood in America, From Colonial Times to the Present.* New York: New Viewpoints, 1975.

RYAN, W., *Blaming the Victim.* New York: Pantheon, 1971.

SAGARIN, EDWARD, "Homosexuality as a Social Movement: First Reports from the Barricades," *The Journal of Sex Research,* 9, no. 4 (November 1973), 289–94.

SAMORA, JULIAN, "The Educational Status of a Minority," *Theory into Pract.,* 2, no. 3 (June 1963), 144–50.

SANDERS, IRWIN T., and EWA T. MORAWSKA, *Polish-American Community Life: A Survey of Research.* Community Sociology Training Program, Boston University, 1975.

SCHAFER, WALTER E., CAROL OLEXA and KENNETH POLK, "Programmed for Social Class: Tracking in High School," *Trans-Action,* 7, no. 12 (October 1970), 29–46, 63.

SCHEFF, T. J., *Being Mentally Ill.* Chicago: Aldine, 1966.

———, "Stereotypes of Insanity," *New Society,* 9, 232 (March 9, 1967), 348–50.

———, ed., *Mental Illness and Social Processes.* New York: Harper & Row, 1967.

SCHERMERHORN, R. A., "Towards a General Theory of Minority Groups," *Phylon,* 25, (1964), 238–46.

———, *Comparative Ethnic Relations: A Framework for Theory and Research.* New York: Random House, 1970.

———, "Minorities and National Integration," *Journal of Social Research,* 13, no. 2 (March 1970), 23–35.

SCHIAVO, G. E., *Italian-American History.* New York: Arno, 1975.

SCHUMAN, HOWARD, and JOHN HARDING, "Prejudice and the Norm of Rationality," *Sociometry,* 27, no. 3 (September 1964), 353–71.

SCHUR, E. M., *Crimes Without Victims—Deviant Behavior and Public Policy: Abortion, Homosexuality, Drug Addiction.* Englewood Cliffs, N.J.: Prentice-Hall, 1965.

SCOTT, R. A., "A Proposed Framework for Analyzing Deviance as a Property of Social Order," in *Theoretical Perspectives on Deviance,* eds. R. A. Scott and J. D. Douglas. New York: Basic Books, 1972, pp. 9–36.

SCOTT, R. A., and J. D. DOUGLAS, eds., *Theoretical Perspectives on Deviance.* New York: Basic Books, 1972.

SEBALD, H., *Adolescence: A Sociological Analysis.* New York: Appleton-Century-Crofts, 1968.

SEGGAR, JOHN F., and PENNY WHEELER, "World of Work on TV: Ethnic and Sex Representation in TV Drama," *Journal of Broadcasting,* 17, no. 2 (Spring 1973), 201–14.

SEIBEL, H. D., "Social Deviance in Comparative Perspective," in *Theoretical Perspectives on Deviance,* eds. R. A. Scott, and J. D. Douglas. New York: Basic Books, 1972, pp. 251–81.

SELIGMAN, BEN B., *Permanent Poverty: An American Syndrome.* New York: Quadrangle Books, 1968.

SENNETT, R., and J. COBB, *The Hidden Injuries of Class.* New York: Knopf, 1973.

SHACK, WILLIAM A., "Black Muslims: A Nativistic Religious Movement Among Negro Americans," *Race,* 3, no. 1 (November 1961), 57–67.

SHANAS, ETHEL, "A Note on Restriction of Life Space: Attitudes of Age Cohorts," *Journal of Health and Social Behavior,* 9, no. 1 (March 1968), 86–90.

———, "What's New in Old Age?" *American Behavioral Scientist,* 14, no. 1 (September-October 1970), 5–12.

———, "Family-Kin Networks and Aging in Cross-Cultural Perspective," *Journal of Marriage and the Family,* 35, no. 3 (August 1973), 505–11.

SHANLEY, MARY L., and VICTORIA SCHUCK, "In Search of Political Woman," *Social Science Quarterly*, 55, no. 3 (December 1974), 632–44.

SHIBUTANI, TAMOTSU and KIAN M. KWAN, *Ethnic Stratification: A Comparative Approach*. New York: The Macmillan Co., 1965.

SHIPMAN, M., *Childhood: A Sociological Perspective*. New York: Humanities, 1972.

SHORT, JAMES F., Jr., "Youth, Gangs, and Society: Micro- and Macrosociological Processes," *The Sociological Quarterly*, 15, no. 1 (Winter 1974), 3–19.

SHORT, JAMES F. Jr., RAMON RIVERA, and HARVEY MARSHALL, "Adult-Adolescent Relations and Gang Delinquency," *Pacific Sociological Review*, 7, no. 2 (Fall 1964), 59–65.

SIEGEL, PAUL M., "On the Cost of Being a Negro," *Sociological Inquiry*, 35, no. 1 (April 1965), 41–57.

SIMON, RITA J., "American Women and Crime," *The Annals of the American Academy of Political and Social Science*, 423 (January 1976), 31–46.

SIMON, WILLIAM, and JOHN H. GAGNON, "Homosexuality: the Formulation of a Sociological Perspective," *Journal of Health and Social Behavior*, 8, no. 3 (September 1967), 177–84.

SIMPSON, G. E., and J. M. YINGER, *Race and Cultural Minorities: An Analysis of Prejudice and Discrimination*, 4th ed., New York: Harper & Row, 1972.

SKLARE, MARSHALL, "Assimilation and the Sociologists," *Commentary*, 39, no. 5 (May 1965), 63–66.

SMITH, ROGER, "Status Politics and the Image of the Addict," *Issues in Criminology*, 2, no. 2 (Fall 1966), 157–76.

SONENSCHUN, DAVID, "The Ethnography of Male Homosexual Relationships," *Journal of Sex Research*, 4, no. 2 (May 1968), 69–83.

SOTOMAYOR, MARTA, "Mexican-American Interaction with Social Systems," *Social Casework*, 52, no. 5 (May 1971), 316–22.

STAPLES, R., *Introduction to Black Sociology*. New York: McGraw-Hill, 1976.

STERNE, RICHARD S., *Delinquent Conduct and Broken Homes*. New Haven, Conn.: College and University Press, 1964.

STOLL, C., *Female and Male: Socialization, Social Roles and Social Structure*. Dubuque: W. C. Brown, 1974.

STRAWBRIDGE, WILLIAM, "Competition as a Cause of Discrimination and Prejudice," *University of Washington Journal of Sociology*, 2, (November 1970), 28–37.

SUCHMAN, EDWARD A., "The 'Hang-Loose' Ethic and the Spirit of Drug Use," *Journal of Health and Social Behavior*, 9, no. 2 (Fall 1966), 157–76.

TABB, WILLIAM K., "Race Relations Models and Social Change," *Social Problems*, 18, no. 4 (Spring 1971), 431–44.

TAPPAN, P., *Crime, Justice, and Correction*. New York: McGraw-Hill, 1960.

TEAHAN, JOHN E., and JAMES HUG, "Status Threat and White Backlash," *Journal of Human Relations*, 12, no. 2 (1970), 939–47.

TEMPLIN, LAWRENCE, "The Pathology of Youth," *Journal of Human Relations*, 16, no. 1 (1968), 113–27.

TIBBITS, CLARK, and WILMA DONAHUE, eds., *Social and Psychological Aspects of Aging Around the World*. New York: Columbia University Press, 1962.

TRIPP, C. A., *Homosexual Matrix*. New York: McGraw-Hill, 1975.

TROLL, LILLIAN E., "'Generation Gap' in Later Life: An Introductory Discussion and some Preliminary Findings," *Sociological Focus*, 5, (1971), 18–28.

TUMIN, MELVIN, ed. *Comparative Perspectives on Race Relations.* Boston: Little Brown, 1969.

TURK, AUSTIN T., "Toward Construction of a Theory of Delinquency," *Journal of Criminal Law, Criminology, and Police Science,* 55, no. 2 (June 1964), 215–29.

——, "Prospects for Theories of Criminal Behavior," *Journal of Criminal Law, Criminology and Police Science,* 55, no. 4 (December 1964), 545–61.

UHLENBERG, PETER, "Marital Instability Among Mexican Americans: Following the Pattern of Blacks," *Social Problems,* 20, no. 1 (Summer 1972), 49–56.

U.S. Bureau of the Census, *Statistical Abstract of the United States: 1974,* (95th ed.), Washington, D.C.: 1974.

VAIRO, PHILIP D., "The Italian Immigrant in the United States," *Indian Sociological Bulletin,* 2, no. 4 (July 1965), 196–205.

VALENTINE, C. A., "Voluntary Ethnicity and Social Change: Classism, Racism, Marginality, Mobility, and Revolution with Special Reference to Afro-American and Other Third World Peoples," *The Journal of Ethnic Studies,* 3, no. 1 (Spring 1975), 1–27.

VAN DEN BERGHE, P. L., *Race and Racism.* New York: Wiley, 1967.

VAN MANEN, GLORIA COUNT, "Father Role and Adolescent Socialization," *Adolescence,* 3, no. 10 (Summer 1968), 139–152.

VECOLI, RUDOLPH J., "European Americans: From Immigrants to Ethnics," *International Migration Review,* 6, no. 4 (Winter 1972), 403–34.

VOGEL, MANFRED, "Some Reflections on the Jewish-Christian Dialogue in the Light of the Six-Day War," *The Annals of the American Academy of Political and Social Science,* 387 (January 1970), 96–108.

VOSS, HARWIN L., "Socioeconomic Status and Reported Delinquent Behavior," *Social Problems,* 13, no. 3 (Winter 1966), 314–24.

WAGLEY, C., and M. HARRIS, *Minorities in the New World.* New York: Columbia University Press, 1958.

WAGNER, STANLEY P., "The Polish-American Vote in 1960," *Polish American Studies,* (January, June 1964), 1–9.

WARD, RICHARD H., "The Labeling Theory: A Critical Analysis," *Criminology,* 9, nos. 2–3 (August–November 1971), 268–90.

WARREN, DONALD I., "Neighborhood Structure and Riot Behavior in Detroit: Some Exploratory Findings," *Social Problems,* 16, no. 4 (Spring 1969), 464–85.

WEINBERG, MARTIN S., "The Male Homosexual: Age-Related Variations in Social and Psychological Characteristics," *Social Problems,* 17, no. 4 (Spring 1970), 527–37.

WEINSTEIN, RAYMOND M., "Patients' Perceptions of Mental Illness: Paradigms for Analysis," *Journal of Health and Social Behavior,* 13, no. 1 (March 1972), 38–47.

WEISS, JONATHAN, "The Law and the Poor," *Journal of Social Issues,* 26, no. 3 (Summer 1970), 59–68.

WELLMAN, BARRY, "Social Identities in Black and White," *Sociological Inquiry,* 41, no. 1 (Winter 1971), 57–66.

WELLS, J. GIPSON, "A Selected Bibliography on the Sociology of Adolescence," *Sociological Symposium,* 7 (Spring 1971), 73–92.

WEST, D. J., "Parental Figures in the Genesis of Male Homosexuality," *International Journal of Social Psychiatry,* 5, no. 2 (Autumn 1959), 97.

WESTIE, F. R., "Race and Ethnic Relations," in *Handbook of Modern Sociology*, ed. R. E. K. Faris. Chicago: Rand McNally, 1964.

WHITE, TERRENCE H., "Minority Groups: Beyond Description," *Wisconsin Sociologist*, 6, no. 1 (Spring-Summer 1968), 25–33.

WHITEHEAD, CARLTON J., and ALBERT S. KING, "Differences in Managers' Attitudes Towards Mexican and Non-Mexican Americans in Organizational Authority Relations," *Social Science Quarterly*, 53, no. 4 (March 1973), 760–71.

WHITING, B. B., and J. W. WHITING, *Children of Six Cultures*. Cambridge: Harvard University, 1974.

WILLARD, WILLIAM, and HARLAND PADFIELD, "Poverty and Social Disorder: Introduction," *Human Organization*, 29, no. 1 (Spring 1970), 1–4.

WILLIAMS, JAY R., and MARTIN GOLD, "From Delinquent Behavior to Official Delinquency," *Social Problems*, 20, no. 2 (Fall 1972), 209–29.

WILLIAMS, JOYCE E., and WILLIAM M. BATES, "Toward a Typology of Female Narcotic Addicts," *Proceedings of the Southwestern Sociological Association*, 18 (March 1967), 152–56.

WILLIAMSON, JOHN B., "Beliefs about the Motivation of the Poor and Attitudes Toward Poverty Policy," *Social Problems*, 21, no. 5 (June 1974), 634–48.

WILLIE, CHARLES V., "The Relative Contribution of Family Status and Economic Status of Juvenile Delinquency," *Social Problems*, 14, no. 3 (Winter 1967), 326–34.

WILLIE, CHARLES V., and ANITA GERSHENOVITZ, "Juvenile Delinquency in Racially Mixed Areas," *American Sociological Review*, 29, no. 5 (October 1964), 740–44.

WINICK, CHARLES, "Prostitutes' Clients' Perception of Themselves," *International Journal of Social Psychiatry*, 8, no. 4 (Autumn 1962), 289–97.

WINICK, CHARLES, and PAUL M. KINSIE, *The Lively Commerce: Prostitution in the United States*. Chicago: Quadrangle Books, 1971.

WIRTH, L., "The Problem of Minority Groups," in R. Linton, ed., *The Science of Man in the World Crisis*. New York: Columbia University Press, 1945.

WITTKOWER, E. D., and GUY DUBREUIL, "Psychocultural Stress in Relation to Mental Illness," *Social Science and Medicine*, 7, no. 9 (September 1973), 691–704.

WOOD, ARTHUR E., *Hamtramck: A Sociological Study of a Polish-American Community*. New Haven: College and University Press, 1955.

WORSLEY, PETER M., "Authority and the Young," *New Society*, 6, no. 147 (July 1965), 10–13.

YELLOWITZ, IRWIN, "Black Militancy and Organized Labor: An Historical Parameter," *Midwest Quarterly*, 13, no. 2 (January 1972), 169–83.

YINGER, J. MILTON, "Social Forces Involved in Group Identification or Withdrawal," *Daedalus*, 90, no. 2 (Spring 1961), 247–62.

YOUNG, D., *American Minority Peoples*. New York: Harper, 1932.

YUAN, D. Y., "Chinatown and Beyond: The Chinese Population in Metropolitan New York," *Phylon*, 27, no. 4 (Winter 1966), 321–32.

ZAGRANICZNY, STANLEY, "Some Reasons for Polish Surname Changes," *Polish-American Studies*, (January–June 1963), 12–14.

ZENIDES, J. P., *The Greeks in America*. San Francisco: R & E Associates, 1972.

Name Index

Subject Index